To Auntie F

with lots of xvv

from

Dave

x

Coal, Goals and Ashes

Fryston Colliery's Pursuit of the
West Riding County FA Challenge Cup

David P. Waddington

First published by Route in 2013
PO Box 167, Pontefract, WF8 4WW
info@route-online.com
www.route-online.com

ISBN: 978-1-901927-57-3

David P. Waddington asserts his moral right to be
identified as the author of this book

A catalogue for this book is available from the British Library

Design:
GOLDEN www.wearegolden.co.uk

Printed and bound by CPI Group (UK) Ltd, Croydon, CR0 4YY

Contents

Dedicated to my parents, Mary and Peter,
and in loving memory of
Tommy, Edie and Melvin Waddington

Foreword
Ian Clayton

This book reminds me of one I read years ago by the maverick Yorkshire writer and publisher, J.L. Carr, called *How Steeple Sinderby Wanderers Won the FA Cup*. The same themes of 'triumph against the odds', 'little un's putting one over the big guys' and 'homespun excellence' pervade both books. Carr's book has a hero in the Captain Alex Slingsby, a mighty athlete just waiting for his moment, and Mr Fangfoss, a manager who likes to be a boss but hasn't got much time for football. Similarly, David Waddington's book has a hero in goal-scoring veteran, Freddie Howard, and a manager who takes the cup home in his car as though it's his own. But there is one big difference: J.L. Carr's book is a work of fiction, this book is all true.

It's all true and it's written from the authentic point of view of one who knows. Professor David Waddington has his roots in the tiny pit community of Fryston and his dad, Peter, was the captain of the village team on their famous day. David states at the very beginning of this book that his motives for writing it are 'purely personal' and fair play to him for that. The best books are purely personal ones and, at a time when football memoirs that purport to be written by stars and so called role-models are ten a penny, this is refreshingly real, down to earth and just damn honest. It's about playing football for the love of it, about mates and their escapades, about people who help – there's a wonderful little vignette about Alf Atack, one of the back-room staff: 'Whenever you turned round he was carrying something or else putting up goalposts.' It's also about camaraderie that starts at work and spills over onto the field of play; about support from wives, girlfriends and neighbours. As such it becomes more than just a football book; it's a social history about a pit village in Yorkshire and how that place was made.

When I was a lad, I played mainly Rugby League. If you come from Featherstone, like I do, it's expected of you. We did play football as well, though, at the top of our street, against two gable ends. On each of these gables, some older lads from the bottom of Girnhill Lane had painted two blue goalposts and, inside these goal posts, were the words 'Stoke City'. I don't think anybody can remember now why it said Stoke City. At the time we thought it was because Gordon Banks played in goal for them, and Gordon Banks was a proper hero who, himself, had started his career with a coal miners' team. I've found something out in this book that might put another meaning on the connection between Staffordshire and Yorkshire pit villages. A lot of men came from that part of the world to find work in the pits round here a century ago. They brought their favourite game with them, so when I was scoring goals between our Stoke City posts, I was doing something that my ancestors had done.

I left football not long after and my heroes became Rugby League giants who played for Featherstone Rovers; men like Vince Farrar, Jimmy Thompson, Keith Bridges and Peter Smith. Local men who you might see buying a loaf of bread from a corner shop on a Friday and then turning out for Great Britain the following day. My lad, though, prefers soccer and decided that Newcastle United would be his team. Alan Shearer – 'a proper old fashioned forward' – was his first hero. Now his Geordie heroes are as likely to come from West Africa as they are from West Auckland. We go up to St James' Park now and again. We saw them recently playing against a Russian team called Anzhi Makhachkala in the Europa League. Anzhi have a player, Samuel Eto'o, who is paid £330,000 a game. I don't know how many times he touched the ball in that game, but it wasn't many.

There are no perfumed millionaire footballers in this book, just muddy, sweaty working lads who wash the muck off their legs in tin buckets – people like Terry Templeman 'who would run all day for the sake of his team'; players like the wonderfully named 'Cobbo' Robinson and 'Agga' Mattison. Then there is the veteran Freddie Howard, who is called upon the day before the final to bring his magic to the front line.

It's a proper book then, about proper blokes, written for proper reasons, that is to say it celebrates, honours and pays tribute to local endeavour. If you get all misty-eyed when you think about the days when footballers wore the numbers one to eleven on their backs and the time when you looked in *The Green Final* to see how your rivals had got on, this is the book for you. And if you're the sort of fan who still goes to a match armed with a flask of tea or you believe that local heroes are always better than manufactured ones, you'll love reading this.

I'll leave the last words to 'Agga' Mattison who helped to organise the Fryston rearguard action on that famous day fifty years ago. 'The majority of 'em were Fryston lads – they were born, worked or lived in Fryston, and for most on us it was all three!'

Introduction
In Pursuit of the Ultimate Prize

Previous page: The Fryston Colliery Welfare team which contested the West Riding County FA Challenge Cup final against Thackley in May 1963. BACK ROW (left to right): J. Simpson (committee member), H. Ward (goalkeeper), T. Templeman, H. Mattison, J. Appleyard, B. Wood, A. Commir (committee member) and A. Atack (committee member). FRONT ROW: B. Robinson, J. Sharp, P. Waddington (captain), C. Braund, F. Howard and T. Ward.

Background and Motives

Wednesday, 22 May 2013 marked the fiftieth anniversary of the day that Fryston Colliery Welfare, then a humble Second Division team in the West Yorkshire League, took on the seemingly invincible Bradford side, Thackley AFC, in the 1963 West Riding County Football Association Challenge Cup final (WRCC Cup). Throughout most of the twentieth century, the WRCC Cup was justifiably regarded as the local equivalent of the FA Cup – the 'ultimate prize' – for amateur teams in the Castleford area. This book utilises newspaper archives and interviews with the players of both sides to explain the full emotional, cultural and historical nature and significance of their famous encounter.

My main motive for writing this book is unashamedly personal: my father, Peter (Pete) Waddington, was captain of the Fryston team that played against Thackley in 1963, and also in the 'return match' between the two sides at the equivalent stage of the following year's competition. I had first considered the possibility of writing a commemorative publication as early as 1985 whilst in the process of researching my earlier book, *One Road In, One Road Out: A People's History of Fryston*,[1] but the project then lay dormant until an article appearing in the *Pontefract and Castleford Express* (hereafter, referred to as the *Express*) proved both captivating and inspirational. The piece in question centred on a photograph of the 1963 team, sent in by a reader, the Castleford-born David Nathan, and an accompanying letter in which he outlined the qualities of a set of players he had clearly idolised when just a boy:

> The goalkeeper Archie Ward was brilliant and would have made David Seaman look ordinary... The defence was rock solid with iron man Brian Wood, Johnny Appleyard and Agga Mattinson [sic]. Jack Sharpe [sic], a man of small stature but huge heart, inspired the team and was the toughest

of competitors. The captain was Pete Waddington, a tough but classy midfielder, and the engine room of the team. Terry Templeman was known as perpetual motion, had a shot like Eusebio and covered every blade of grass. Up front were Fred Howard, stylish Cliff Braund and goal-scoring left-winger Trevor Ward. There was also the George Best-type right-winger, Barry Robinson, the team pin-up. Collectively they were Castleford's best ever football team.[2]

My reaction was instantaneous. I asked my dad to compile a list of the contact details of all his former Fryston team-mates. He and my daughter, Laura, then helped me obtain photocopies of all of Fryston's 1962-63 season's match reports from the *Express* archives, which exist on microfilm in the Pontefract Library. However, this early momentum soon stalled as it became apparent that things were likely to prove far more difficult than first imagined. I already knew, for example, that two players from the 1963 team (Johnny Appleyard and Freddie Howard) had since died. I was then told that Cliff Braund and Archie Ward had emigrated, to New Zealand and Australia respectively, and that no-one quite knew the whereabouts of Barry 'Cobbo' Robinson, who was understood to have opened a chip shop 'somewhere out in Bradford'. To crown it all, for some reason Trevor Ward never seemed willing or able to answer his phone. The growing feeling that there were far too many potential obstacles to overcome was compounded when I developed a heart condition in the summer of 2004 which eventually required surgery. Hence the project was shelved – albeit temporarily.

My interest and enthusiasm was subsequently rekindled as a result of reading several football books which had each been written to commemorate major milestones in the professional game. No-one could convince me that the exploits and accomplishments of my own dad and his former Fryston team-mates were any less relevant, valid or interesting – certainly to their families, friends and, indeed, the town of Castleford – than their supposedly more illustrious contemporaries of the professional game.

One of these books was Simon Hattenstone's *The Best of Times: What Became of the Heroes of '66?*[3] in which he spoke to members of England's 1966 World Cup-winning team, forty years on from their triumph over West Germany. A second book, *The Lost Babes: Manchester United and the Forgotten Victims of Munich*,[4] by Jeff Connor, comprises a fiftieth-anniversary reflection on the nature and consequences of the

1958 Munich air disaster in which the majority of Matt Busby's great side tragically lost their lives. Whilst each of these commemorative texts was undoubtedly inspirational, it was a third book, *Johnny the Forgotten Babe: Memories of Manchester and Manchester United in the 1950s*,[5] written by Neil Berry, son of Johnny Berry, the United right-winger and survivor of the Munich plane crash, which had the most powerfully resonant and animating effect. I was therefore now hell-bent on producing a commemorative publication to coincide with the fiftieth anniversary of the final.

I set about this task in two ways: firstly, by delving back into newspaper reports of earlier seasons in the club's history; and second, by interviewing as many surviving members of the Fryston and Thackley teams as I was able to track down. I was initially intent on writing nothing more than a succinct 'journalistic' article on the final, based on relevant press accounts and the recollections of these former players. However, the more I began to excavate the newspaper reports, the more I became aware of the extent to which such knowledge was necessary to appreciating the full significance of Fryston's appearance in the 1963 final, and of how it also provided a fascinating insight into a remarkable, virtually forgotten and hitherto undocumented local football culture. Thus, between August 2010 and the winter of 2012-13, Fryston Colliery's pursuit of the 'ultimate prize' became transformed into an obsessive pursuit of my own.

Methods of Research

The archival research on which this book is based involved going back through all weekly editions of the *Express* from 1895 to 1992. This often proved a very discouraging and exasperating experience, primarily because, for some seasons in particular, Fryston's match reports appeared only sporadically, and in others not at all. Inexplicably, there was no guarantee that an account of Fryston's semi-final victory appearing one week would be followed by details of the final in subsequent editions of the paper. Sometimes, the library archive contained only *Pontefract* editions of back-copies of the *Express*. Attempts to overcome this problem by tracking down corresponding *Castleford* editions from Castleford Library were stymied by the fact that the library was in the process of relocating to different premises for the duration of the research period. Similar attempts to fill in the gaps and/or supplement existing knowledge by consulting back-copies of newspapers like the *Leeds Mercury*, *Yorkshire Post* and *Yorkshire Evening Post* were often only partially successful and invariably hampered by a similar range of problems.

Most frustrating of all was the lack of archival material available from the local football associations. Few relevant records have been kept, either by the Castleford and District Football Association, or its Leeds and District counterpart. A request to the West Yorkshire Football Association for access to its yearbooks was declined on the grounds that the set of copies belonging to the current FA secretary constituted the only one in existence, and was therefore 'not for public use'. One particular appeal for an especially important piece of information was subsequently granted, but only on the understanding that there would be no further requests of that nature. Due to the unavailability of such relevant detail, it was necessary to turn to fellow amateur football historians and benevolent library staff (see 'Acknowledgements') who invariably did their best to plug the missing gaps.

The interview content used in this book comes from two principal sources. In a minority of cases, it derives from research carried out as part of the *One Road In, One Road Out* project. These include conversations recorded in 1985 or 1986 with such respondents as: the former pit managers, Jim Bullock OBE and Edgar Williams; village residents like Bill Astbury, Cath Betteridge and Jack Hulme; the former Fryston players, Tommy Templeman and Jabie Foulkes; and the life-long Fryston supporter (and club life-member), Ronnie Foulkes, whose father, Dick, was a former Fryston player of the 1920s and coach of the 1963 cup-final team. It was Ronnie who was kind enough to present me with a tape-recorded conversation from the early 1980s between his father and the then Fryston club secretary (Barry Bennett), which is used here with the permission of both parties.

The majority of the remaining interviews were carried out in 2010 or 2011. Given his compendious knowledge of the club's history, I chose to begin by re-interviewing Ronnie. In the same two-week period in August 2010, I conducted further interviews with such participants in the 1963 final as Harold 'Agga' Mattison, Jack (or 'Jackie') Sharp, Terry Templeman and Brian Wood, and with other key

Fryston players of that era, like Frank Isles and David Rotherforth. As if to reinforce my growing optimism, Trevor Ward finally picked up his phone and cheerfully reassured me that, far from deliberately avoiding me, he had been working unsociable hours as a security man for the University of Leeds. Now that he had retired, he would be only too glad to talk.

Just as encouraging was Ward's disclosure that he had stayed friends with Cliff Braund ever since their Fryston days, and was due to visit him in Australia in the spring of 2011. Ward was therefore able to pass on Braund's contact details, and eventually enable me to interview him by phone. Then, just as I was starting to believe the persistent rumour that Archie Ward had died while out in his adoptive Australia, I received an unexpected phone call from his brother, Frank, who helped stage a long-distance interview with the charismatic ex-Fryston 'keeper.

Similar good fortune surrounded my attempt to get in touch with Freddie Howard's brother, Stan, in a bid to get to know a bit about the deceased, free-scoring ex-Fryston centre-forward's childhood, family background and footballing career. It seemed for an uncomfortably long time as if no-one could inform me of Stan's precise whereabouts; but then one day Jack Sharp bumped into him by chance and I was given permission to contact him. A very productive interview was arranged, involving, not only myself and Mr Howard, but also Freddie's daughter, Susan, and his son-in-law, Trevor. Subsequently, Stan also put me in touch with the former Fryston striker, J.C. 'Charlie' Barnett, who was a life-long friend of Freddie's.

For a former chip shop owner, Barry Robinson proved an especially difficult fish to land. No-one had the remotest idea of his whereabouts and I was forced into the desperate last resort of 'cold-calling' every listed 'chippy' in the Bradford area in the hope of tracking him down. There were only two phone numbers left on my list when the proprietor of the last but one charitably suggested that I phone a sandwich shop up the road. He explained that the owners of it used to run the chip shop next door as well, but had recently closed it down. He was sure their name was Robinson. I held my breath and dialled the number he had given me. A woman answered. I explained who I was and why I was looking for Cobbo Robinson. There was a long, unnerving silence before she let out a revealing laugh and replied: 'Yes, I know Mr Robinson. I also know his wife. In fact, she's standing no more than three feet away from where I am now.' Three hours later, I was speaking to Mr Robinson directly on the phone. 'Cobbo,' I said to him only half-jokingly, 'I don't care whether you're George Best, the "fifth Beatle" or what. *Where in hell's name* have you been hiding yourself?' Having finally 'landed' Cobbo, I got round to interviewing my dad. I had deliberately saved this conversation until last. There was something about the fact that he was team captain that told me it should be his prerogative to have the final word. In purely practical terms, it also gave me an excuse to give him a good leg-pulling about some of the things his team-mates had been saying about him. In truth, it was an exceptionally emotional experience: I took great pride in recounting some of the warm tributes his ex-colleagues had paid him; and I was glad to discover that no-one was more generous or warm-hearted than he in reminiscing about his former comrades.

In the meantime, I had approached the current Thackley club secretary, Chris Frank, to see whether he might consider putting me in touch with some of their former players. His enquiries soon revealed that, of the team opposing Fryston, two had since died, the whereabouts of two more were unknown, their former captain was now living in Australia, and a fifth was unwilling to be interviewed. That still left a total of six willing respondents – five ex-players (in Ray Cole, John Gunnell, Ken Hill, Barry Holmes and Jack Walker) and their ex-manager, Peter Glover – whom I arranged to interview as a group at Hill's place on the outskirts of Wyke. Glover subsequently gave me the telephone number of the club's former centre-half and captain (who, by a remarkable freak of coincidence, also goes by the name of David Waddington), with the result that I was able to call him up in Sydney.

Almost a full year passed by before I conducted the next and, as it turned out, penultimate interview. For reasons soon to become apparent, I considered it essential that I talk to the former Bradford Park Avenue and Manchester United midfield star, Johnny Downie, who had worked as a 'Bevin Boy' at Fryston pit during the Second World War. It was well-known that Downie (who was 86-years-old by this time) had run a newsagent's shop in the Lidget Green area of Bradford following his retirement from the game in the 1960s. However, a Wikipedia reference suggested that he had been spending his retirement in Tynemouth in the north east of England.

I therefore re-adopted the strategy I had used with Cobbo Robinson by cold-calling the local numbers listed for 'Downie'. I had all but given up when I suddenly had the brainwave of calling up newsagents in the Tynemouth area to see whether his name and address might feature on their rounds. I had only made two such calls when the second respondent was kind enough to volunteer Mr Downie's address. After some brief correspondence between myself and Mr Downie's wife, Sheila, my own wife (Joanna) and I travelled up to Tynemouth to spend a day in their company. I had been warned in advance that Mr Downie suffered from Alzheimer's and was apt to be very forgetful, but he actually remembered a vast amount of relevant detail and Sheila invariably filled in the missing information.

That left only one interview to carry out. My research was finally completed in the New Year of 2013 when I spoke to Carol Woolley, the widow of Johnny Appleyard who had died in 1968 while still in his early twenties. It had always been my intention to delay talking to Carol until I was in a position to show her a draft of all the things I might have written about Johnny. It was imperative, of course, that Carol should feel comfortable about whatever ex-colleagues might have said about her husband and the manner and circumstances of his death. Her co-operation was therefore especially appreciated.

Contents and Scope

By now, I was embarked on a desperate race against time. There was a danger that the book's symbolic significance would automatically diminish in the event of my failure to see it published in time for the day marking the fiftieth anniversary of the final. As if to further emphasise the urgency of my task, I learned in the autumn of 2011 that Archie Ward had died of a heart attack. During 2012, both my dad and Cliff Braund underwent heart bypass operations, with the latter also suffering a post-operative stroke. Finally, in February 2013, I learned that Johnny Downie had sadly just passed away.

This increasingly pressing need to prepare the book for final publication, combined with the unavailability or deficiency of match reports, have made it inevitable that what follows is an incomplete and occasionally flawed historical account of Fryston's pursuit of the WRCC trophy. I remain satisfied, however, that the following chapters constitute as comprehensive and well-documented an account as it was possible to produce in the face of such impediments. I will not try to conceal my intense emotional attachment to this project, or pretend that it is not fundamentally concerned with my own personal heritage. The historical narrative which follows is deliberately intended to document and commemorate what I personally consider to be the remarkable and even heroic accomplishments of a team of 'ordinary', working-class men. It is because I also firmly believe that such a claim is best served by eschewing the temptation to exaggerate, disguise or over-romanticise, that the emphasis throughout this volume will be on the presentation of substantive evidence ('warts and all') which will hopefully speak for itself and be all the more potent for that.

The book begins by charting the origins and development of Fryston as a pit village, with a view to establishing the part played by early industrial conflict and the related influx of miners (most notably from Staffordshire) in helping to implant and cultivate the fervent footballing culture that provided the engine for Fryston's pioneering involvement in county competition, and sustained its future ambitions to lift the trophy. It will become apparent that the historical development of the football team is inseparable from parallel activities in the mining industry, in the affairs of Fryston pit, and in the contrasting styles and interventions of local colliery managers.

Chapters 2, 3 and 4 focus on Fryston's attempts to win the WRCC trophy in the pre-First World War, inter-war, and Second World War eras, respectively. We shall see how, within this period (1910-1945), the club contested four county finals. Particular individuals with ancestral roots in the Staffordshire coalfield (notably representatives of the Foulkes and Astbury families) were especially prominent and influential in the course of the four decades in question. Of further significance in this period was the impact of Fryston's 'Bevin Boys', professional footballers such as Len Shackleton and Johnny Downie who opted to work down the pit in preference to joining the armed services.

In chapters 5 to 8 inclusive, our attention shifts onto the seasons spanning 1946 to 1962 in which Fryston experienced a comparatively barren period and failed to progress beyond the preliminary rounds of the county trophy. The primary purpose of these chapters is to trace the evolution of the team which eventually graced the 1963 final against Thackley. Chapters 6 and 7 focus on the exploits of one Fryston player in particular – the club's record goal-scoring phenomenon, Freddie Howard, who was to play a significant role in that final.

Chapters 9, 10 and 11 outline the build-up to the Fryston-Thackley encounter in the context of Fryston's attempt to bring off a league and cup 'double', characterise the players representing the two teams and relate the main events of the final itself. Chapter 12 constitutes a briefer, though similarly structured narrative, only this time in relation to the 'repeat contest' of the following year. The penultimate chapter comprises a summary of Fryston's progress in the WRCC Cup in the subsequent 30 years.

The final chapter not only reiterates the significance of Fryston's footballing accomplishments, but also reflects on 'what has become' of the players who represented them in that final of a full half-century ago. It is in this last regard that the underlying meaning of the enigmatic reference to 'ashes' in the title *Coal, Goals and Ashes* will finally be disclosed. To prematurely explain such meaning risks spoiling an inherently romantic aspect of the story of eleven men who arguably comprised 'Castleford's best ever football team'.

Chapter 1
Strikers and Substitutes

Previous page: Fryston and Wheldale strikers at the forefront of a rally involving 95 branches of the Yorkshire Mining Association, held in Castleford in June 1903. The strike lasted from October 1902 to early 1904 and resulted in scores of miners and their families being evicted from colliery-owned properties.

In Keeping with Tradition

The triumphant yells of eleven players, a handful of officials and 30 hardy spectators rang out as one in the cold, mid-morning air in Ferry Fryston, Castleford, on Sunday 4 November 2012. The goal they were collectively celebrating was the third – and arguably the pick – of five scored by James Lister in Fryston AFC's 6-0 third-round West Riding County FA Sunday Challenge Cup win at home to Queensbury of the Bradford Sunday Alliance League.

The scorer's surname was one already immortalised in the annals of Fryston's footballing history. Ronnie 'Chunner' Lister had been a stalwart centre-half for Fryston Colliery Welfare in the late 1940s and 1950s, and was coach of the colliery team that progressed to the final of the WRCC Cup in 1963. Fryston's current Lister was unrelated to his celebrated namesake, and it is probable that he had never even heard of Chunner, let alone the cup final with which he will forever be associated. By contrast, older spectators may have knowingly reflected how the young man's hat-trick goal (described as follows by a local news reporter) was strongly reminiscent of a key moment that figured in the final of almost half-a-century earlier:

> More fantastic play followed, this time from [Tom] Bryan, which saw him feed Lister on the right of the 19-yard box. The striker moved forward and shaped to square the ball across the area, but instead of passing, he smashed a shot past the 'keeper, beating him at his near post.[1]

Since recently reforming in 2008, Fryston AFC had won promotion from the First Division of the Castleford and District FA Sunday League, and been runners-up in the league's Premier Division in 2011-12. The club's inaugural appearance in the 2012-13 Sunday County Challenge Cup was indicative of the strength of its ambition, and of its determination to reassert its ancestral roots. For most of its history –

starting from its inception in 1910 and ending in its temporary demise in 1993 – the club was known as 'Fryston Colliery' or 'Fryston Colliery Welfare', in recognition of its attachment to the local mine. Indeed, Fryston AFC's home ground on Askham Road forms part of Fryston Miners' Welfare, while their nickname, 'The Colliers', alludes to a mining heritage that is still physically apparent in what little remains of the village of Fryston and its former pit environs.

Less than one mile away from where the match was taking place, the congregation of the Holy Cross Church, Airedale, was undoubtedly preoccupied with a different form of resurrection. This majestic place of worship backs on to the recently expanded Airedale Library and overlooks the bus terminus and row of local shops comprising what is known as 'the Square', or more colloquially 'the Magnet', in honour of the former public house of that name, now converted into a supermarket.

Since 1932, the 'Holy Cross' has bisected the mile-long Fryston Road that forms the backbone of the Airedale council-house estate. The top half of the road extends to the Airedale Hotel, which sits at a road junction going left to Townville and Pontefract, or right towards Glass Houghton and Castleford town centre. Its lower half descends down a steep hill to where a similar road junction, once occupied by the corresponding Fryston Hotel, goes left along Wheldon Road (past the Castleford Tigers Rugby League ground) into the town centre, or right into what remains of Fryston village.

Fryston: 'A Mining Shangri-la'

This small, isolated West Yorkshire ex-mining community is accessible by no other means than a narrow railway bridge. While new visitors to Fryston might be forgiven for deducing from its wide-open spaces and few remaining terraces of housing that the village constitutes a pale shadow of its former self, it would be all too easy to underestimate the extent of recent attempts, led by the charitable Castleford Heritage Trust, to regenerate the village and revitalise its cultural traditions.

Such attempts are epitomised by the specially commissioned wall sculpture ('Fryston above and below ground') adorning one of the outer sides of the bridge leading in and out of the village. The sculpture, which was produced by the former Fryston miner, Harry Malkin, is modelled on two well-known pictures by the celebrated Fryston-born amateur photographer, Jack Hulme.[2] Neatly standing opposite is a cluster of recently renovated terraced housing, comprising South View and William Street. Slightly further into the village there lies an expansive children's play area, set in a stepped amphitheatre. Conspicuous within this area is a piece of cairn sculpture resembling a crooked finger pointing skyward. Both this and the amphitheatre itself are the work of the Brooklyn-born sculptress, Martha Schwartz.[3] Only two other streets remain intact: North Street and the more elevated Brook Street to its rear, from which it is possible to look across the River Aire to the nearby former mining village of Fairburn.

Public transport entering the village is obliged to make a full rotation round the 'Bullring', a circular, fenced-off area containing a street light, which was built to commemorate the opening of the colliery's pit-head baths in 1932. This modest but iconic feature recalls a particular village heyday when the four streets just mentioned, in addition to rows of terraces on Smith Street, School Street, Hope Street and Wheldon Road, and the back-to-back houses on Castle Street, Oxford Street and Wellington Street, accommodated a thriving population of between 1,500 and 2,000 people, while the local colliery employed as many as 1,300 men. The fact that it was such a cut-off, tightly-knit and essentially self-sustaining community gave Fryston an almost mythical reputation, which prompted Frank Metcalfe of the *Yorkshire Evening Post* to call it 'a mining Shangri-la':

A self-contained community, it had a pub, the Milnes Arms, butcher's shop, general store, post office, drapers, fruit and vegetables, fish and chips. Above three of the shops on Wheldon Road was the 'Civic Hall,' where the old men had a reading and games room, where various committees met to run all the village events. There were flower and vegetable shows, whippet and pigeon racing. There was a well-filled school, a well-filled chapel. If you were born there the same two ladies who laid out the village dead were at the bedside as midwives… For the people of Fryston, virtually their whole world revolved within the village boundaries, many of them rarely crossing the bridge to visit Castleford. There was really no need to leave it. It had everything. It had real life.[4]

Social and Geographical Origins

The seminal Fryston Coal Company was formed in the early 1870s with the intention of exploiting the rich strata underlying the Fryston Hall Estate, which then belonged to the famous politician and literary figure, Richard Monckton Milnes, the first Lord Houghton.[5] The company rented 2,000 acres of land from Lord Houghton and it was his son, the future Marquess of Crewe, who 'turned the first sod' in anticipation of the sinking of the new Fryston Colliery. Crewe was quoted as saying 'that he hoped the undertaking would tend to increase the activity and comfort the population in that neighbourhood, and improve the N.E. portion of the West Riding... He sincerely hoped that the proprietors of that colliery would show the surrounding collieries an example of how to work amicably with their men.'[6]

Such hopes were not subsequently realised, an outcome which had important implications for the emergence of local sport. Indeed, the conflictual relations between management and men that were such a feature of the pit's early existence are fundamental to explanations of the origins, both of the village population and a sporting culture which fuelled Fryston's development as one of the pioneering, and subsequently most renowned, colliery-based football teams in the whole of West Yorkshire.

In her splendid history of the Yorkshire miners, Baylies[7] explains how the majority of early West Riding mines were sunk in close proximity to existing villages, into which the miners and their families were assimilated. Failing that, entire streets were added to include rows of miners' cottages, as occurred shortly after the sinking of the West Riding Colliery at Altofts (near Normanton), the Sharlston Colliery (between Pontefract and Wakefield), and Denaby Main (between Doncaster and Rotherham). Baylies makes the additional point that, during the 'boom years' of the 1860s and 1870s, when pits were being established in more remote rural areas, it became necessary to recruit workers from further afield and accommodate them in relatively isolated mining communities. She makes the crucial observation that:

> The ultimate destination of miners coming to Yorkshire was often serendipitous, but, as with most patterns of migration, once some had initially ventured forth, others followed to a place where a friend or relative had settled and reported on favourably... In some instances the

concentration can be traced to a specific cause or event. Attempts were not infrequently made, for example, to break strikes by recruiting from outside the county on the assumption that distance would make for ignorance among potential recruits as to the sudden need for their labour and that the very trauma of a break once made might prevent what would otherwise have been a strong resistance to gain work through blacklegging. But there were also cases of a group of miners from a certain area being brought in to help open up a new mine.[8]

There is plentiful evidence to suggest that several of these motives may have been relevant to the workers and their families forming the early population of Fryston village.

In my book *One Road In, One Road Out: A People's History of Fryston*, I quote one Fryston woman who claimed to be the granddaughter of a Staffordshire man called Charles Poundsford, who came up from Kingswinford, Stourbridge, with his two brothers, to sink the original shaft at Fryston.[9] While some Fryston miners undoubtedly came from the Castleford area and other parts of Yorkshire, there is evidence to suggest that others arrived (whether intentionally or unwittingly) as strike-breakers, or on the coat tails of such men, notably from Staffordshire, and in smaller numbers from other Midland counties like Derbyshire. Belcher[10] maintains that the 'moderate' sensibilities of Staffordshire miners is 'legendary – or notorious – depending on one's viewpoint. There are many documented examples of the strike-breaking activities of Staffordshire men and local unions were often poorly supported.' Numerous instances are reported by Machin[11] and Baylies[12] of Staffordshire miners being brought in to replace (and displace) striking miners. Often, as was certainly the case of pit villages like Altofts, Denaby and Sharlston, these 'black sheep' took over the homes of striking miners and their families who found themselves evicted from colliery-owned properties. This practice also appears to have been a strong feature of the early development of Fryston Colliery.

Baylies points out that, for the first three decades of its existence, Fryston was an extremely dispute-prone colliery, with major strikes and/ or 'lockouts' occurring, for example, in 1884, 1885, 1896, and in two especially prolonged cases between 1897 and 1899, and 1902 to 1904.[13] As a rule, these disputes stemmed from grievances relating to workforce perceptions that enforced changes in wages or working conditions were disadvantageous in comparison to those that already existed, or that were known to be enjoyed by employees at neighbouring pits. They invariably involved the coercive use by management of such tactics as lockouts, evictions and the introduction of strike-breakers.

One early major example of this relates to a strike caused by the removal of a check-weighman – a trade union official whose primary function was to ensure on behalf of miners that coal coming out of the pit was fairly weighed and that no tubs were unnecessarily confiscated on the grounds that they contained unacceptable quantities of 'muck'.[14] On 26 September 1885, the *Leeds Mercury* reported from the trial at Sherburn Petty Sessions of the check-weighman concerned, a Mr William Askew, and a second miner, who were both charged with 'besetting' the house of a working Fryston miner with the intention of preventing him from working.

> The case for the prosecution was that the complainant was in the employ of the Fryston Colliery Company, and in consequence of the strike at their collieries had been into Staffordshire to employ hands to work the colliery. On the morning in question, at about four o'clock, the defendants went to Jones' house, and, knocking him up, asked where the Staffordshire men were, and made use of threats towards him, stating that they would not allow him or them to go to work. There were about 200 persons outside on the road at the time, and the three defendants were amongst those who went to the door of Jones' house and made use of the threats.[15]

The defendants were each fined £1 and required to pay costs but this was not the end of the matter.

Things came to a head on 17 January 1886, by which time substantial numbers of black sheep had been brought in from Staffordshire to replace striking miners, with the result that: 'A great deal of ill-feeling existed between the new and the old hands and many summonses for assault had been issued.'[16] Most of the strike-breakers were resident in Newton, while most of the old hands lived three miles away in Brotherton. Having grown tired of being on the receiving end of such threats, a 40- to 50-strong delegation of former Staffordshire miners now working at Fryston Colliery marched with sticks and staves in their hands into Brotherton. There, they were confronted by some 200 strikers who bombarded them with stones before chasing them off into Fairburn. It was at this point that two of the working miners drew revolvers and fired them into the crowd, hitting at least one striker and police officer in the process. Each of these 'gunmen' was subsequently imprisoned and the strike was settled one month later to the apparent satisfaction of both sides.[17]

The eighteen-month-long strike which started in the summer of 1897 concerned the introduction by the employer of safety lamps, which the men objected to on the grounds that they hampered the winning of coal and detracted from attempts to examine roofs with the requisite degree of thoroughness. Compensatory 'lamp money' allowance was conceded by many local employers, but not at Fryston, where the Yorkshire Miners' Association (YMA) branches unsuccessfully requested a payment of one penny per ton in lamp money to bring them into line with those of neighbouring pits. In mid-July 1897, 950 workers came out on a strike which went unresolved until early 1899.

A programme of evictions was put into operation by management. By March 1898, the *Yorkshire Evening Post* was talking of Fryston having seemingly been deserted: 'At no time does it boast of more than perhaps a thousand inhabitants, but now that over one hundred houses are shut up, there is a graveyard quiet about it.'[18] Due to their inability to pay rent, many employees had been served notices to quit and gone to live on Wheldale Lane. Some strikers had taken advantage of the healthy economic climate by taking on jobs at neighbouring collieries, like Wheldale. By December 1898, approximately 150 miners were working at the Fryston coal face: 'But rather than form a break in the ranks of those still out, this had been achieved by recruitment from other counties, which the YMA proved unable to stem.'[19] The *Yorkshire Herald* reported on 9 February 1899 that the dispute had been settled the day before, with 'the miners having been met half-way by the masters'. However, of the 800 miners formerly employed by the colliery, 'only three hundred now remain in the district'.[20]

An even more protracted example occurred in 1902, when Fryston miners sympathetically came out on strike in support of their colleagues at the neighbouring Wheldale Colliery, where a considerable thinning of coal seams and corresponding thickening of dirt meant that workers were having to toil much harder for diminishing returns. However, the owners' section of the West Yorkshire joint committee maintained that Wheldale miners were not making poor enough earnings relative to the district average to warrant an adjustment in rates of pay. In the absence of any compromise, the strike began on 16 October 1902 and lasted until early 1904, and once again entailed the use of evictions and strike-breakers by management. The full extent of the strategic advantage enjoyed by the colliery owners was set out in an *Express* article for 15 June 1903, which emphasised that:

> The Colliery Company are the owners of practically the whole village of Fryston with the exception of the public buildings – The Board Schools and the Wesleyan Chapel – and a few houses occupied by servants of the North Eastern Railway Company, the total number of the Colliery Company's cottages being over 150. For some time 50 of these have been standing empty, the tenants having gradually left the village, as the breadwinners have found work elsewhere. About another 50 are in the occupation of deputies and topmen who have continued at work at the colliery. The remainder are tenanted by miners who are out on strike. The Company are also owners of 24 houses in the village of Fairburn on the other side of the river, but half of these are in the occupation of miners of neighbouring collieries and others, and the remaining twelve are Fryston miners on strike. Nearly 50 houses in Wheldale Road also belong to the Company.

The article revealed that between 50 and 60 'notices to quit' had already been served on striking miners occupying company cottages in Fryston and Fairburn, and that 'a few miners from outside districts have been engaged and are at work'.

A dramatic change of mood occurred in late September 1903 when, according to the *Sheffield Daily Telegraph*, a fracas involving stone-throwing and revolver shots occurred in Fryston. The *Telegraph* began by emphasising how, in the twelve months since the strike began, 'anything approaching serious trouble has been averted until quite recently, when more new hands have been imported into the district, and set to work at the old rates of pay'. The pit was by this time 'almost, if not quite, completely manned', and the trouble occurred when two striking miners who claimed to be taking a short cut through the village with the intention of reaching Fairburn were regarded with suspicion. On the return leg of their visit, the men 'found themselves the centre of a rapidly increasing throng, whose demeanour was far from friendly'. Before long, rival factions numbering several hundred strong were lining the banks of the river and, at one stage, stones were thrown and revolver shots fired before police arrived on bicycles to disperse everyone concerned.[21]

By late January 1904, all remaining strikers voted to present themselves for work. The situation at Fryston was that about two-thirds of the workforce necessary to produce full output had now returned to work. These were 'chiefly new hands', but also included a fair proportion of existing employees.[22] The strike having crumbled, the YMA 'was reduced to requesting the joint committee that "old hands" should be set on before "strangers"'. However, owners' representatives replied that they 'had given an undertaking that the company's hands should not be tied'.[23]

There is plentiful anecdotal evidence to suggest that there was an influx into Fryston of Staffordshire miners and their families from places like Pelsall and Fenton around 1903. Added to this was a sprinkling of families arriving from neighbouring counties like Derbyshire. In *One Road In, One Road Out* I quote an 'ex-Fryston woman' who was brought up to Fryston from Staffordshire as a three-year-old in 1903. Her father had lodged with a local Fryston family for four months before sending back for her mother and herself.[24] An 'ex-Fryston man' (actually Jack Hulme) likewise reveals how his parents moved up from Fenton in 1903, and immediately settled into a ready-furnished back-to-back house. One local woman mentions on her family history website how her father's family first settled in Fryston in 1903, having arrived from Beighton near Chesterfield, North Derbyshire. They then lodged for a while at nearby Wheldale Farm, before taking up residence in a village consisting of rows of very basic houses, which lacked such facilities as hot water. Revealingly, she recollects how 'Only colliery employees were allowed to live in the houses. Leave the pit, leave the house. Get behind with the rent, be evicted. Those who were evicted would move into huts on Wheldale Road and manage as best as they could.'[25]

This migratory trend continued for several years afterwards. As one Fryston woman explained:

All my relatives worked down Fryston pit. My dad was an Irishman, but I think he came to Fryston from having previously settled in Castleford. My mother's side were all from Staffordshire. They came from somewhere near Pelsall. At one time, I should think there were more Staffordshire people in Fryston than anybody else. My mother was thirteen when she came. She's been dead twenty years and she died when she was 72. So, it would have been 1907 when she came to Fryston.[26]

Not surprisingly, the influx of migrants included several families whose current male relatives and their descendants would form the nucleus of the future Fryston football teams. This was undoubtedly true, for example, of the huge Astbury contingent, and their relatives, the Foulkes, who came up from Pelsall around 1905-06. As we shall see in later chapters, descendants of these families were to become some of the village's most influential players.

Spawning a New Football Culture

The Altofts FC website raises some very interesting speculation regarding the pivotal role of Staffordshire miners in the club's late-nineteenth and early-twentieth-century domination of the local game.[27] It refers to the fact that the early 1880s heralded a radical shift in the composition of the local population, tied in with the inward migration of miners who had settled down on the long 'Silkstone Row' of terraced houses that had been specially constructed to accommodate them. It was at this point that sport became a major pastime. However, 'Whilst Rugby was perhaps the main sport in the rest of the West Riding, Association Football dominated in the Altofts area. This maybe was due to the fact that much of the new workforce had come from Staffordshire, which was very much a footballing county.'[28] Altofts became one of the founder-members (in 1894) of the West Yorkshire League, which was soon to include: Bradford, Castleford Town, Ferrybridge, Hunslet, Normanton, Oulton (Leeds), Pontefract, Pontefract Barracks and Rothwell. It is a measure of their standing in the local game that, between 1902 and 1904, Altofts won the West Riding FA Cup in three successive seasons.

This line of explanation might help to explain the corresponding development of a strong football culture in Fryston. Official records are non-existent for this period and newspaper reports extremely hit and miss. Nevertheless, there is fleeting evidence of Fryston having played in the West Yorkshire Amateur League in the 1896-97 season, when they beat Altofts 3-2 at home, but lost the corresponding away fixture 6-0. More intriguingly still, Fryston went down 5-2 at Bradford in the third round of the West Riding FA Cup. A report of the first half of this contest in *Yorkshire Evening Post* shows Fryston to have been sporting a 2-1 half-time lead:

At Park Avenue, Bradford, this afternoon, before a good gate, after some fairly even play the Bradford men commenced to attack, and after a short spell of kicking, Thompson sent the ball through for them. Bradford still kept up the attack, and the visitors [were penned in their own half]. Finally, however, [Fryston] rushed the ball down the field, and Pearce shot a goal. Pearce added a second goal. Half-time score – Fryston 2 goals, Bradford 1 goal.[29]

Grillo[30] explains that Bradford were then beaten 2-1 by Hunslet (the forerunners of Leeds City/Leeds United), who went on to beat Halifax in the first-ever final of the competition at Valley Parade, Bradford. The only available details of the 1897-98 season reveal that Fryston were beaten by Ossett 3-2 in the first round of the West Riding FA Cup. At this point, the club temporarily folded (possibly, in consequence of the eighteen-month strike referred to above) before resurfacing in the 1901-02 season in the Leeds and District League under the name of Fryston Recreation. The club appears to have performed with great credit, since a league table appearing in the *Express* has them appearing fourth (behind Oulton, Altofts and Rothwell) in a league of nine teams, having won 8, drawn 4 and lost 1 of their 13 games.[31]

Grillo includes a priceless newspaper report of Fryston's West Riding FA Cup first-round tie against Airedale at Undercliffe on 1 February 1902, which resulted in a 2-2 draw:

Just at the commencement the home team had slightly the better of the argument, but Fryston played some good combination on the left and centre, and some very steady work by A. Stone and Parkinson at the back was too much for the opposing forwards, who were constantly being beaten by the pace at which the ball travelled. Ultimately the Fryston right-wing acquired possession, and the forward line, beating up skilfully against the wind, secured a corner, from which Ward scored.[32]

Boocock equalised for Airedale to make the half-time score 1-1. After the interval, 'Fryston at once developed a strong attack, during which Bouchier brought down an opponent foully, and a goal to the visitors followed from the penalty kick.' A breakaway move by Airedale, following strong Fryston pressure, resulted in Dennison being fouled in the area, and Boocock equalised once more from the ensuing spot kick. Though Fryston 'continued to have the better of the argument', the game ended in a draw. Wharton confirms that it was Airedale who progressed to the next round,[33] although there is no indication of the score in their replayed match with Fryston. It is possible, however, that the 1-0 defeat of Fryston by Airedale in the 'ordinary match' referred to by the *Express* on 15 February 1902 was the result of the replay in question.

A year later, Fryston Recreation started their league campaign in style, with early home victories over Pontefract, Beckett Clarence and Oulton. By late October, they topped the league, with six wins and one draw out of seven played, although Upper Armley CC in second could boast six straight wins. Indeed, while Fryston subsequently went on to lose a handful of games, Armley remained undefeated all season. Their 3-0 end-of-season home win over Fryston merely reinforced their superiority. There are no records of Fryston having played in that year's West Riding Cup, although they did reach the semi-final of the Leeds Workpeople's Hospital Cup, only to lose 2-1 to Beeston Hill Parish Church.

There are no indications either of Fryston Recreation (or any other Fryston team for that matter) having played in the 1903-04 season (once again, the occurrence of a prolonged strike may help to explain their absence). However, in 1904-05, 'Fryston United' appeared in the Castleford and District Association Football League, where their final record of played 20, won 6, lost 11 and drew 3 placed them second-bottom of a league won by Pontefract Garrison. Fryston fared no better in the following season's league competition, having won only three and drawn three of seventeen matches (one of which they lost 11-0 at Allerton) before they withdrew from the competition. Fryston made a fleeting return to the Castleford and District Association Football League in the 1908-09 season, briefly topping the table in early November, with a record of won five and lost two of their first seven matches. However, they eventually slipped down to fifth place (having had four points deducted for a 'breach of the rules') in a league dominated by Goole Town Reserves.

Nevertheless, there were signs of a distinctive footballing culture having been established which would begin to see fruition in the years leading up to World War I. One descendant of the Astbury and Foulkes families referred to earlier makes the point that:

> By the time of the 1911 Census, 13 more children had been born to the families. Fryston appears to have been a happy village and no doubt the Pelsall people injected a boost to the life of the village. I believe the locals

called the village Little Staffordshire. Fryston Colliery football teams were filled with Pelsall players including a number of the Astbury family and did very well against the local clubs.[34]

Perhaps the key to this statement lies in its reference to the '*colliery* football teams'. As we are about to discover, the first *pit-sponsored* football team bearing the name of 'Fryston Colliery' did not come into being until 1910-11. It is possible that the working conditions experienced by Fryston miners, combined with their relative isolation as a community, may have helped create a footballing culture in which values of toughness and togetherness were pervasive. As a future manager of Fryston pit, Jim Bullock OBE had started working there as a pony boy, just transferred from nearby Bowers Row. His new pit was three times as big again and employed 500 per cent more miners:

> It was certainly the hottest pit in Yorkshire and the wildest set of men and lads I had ever met. The atmosphere underground was stifling. When you went on some of the working faces it was like going inside a Lancashire boiler. Everyone underground worked practically naked. I had heard swearing before but had never heard swearing with such venom and accompanied by such foul oaths as I heard here. The conditions down the pit were inhuman and the men had made themselves fit their environment. I couldn't believe such conditions could exist.[35]

Baylies makes the related point that the 'migrant' mining communities of West Yorkshire were sometimes characterised by a 'frontier quality' and tendency to 'turn in on themselves' in such a way as to be deemed 'different' or 'inferior' by neighbouring communities.[36] Perhaps it was this kind of 'siege mentality' and inherent toughness that imbued the first ever Fryston Colliery football team with both the physical and mental capacity required to compete so tenaciously in the five-year period from 1910 to 1915 for the prestigious West Riding County FA Challenge Cup.

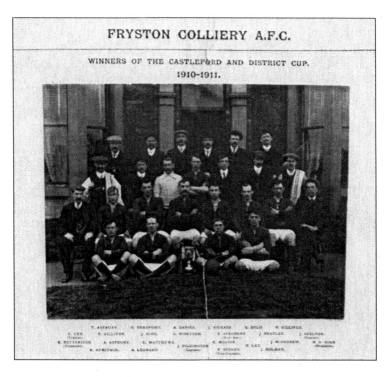

FRYSTON COLLIERY A.F.C.

WINNERS OF THE CASTLEFORD AND DISTRICT CUP.
1910-1911.

Chapter 2
Fryston's 'Colliery' Association

Previous page: The newly-formed Fryston Colliery AFC, winners of the Castleford and District FA Challenge Cup for 1910-11.

Well-Founded Optimism

'Football Club Formed' was the historic proclamation appearing in the 5 August 1910 edition of the *Express*. Earlier that week, a meeting had been held in the Fryston Reading Room to discuss the possibility of establishing a village football team. Attendance had been so overwhelming that it was necessary to re-convene in a larger recreation room, where 'much enthusiasm was manifested in the proposal, and it was unanimously resolved that a club be formed under the name of the Fryston Colliery Association FC and further that application be made to the secretary of the Castleford and District League for inclusion in that league'.[1] Affirming his commitment to establishing Association Football in the village, the Colliery Manager, Mr H.G. Soar, was elected as club president, Mr J. Clark as its vice-president, Mr R. Betteridge treasurer, and Mr T. Stephens secretary. The club also boasted an impressive list of 50 founding members.

A subsequent *Express* article emphasised that the new league could reasonably be regarded as one of the strongest in the entire West Riding:

> The pick of the Leeds and District Senior League have thrown in their lot, together with the best of last year's Castleford and District League teams, and he would be a bold man who would predict which of the clubs will play-off for the championship at the end of the season... The innovation of the top two clubs playing off for the championship at the end of the season will stimulate interest throughout, medals being offered to both teams and the Ambler shield for the victors.[2]

The article also confirmed that Fryston Colliery would be entering their first team into the Senior Division and their reserves into the corresponding Junior League. 'They will meet some good clubs in the league,' the *Express* remarked, 'but intend to make a bold bid for a high position in the table.' Few could have imagined at this early stage that Fryston would quickly develop into a major force in county amateur football and soon figure prominently in the final rounds of the WRCC Cup.

Fryston's confidence of faring well in the league was soon vindicated. Wearing what would soon become their traditional colours of blue and white vertical stripes, the colliery's first eleven emphatically won their first-ever match, scoring six without reply at neighbouring Brotherton. They then recorded six further wins (including another 6-0 thrashing of Brotherton and a 9-0 annihilation of Castleford Territorials), a 1-1 home draw against Cutsyke, and only one defeat (3-1 at Altofts Wesleyans) in their next eight matches to enter the New Year as joint league leaders on thirteen points with Cutsyke and unbeaten Allerton Bywater. In mid-January, they showed further evidence of their calibre by beating Allerton 3-1 in the quarter-final of the Castleford and District FA Challenge Cup (henceforth: Cas and District Cup).

In their first outing in the WRCC Cup as The Colliers, they played New Wortley Gasworks in the fourth round. The tie was played in front of a good-sized crowd in Armley, Leeds. The teams were well-matched and New Wortley had an early goal disallowed for offside. Afterwards, though:

> The Fryston forwards soon became prominent again, Rudge and Clayton in particular, and an attack by the visitors' left put Dicky Morris, Welsh international, in possession within range of goal, and he scored a beauty… Rudge was injured and he had to leave the field for the rest of the game. Still the visitors attacked, and Morris gave to [Frank] Stones at the right moment, the latter netting finely. The Wortley men attacked, but Matthews and Astbury troubled them considerably with their tackling. At half time Fryston led by 2 goals.[3]

In the second half, Fryston started to feel the disadvantage of being a man short and Wortley gradually reduced their two-goal arrears. The visitors withstood late Wortley pressure, during which they almost scored from a goalmouth melee, to hold out for a well-deserved two-all draw.

For the replay, Fryston's captain, J. Pilkington, was absent due to illness; but this made no discernible difference. In the early stages, Fryston's centre-half (McAndrew) and wing-half (Coates) 'fed [their] front ranks well, and Stones looked like a likely scorer on one or two occasions, one of his shots just missing the posts'.[4] With their wingers, Clayton and Holmes, playing especially well, Fryston established a 3-1 half-time lead, through goals by Stones, Clayton and an unnamed third player. The colliery eleven began the second half in equally determined manner, with Morris running through the entire opposition ranks only to be thwarted by a great save. Wortley pulled one back against the run of play but further goals by Clayton, the half-back, G. Whetton, and Morris soon put the result beyond doubt and the team ran out easy winners, 6-2.

'Wretched weather' was to blame for the disappointingly small crowd which turned out at the Mirfield United ground, near Dewsbury, for Fryston's difficult away fifth-round tie. The eventual scoreline of 4-1 in Mirfield's favour gave a false impression of the match. Fryston had enjoyed some two-thirds of the play in the first half, only to find themselves 2-0 down to goals conceded in the first minute and close on half time. Early in the second half, 'Fryston attacked in promising fashion and after tricky play by the forwards Morris scored [their] only goal.'[5] However, they were subsequently overpowered as Mirfield's strong team of semi-professionals added two more goals to its tally. Fryston's defeat was certainly no disgrace. Indeed, it was a measure of Mirfield's prowess that they went on to beat Morley 2-0 in the fourth replay of that season's semi-final, before running out 5-1 winners against Allerton Bywater. Three of the Mirfield players appearing in that final – Trenham at full-back, Cotterill (half-back) and Doggart (forward) – could claim Football League experience.

In the end-of-season run-in of the Castleford and District League for 1910-11, there were some crucial matches in early April, with the top four teams of the nine entered vying for the two play-off positions:

	P	W	L	D	Pts
Cutsyke United	12	7	1	4	18
Allerton Bywater	10	8	1	1	17
Fryston Colliery	10	6	2	2	14
Altofts Wesleyans	11	6	5	0	12

Fryston clearly needed a win at home to Allerton to have any chance of reducing the gap. Allerton had already beaten Fryston 2-0 in the corresponding away match four weeks earlier. Playing into a stiff breeze in the return fixture, Fryston found themselves two down at half time to goals scored in the twentieth and thirtieth minutes. The second half commenced with Fryston now playing with the wind behind them, and they gradually drew level with goals by Rudge and Edwards. Indeed, they would have run out winners had Whetton not missed a penalty. Fryston then lost 2-1 in an equally crucial game at Cutsyke, who proceeded to lose by the same score to Allerton in the final play-off.

The Colliers were therefore forced to look to their Cas and District Cup final against Altofts Wesleyans for their sole chance of winning a trophy in their debut season. Having beaten Allerton 2-0 in an earlier round, Fryston had initially been held to a 2-2 draw in their semi-final against Fairburn, but had easily won the replay by three goals to nil. The final was played on a sunny Good Friday afternoon before a large crowd on Castleford Town's Wheldon Road ground, where Fryston lacked centre-forward, Morris, through illness. After an even first half, Altofts had a goal disallowed for offside, but 'The Fryston forwards eventually wore their opponents down and Lee scored from a beautiful pass by Clayton. The Wesleyan goalie had touched the ball but he was unable to divert it from its course.'[6] Fryston played out time for a deserved 1-0 win to provide a fitting climax to what had been an immensely promising first season.

Meeting Old Foes

The following year, Fryston entered their first team in the extremely strong and prestigious Yorkshire Combination League, while their second team occupied their old place in the Castleford and District League. The Combination was made up of several reserve teams from professional clubs (Bradford City, Park Avenue, Leeds City, Halifax Town, York City), playing alongside some of the county's major semi-professional teams, like Goole Town, Morley and Mirfield United.

Fryston signed on two new players – Stead, the ex-Pontefract Garrison goalkeeper, and Laidlow, a promising outside-left from Aberford. Fryston teams of this era comprised a mixture of home-grown personnel (e.g. Whetton and Soar) alongside 'imported' players with Football League and, in some cases, international experience, e.g. Dicky Morris (Wales) and Mickey Leonard (Ireland). A typical line-up for the season would be: Stead, Armitage, Millership, Matthews, Andrews, Whetton, Soar, Leonard, Morris, Edwards and Laidlaw (Stones, Clayton and Gedney also figured prominently that year). Fryston started the season reasonably well, opening with a 3-1 home win against Leeds City, before suffering a narrow 3-2 defeat at Knaresborough. The club's humbling 8-1 setback at Valley Parade against Bradford City in the Bradford Charity Cup established something of a yo-yo sequence of results for the remainder of the season. Fryston could feel reasonably satisfied with a final league position of tenth out of fourteen (having played 26, won 9, drawn 1, lost 16 = 19 points) in a table headed by Bradford City, with Park Avenue second, Goole Town third, Scarborough fourth and Morley and Mirfield United fifth and sixth respectively.

Fryston fared better in local cup competitions, reaching the semi-final stage both of the Leeds Hospital Workpeople's Cup and Cas and District Cup, where they met their old rivals, Allerton Bywater, on both occasions. In the former match, played on a bitterly cold day at Wheldon Road, Gedney put in a sparkling display on the Fryston wing as The Colliers came back from being 3-2 down to win 6-3, thanks to a hat-trick by Morris and further goals from Stones (2) and Edwards. The *Express* report of the match emphasised that the 6-3 scoreline was flattering to Fryston, especially as Allerton had played the second half a man short due to injury. It further maintained, however, that, 'Considering the local rivalry between the two clubs, the game was played in a good spirit,' and that the game was well into its final stages before the referee saw fit to have words with any of the players.[7] There was to be no trophy though, as Fryston were comfortably beaten 3-0 by Clarence Ironworks in the final, played on Leeds City's Elland Road ground.

The next match in the Allerton–Fryston saga took place in mid-March, when another big crowd gathered at Wheldon Road in anticipation of a second keenly contested semi-final. Though lacking Gedney, Fryston took early lead through Edwards. However, with the slope acting to their advantage, Allerton quickly established superiority by building up a virtually unassailable 4-1 half-time lead. All that Fryston had to offer in return was a shot by their star full-back, Harry Millership, that went just wide of the post. A second-half penalty by Morris gave Fryston brief reason to hope, but this was soon extinguished by a fifth Allerton score, which left them the deserving 5-2 winners.

Fryston also enjoyed an extended run in the WRCC Cup, thrashing Rothwell White Rose 8-0 (with two goals each by Gedney, Morris, Edwards and Clayton), before winning a much tighter game at Calverley. With only fifteen minutes gone, Whitham opened the scoring for the home side with a penalty. However:

> After a clever individual effort, Leonard equalised. In the second half Fryston attacked early on, Soar coming near to scoring [and] Whitham missed a glorious opportunity, having no one to beat but the goalkeeper. However, before the close Fryston obtained the winning goal.[8]

At the fifth-round (quarter-final) stage, Fryston easily saw off the Huddersfield side, Marsden, by beating them 4-0 at home. The colliery team made the most of a helpful first-half breeze to take a 3-0 interval lead, with goals by Gedney, Coates and Soar. After half time, 'Marsden were playing much better than they did in the first portion of the game, and they made great efforts to score, but in Millership and Morris they found a couple of sterling defenders.'[9] Fryston added another goal close to the end of the match to enter the semi-final, where an old adversary, Mirfield United, lay in wait.

The semi-final took place on the Goole Town ground where, despite 'railway difficulties', both sides were well supported. A close game ensued in which Harry Millership was prominent in a generally outstanding defensive performance by Fryston:

> Mirfield had the advantage of a strong wind in the first half, and the Fryston defenders had a warm time of it, but Millership and Stead were equal to all demands. They kept out their opponents until just before the interval, when Moon scored a good goal from a centre by Doggart. This proved to be the only score of the match, and although beaten, Fryston played well, in that the backs were a better set than the Mirfield division. Morris and Soar were absent from the forward line owing to injuries received in practise. Millership was in great form.[10]

Once again, Fryston had the misfortune (and satisfaction) of knowing that they had been beaten by the eventual winners, albeit in a closer contest than that of the previous year, with Mirfield prevailing 2-0 over Halifax Town in the 1912 final.

Given the previous year's laudable performance as underdogs in an extremely competitive league, Fryston had good reason to feel more confident about their chances as they entered the 1912-13 league season, despite the loss of Millership to Blackpool in the close season. Such optimism soon appeared justified as Fryston inflicted two early-season drubbings away and home to York (4-0 and 6-0, respectively). However, by late November, defensive frailties were becoming increasingly evident as Fryston crashed to a 6-0 loss at Huddersfield Town, which underlined the extent to which they were feeling the recent loss of arguably their most valuable and reliable player:

> Since the departure [in July] of Millership to Blackpool the Colliery men have been unlucky with their backs, for Stones has since been injured, and capable substitutes for these strong defenders have not yet been secured, although it is understood that this difficulty will soon be overcome.[11]

The wheel appeared to have come off completely two weeks later when Fryston were destroyed 12-0 at Bradford Park Avenue. However, thanks to the scoring exploits of Dyer, who had a strike-rate of one goal per game, and another free-scoring player in Burt, Fryston entered the second half of the season in much better form. This was exemplified by the club's 2-0 home victory over Mirfield in late February. Here, Burt scored twice to inflict on the league leaders their only defeat so far that season. Fryston then went on to draw the return fixture 0-0. In their penultimate league game, Fryston went down 3-1 at Goole in a match attended by over 3,000 spectators. However, the 2-1 revenge victory they achieved one week later ensured Fryston fourth spot in the table, their impressive record of played 24, won 15, drawn 2, lost 7 = 32 points leaving them behind Huddersfield Town, Bradford Park Avenue and Mirfield United, but one place ahead of Goole.

The club's performance in the WRCC Cup competition was very disappointing by comparison, especially in light of the raised expectations resulting in the previous year's appearance in the semi-final. Having easily beaten Benson Lane 6-0 (with goals by Burt 2, Gedney, Burns, Stones and Dyer), Fryston's progress was derailed by Allerton Bywater, who narrowly beat them 2-1, with Stones scoring the solitary goal.

Fryston exacted revenge by beating Allerton 2-0 in the final of the

Cas and District Cup. Gedney and Burt were Fryston's scorers in a game watched by well over 2,000 people at Wheldon Road.

Getting Closer

Fryston had begun their reduced league programme of only eighteen games in the 1913-14 season by registering a 2-2 draw against their old rivals, Mirfield; but variable form and occasional ill-luck thereafter cost The Colliers the higher league position that their talents undoubtedly deserved. For example, they lost the return fixture against Mirfield after several of their players somehow missed the train. Fryston did, however, do the 'double' over the champions, Bradford Park Avenue, winning 2-0 home and away, in the course of finishing fourth out of ten in the table.

This season also saw Fryston make their inaugural appearence in the English Cup. They produced a commanding performance in the extra preliminary round to beat Brigg (Lincolnshire) 8-0 away, with goals by Burt (4), Biggins (2), Burnill and Gedney. Prior to their next tie, away to Cleethorpes, Fryston lost Burt, who had sustained a fractured collarbone in a 2-0 home league win against Heckmondwike. The visit to Lincolnshire was an uncomfortable experience, in which Fryston came from behind to draw 1-1 through a penalty by Baker:

> The game was by no means a pleasant one, there being too much roughness. Fryston claim that the home men were the aggressors, and the fact that both Burns and Gedney were so severely kicked about the legs that they are doubtful starters for the replay bears out this assertion to a certain extent.[12]

It came as some relief to Fryston when, on the morning of the replay, the Cleethorpes secretary informed them that his club were being forced to 'scratch' the tie 'owing to a strike at the town'. However, Fryston's English Cup adventure was ended when they travelled yet again into Lincolnshire to be defeated 2-0 by Grimsby Heythorpe Rovers in another ill-tempered match which showed The Colliers' readiness to 'mix it' with the opposition should circumstances dictate it necessary.

Given that Fryston had taken three points out of four in their two league matches against Heckmondwike, the 2-1 defeat they suffered in the final of that year's Leeds Hospital Workpeople's Cup was unexpected to say the least – especially as they had been so dominant in the earlier rounds (beating Great Woodhouse Britannia 7-1, for example, in the semi-final at Wheldon Road). Heckmondwike went into the second half of the final with a much-deserved 2-0 lead under their belts. Gedney pulled one back for The Colliers but Burt missed two easy chances as the Dewsbury team held on gamely to win.

Fryston's chances of going one step better than they had two years earlier by actually contesting the final of the WRCC Cup were considerably improved when they easily overcame their local rivals, Methley Perseverance, 5-1 in the second round, although the four-goal margin flattered them:

> The homesters were two goals to the good at the interval, both these having been obtained by Wall, their outside-right. The first was one of the best seen on the ground this season, the player taking the ball almost half the length of the field, and by a fine individual effort netting with a high shot, the ball passing in just under the crossbar. The second goal was gained from a scramble, a shot having previously hit the upright. Frank Stones found the objective with a good shot from just outside the penalty area on resuming, and J. Burt went through the opposition on receiving a good pass from the centre-half, Dyer, bringing the total up to five from a melee in the goalmouth. Methley died game, however, Abrams hitting the upright close on time, and scoring from the rebound.[13]

In the following round, Fryston renewed their rivalry with Allerton Bywater. The Colliers began the match with the benefits of a downward slope and following wind to add to home advantage; but by half time, they only had a goal by Frank Stones to show for all their pressure. Simpson's prominence in the Allerton attack was rewarded when he struck the equalising goal. However, it was Fryston who eventually prevailed in a close contest, with Stones contributing a second vital goal.

Fryston's 5-1 quarter-final victory at home to Brotherton Institute was not as one-sided as the score suggested. They only led by a solitary goal at the interval, and it was not until the final quarter-of-an-hour, following the sendings off of Price (Brotherton) and Gedney (Fryston) for fighting, that 'the home lot seemed to lose their heads, and Fryston netted four times in quick succession'.[14]

The semi-final was a different kettle of fish, with Fryston's five-goal feast against Norland (Halifax) this time being justly deserved:

Fryston were undoubtedly the better team, and from the start they attacked in a determined manner… Dyer was the first to find the net, and Burns was conspicuous with a brilliant individual effort, which he spoiled by shooting wide. He made amends before long by scoring a fine goal, and later he made the game practically safe for Fryston by getting their third goal.[15]

Two more goals after the interval meant that Fryston would now contest the final against Horsforth of Leeds, which took place on Good Friday on the Leeds City ground.

Play was good until a rain-storm swept the field, and the game afterwards deteriorated owing to the greasy state of the turf. Horsforth won by the only goal scored, this in the second half, but if Fryston had taken advantage of half the chances which presented themselves, they would doubtless have been the winners. Burns and Gedney failed in this particular [regard] early on, and Burt on one occasion all but succeeded. Dyer shot wide on resuming, and Fryston made the running for about 25 minutes, but Isles then [stole] between the Fryston backs and headed into the net.[16]

This once again left the Cas and District Cup as Fryston's only possible reward for yet another exhilarating season. Fryston beat Glass Houghton Colliery by the reasonably comfortable score of 3-1 in the semi-final. Stones gave them an early lead but Glass Houghton deservedly equalised shortly after. Burt scored Fryston's second just before the interval, and as The Colliers gradually asserted their superiority, he also added the third with a 'well-placed header'. The final itself was played before a big crowd at Wheldon Road, with Goole fielding two members of their Midland League side. It was Goole who coped better with the strong wind, and they dominated the first half without actually scoring. The pressure eventually told. They had already struck the angle of the upright and crossbar when:

Burnill made a clever clearance from the feet of the inside-forwards, and then Butler seized an opportunity to break away, and racing down the touch-line side he put across a splendid centre, from which Thompson netted, sending the ball quite out of Stead's reach. After this there seemed to be every prospect of Goole taking the cup away with them, but they badly bungled a number of excellent chances to make their position secure, and a minute from time, in a strong forward rush, Burt delighted his team and supporters by equalising in a scene of wild excitement.[17]

Fryston begun the replay at Wheldon Road in fine fashion and it was they, through Plant, who opened the scoring on the half-hour mark. Having missed an early-second-half penalty, Goole equalised shortly after from a direct free kick; then a subsequent slip-up in the Fryston defence let in the opposition for what proved to be the decisive goal. The cup and medals were presented by the Chair of the Castleford Executive, who overlooked the 'little display of temper' he had witnessed to congratulate both teams on the sportsmanlike manner in which they had contested the final.

Crime and Punishment

In the 1914-15 season, Fryston were entered in the Leeds Senior League, emphasising the more parochial nature of the game following the outbreak of World War I. The club sported three new players in Stockdale of Brotherton, Hebden (ex-Lock Lane Woodville) and Lockyer (ex-Goole Town) and they got off to a good start with Dyer scoring the winner in a 1-0 victory at Calverley. Fryston's subsequent invincibility in the league was exemplified by their 8-1 win against Mirfield United in which Burt scored the first four of The Colliers goals.

The club appeared to be enjoying equally smooth progress in the English Cup competition, having beaten both Rothwell Parish Church and Calverley at home (1-0 and 2-0), before facing South Kirkby away. It was at this point that they came a cropper, losing by the odd goal in three — a result that hardly seemed credible on the basis of the *Express* headline for the match: 'South Kirkby again victorious: Fryston Colliery Outclassed'.

Saturday's game was visibly enjoyed by the large crowd which assembled, and was admitted by one and all to be one of the finest there has ever been witnessed on the South Kirkby ground. Although beaten, Fryston are not to be despised or spoken of lightly. They had not suffered a defeat this season, and came to South Kirkby accompanied by a large and enthusiastic band of supporters. They were a splendid team, being far bigger and heavier than South Kirkby, and at the beginning of both halves they completely outmatched the home team for the first quarter of an hour before Kirkby began to make themselves felt.[18]

Despite the efforts of Frost, a centre-half who 'fed his forwards in a very praiseworthy manner, and worked like a Trojan', Kirkby went ahead in the sixteenth minute and took complete control thereafter. After briefly getting back in the game at the start of the second half, Fryston conceded a second, decisive goal. Their own entry on the score-sheet – a scrappy attempt resulting from a goalmouth melee – was nothing more than a consolation goal.

Fryston fared much better in other cup competitions. They easily defeated Woodhouse Britannia 3-0 in the semi-final of the Leeds Hospital Workpeople's Cup to set up a repeat of the 1913 final, which they had lost to Clarence Ironworks. The final was played at Methley. The colliery men took a first-half lead due to an opposition own-goal, only for the Ironworkers to overturn this advantage by striking back twice. It was only two late second-half goals by Burt and a last-minute clincher by Brandon which secured a 4-2 victory and the cup for Fryston.

In the WRCC Cup, Fryston had easily disposed of Preston White Rose, 4-0 at home, when they were informed that they were to be given a walk-over in the next round because their scheduled opponents, New Wortley, could not raise a team. Fryston put up a highly impressive display in the semi-final against Huddersfield Town at Goole, when Dyer was sent off early in the game for kicking an opponent. The Colliers withstood the disadvantage of a strong first-half wind and intense Huddersfield pressure to reach the interval with a clean sheet. In a second half characterised by growing roughness on both sides, 'Fryston were kept pretty much in their own quarters, but in one incursion into their opponents' goal area a player was fouled and a penalty was given, Gedney giving his side the victory with a capital shot.'[19] This goal earned The Colliers the right to play their old adversaries, Goole Town, who had beaten Castleford Town 2-1 in the corresponding semi-final.

It was Fryston and Goole who contested the final of the Cas and District Cup for 1914-15. Fryston had beaten Lock Lane Woodville 3-1 in the semi-final and it was a large Easter holiday crowd that gathered at Wheldon Road to witness the visit of Goole. Fryston could count themselves fortunate that the Midland League team had another game against Castleford Town and therefore only fielded two of their first-team regulars, the remainder being amateurs. An exciting first half resulted in a stalemate between the two sides. On the resumption, it was Fryston who made most of the running and they were unlucky not to score from several good chances. The Goole goalkeeper, Garner, had hitherto coped well with all Fryston efforts on goal:

> The custodian also saved from Gedney, but the rules were infringed in the subsequent melee, and Dyer took the penalty kick and netted with a grand shot. Wilson had a golden opportunity to equalise a little later, a miskick by one of the Fryston backs putting him in possession right in front of the goal, but he sent woefully wide. Fryston then again took up the running, and another goal was quickly forthcoming, Brandon giving Garner absolutely no chance to save. Goole played up gamely, but were unable to penetrate the stubborn defence of the Fryston back division. Close on time a shot from Burt was kept out, and the game ended in a highly creditable win for Fryston by 2 goals to nil.[20]

This raised the intriguing possibility that Fryston might now achieve a momentous cup 'double' at the expense of their more celebrated Midland League opponents. First, they had to face Rothwell Parish Church in the semi-final of the Lubelski Shield. This match also took place at Wheldon Road before yet another large crowd. Following a goalless, evenly-matched first half, it was Fryston who took an early second-half lead through Dyer. This was cancelled out, however, with only fifteen minutes remaining, and the match remained all-square to the end of normal time. It was not until the second period of extra time that Fryston established a winning 2-1 lead with a 'beautiful header by Burt'[21] from a perfect corner by Bradley.

Fryston then faced up to what the *Express* referred to as the 'severest trial in the cup finals in which they have recently been engaged'[22] in confronting Goole Town's full Midland League eleven for the WRCC Cup final at Wheldon Road on Wednesday evening. The colliery men took to the field without their skipper, Gedney, who was injured in the Rothwell match. Their side did include Soar and Frost, however, who had been granted leave from their military duties at Doncaster, and Whetton who had been exempted from similar duties at York.

It was Goole who started the stronger. They subjected Fryston to constant early pressure and were awarded two penalty kicks, the first of which was saved by Grace in the Fryston goal, and the second placed just wide of the post by the normally reliable Spavin. According to the *Express*, 'The Goole forwards were playing pretty football but

Fryston's bustling style frequently upset their calculations, though generally speaking Goole were having the better of matters.'[23] Fryston were handicapped by the loss of Frost, who was carried off injured just before half time. He re-entered the fray early in the second half, only to have to retire again through injury. Ironically, it was his foul on a Goole player which resulted in a third penalty of the match. Once again, Grace brought off a fine save. Generally speaking he 'was always there when he was needed',[24] but even he was powerless to prevent Goole's overwhelming superiority from ultimately telling in a game of increasing brutality:

Following an exciting melee in the Goole goal-mouth, the Goole forwards burst away, and Ford was roughly stopped by Hebden in the penalty area. The Goole player was badly injured, and had to be carried off, and Fryston being penalised, Maynell scored with a shot which gave Grace no chance. Hebden's action therefore cost his side dearly. Unnecessary roughness was introduced on the re-start, and this resulted in T. Garbutt receiving marching orders. Play was contested for some time in mid-field. The Fryston goal had a narrow escape soon afterwards, Spavin shooting and striking the crossbar when he might easily have dribbled the ball into the net. In the closing stages Morley put Goole further ahead with a stinging drive from close quarters, and gave his side the victory by two clear goals.[25]

This was not the end of the matter, though. In the last week of April, the West Riding Football Association Executive committee met in Leeds to discuss the alleged 'rough play and ungentlemanly conduct'[26] by Fryston players and their club secretary during and after their county cup final. The Executive considered the written reports and testimonies of the referee (Mr Melville), a representative of the Goole Town club (a Mr Randall), and the Fryston secretary, Mr J. Bradley.

The Goole representative complained of the extent of the injuries inflicted on his players, several of whom were reputed to be 'a mass of bruises'.[27] He maintained that he had been too intimidated to complain directly after the match to the Fryston secretary for fear of receiving a 'thick eye', and insisted that, should Fryston be allowed to enter the competition again, his team would deliberately lose their first tie, rather than expose their players to the risk of further injury.

Mr Melville elaborated on the contents of his written report by maintaining that Fryston had started to 'rough it' right from the outset of the match:

He asked them to play the game, but several of the Fryston players, notably Burt and Dyer, used bad language, though not directly at the referee. The right half-back for Fryston shouted 'I am out for blood. Some --------- is going to get killed'. When at half time he appealed again to the Fryston players to act like sportsmen they merely laughed at him. He decided that the Fryston team did not intend to play football. Dyer said to him, 'You are like all the rest. You think Fryston is the dirtiest team in the country.' Curiously, the outside-right, Soar, whom he sent off the field for deliberately kicking a Goole player, was, along with Brandon, the Fryston outside-left, the most gentlemanly player on his side. Brandon once cried to his club-mates, 'For God's sake lads let's play the game like sportsmen.' He blamed Burt and Dyer for the trouble.[28]

Mr Melville alleged that once he had boarded the charabanc after the match, he was accosted by Mr Bradley and accused both of having received a bribe and made money by betting on the outcome.

Little credence was given to Bradley's protestation that Fryston had been guilty of nothing more than playing 'good Cup-tie football'.[29] Indeed, the Chair of the committee described the game as 'the most disgraceful exhibition of football – if it could be called football – that he had ever seen or heard of'.[30] The Executive's final decision reflected such displeasure:

The Fryston Club and Mr J. Bradley, the secretary, with the exception of Soar and Brandon, to be suspended during the whole of the next playing season. Soar to be suspended for the remainder of the present season and for a month from the opening of the next playing season. Dyer and Burt to be suspended sine die. The Fryston Club to pay the expenses of that meeting and to have their share of the gate receipts for the final cup tie confiscated.[31]

With an absence of subsequent reports of the Lubelski Shield final perhaps indicating that Fryston had also been banned from competing any further in that competition, the season – and, indeed, the entire first era in the history of Fryston Colliery – had ended ignominiously. There could be no denying, however, that the Fryston team (albeit one containing its fair share of imported playing talent) had quickly developed a formidable reputation among the county's footballing elite, and already established a proud tradition for subsequent generations to try and emulate. Twice in the past two years they had come within touching distance of winning the hallowed WRCC trophy, only to now face expulsion from their league and find themselves branded for the 'dirty' nature of their play. Another ten years would pass before they would realise another opportunity to soothe the disappointment and atone for the disgrace they undoubtedly would have felt as their progress was halted both by suspension and the escalation of World War I.

Chapter 3
Between the Wars

Previous page: The Fryston-born 'wizard of the dribble', Jabie Foulkes, who starred on the right wing for Stockport County, Bradford Park Avenue, Halifax Town and Crewe Alexandra before returning to play in the West Yorkshire League for his home team.

Introducing Dick Foulkes

With the resumption of organised amateur league football after the war, for the 1919-20 season Fryston entered their first eleven in the Senior section of the Castleford and District League, and their second team in the Juniors. The club switched from playing their matches at the bottom of Fryston Road to the 'Hoss [Horse] Field', where resting pit ponies were tethered, closer to the actual colliery. The senior team enjoyed only moderate success as they tried to re-establish themselves after the trauma of 1915, finishing mid-table in a league that included such teams as Knottingley Rovers, Brotherton, Potteries United and Allerton Bywater, who finished runners-up behind Goole Shipyards. It was their junior side, consisting entirely of Fryston miners, which led the way.

The undoubted star of the juniors was the talented and tough-tackling Dick Foulkes, who played at wing- or centre-half, but was equally adept at inside- or centre-forward. Foulkes had moved to Fryston as a three-year-old in 1906, with his parents and one-year-old brother, Charlie, from Pelsall, as part of the Staffordshire influx into the village. Dick attended the Fryston village school, where J.S. Rickaby was headmaster and Tom Stephens sports master, before joining the pit aged thirteen. By the age of sixteen, he was a virtual regular in the senior side but frequently turned out in cup competitions for the juniors.

In the Castleford and District FA Junior Challenge Cup, Fryston easily disposed of all opposition on the way to a 7-0 semi-final win over High Ackworth at Wheldon Road (a ground which would eventually become occupied by Castleford RLFC when Castleford Town slipped out of the Midland League in 1927). The final, against Pontefract YMI, went to two replays. The first game, played at Wheldon Road on Good Friday morning, ended 1-1 after extra time, with Tommy Owens equalising for Fryston. According to Foulkes, Owens was one of three 'wrong 'uns' (players not formally registered with Fryston) who played on the day. The match was replayed at the same ground on Saturday afternoon, 17 April, in the presence of about 2,000 spectators, only to result in another draw. The second replay also took place at Wheldon Road, in the first week of May, before another crowd of over 1,000 people. This time, the tie was decided in Fryston's favour by a Billy Bilton goal in the last few minutes of an hour-long period of extra time.

During the close season, Mr E. Purcell took over from the long-serving Mr Soar as the pit manager. It was soon clear that the new 'boss' would continue to support and encourage the colliery football team with all the enthusiasm of his predecessor. Almost in an instant, the club became one of the founder-members of the Yorkshire League. According to the *Express*:

> The committee of the Fryston Colliery Club have felt that they would be justified in running a team in a higher class of football than was the case last winter, and accordingly they have joined the new Yorkshire League, and have an attractive programme, the league comprising such clubs as Wombwell, Dewsbury and Savile, Bradford Park Avenue, Harrogate, Selby Town, Wakefield City, and Yorkshire Amateurs, and the club will also take part in the West Riding and the local cup competitions. A team has been got together which would be capable of holding its own against all-comers.[1]

The *Express* revealed that, in addition to re-engaging several established players, the club had already signed on a number of newcomers, such as: J.T. Peplow, a full-back or outside-right, who had played for Bristol Rovers and Burslem Port Vale before the war; W. Garbett, of Castleford Town Reserves; P. Stockdale, L. Bradley and J. Hunter, all of Brotherton; E. Armitage (Ferrybridge United); F.W. Bilton (Glass Houghton Juniors); the former Fryston and Castleford Town wing-half, F.W. Stones, who would be taking over as captain; and the Fryston-born Cyril Soar of Selby Town, who was the son of the former Colliery Manager.

Fryston made a promising start to the season by seeing off Dewsbury and Savile 2-1 at home, thanks to excellent defending by Peplow and Astbury, and two goals by Garbett. Indeed, 'the margin ought to have been more, but they had an element of ill-luck on two or three occasions after the ball had been nicely manoeuvred into position'.[2]

It was to prove a difficult campaign, however. For example, Fryston suffered heavy defeats, home and away, to Harrogate Town. At Fryston in November, they were beaten 4-0 by a Town side containing five ex-Castleford Town or other local players. This was followed by an 8-1 hammering at Harrogate in January, when ex-Fryston players, Dyer and Gedney, were among those who scored five second-half goals for the home side. Fryston fared little better against the eventual champions, Bradford Park Avenue Reserves, losing 3-0 away and 7-3 at home, in the course of finishing tenth out of thirteen in the league.

The club's most humiliating setback of the season came in the third round of the WRCC Cup, when Fryston visited the reigning champions, Altofts West Riding Colliery. In an early December fixture, played on 'a bleak, wind-swept playing field, more like a moorland bog after the rain than a decent, respectable football ground', Fryston proved no match for their lower-league opposition:

> From the very start Altofts controlled the game, and though at first materially helped by the gale, it was quite evident they were by far the smarter team of the two. Play was kept almost exclusively in the visitors' half, and we believe Sillito had to handle the ball about once each half! For the rest of the game he and Bastow – Altofts were playing the one back game – were practically 'passengers'! Altofts put in some strenuous passing, and indeed so tired out their opponents that before the game should properly have finished they 'threw up the sponge,' leaving Altofts victors by nine goals to nil... Altofts were far more sure-footed than their opponents, and in ploughing through the mud made rings round Fryston, whose players could not keep on their feet.[3]

Dick Foulkes had become established in the Fryston team by now as a hard, no-nonsense centre- or wing-half, but the next season he left Fryston Colliery for Frickley, shortly after he and other miners had returned to work following the thirteen-week strike of 1921. Foulkes had emerged from a wage-related argument with a check-weighman vowing never to work down Fryston pit again. Coincidentally, he had just received an offer to play for Frickley.

> Well, tha sees, I'd had a letter from Frickley Colliery, asking me to go there. They had a good team at Frickley, but they played in t'Sheff [Sheffield] Association. So that same Saturday, I went and asked for the secretary of the team. They called him Bert Holmes and he had the post office, and I asked him if they had anything doing. The right-half who played for them was

a Frystoner and had got his kneecap broken. He says, 'Tha'll get my place.'
When we were on t'road [to Frickley], our old fella says, 'I won't give thee a
fortnight before tha's back home,' but I was there two years. (Dick Foulkes)

Foulkes' absence from the team for the 1921-22 season did not
prove markedly detrimental. Despite losing eight and drawing one of
their first nine matches, Fryston finished a creditable eleventh out of
seventeen in the league. Fryston consolidated their lower-mid-table
standing in 1922-23 by rallying once again after another indifferent
start to the season. They had their best run in the WRCC Cup since
1914-15, beating Halton 4-1 away, and Rothwell after two replays,
before losing 3-1 at Apperley Bridge, who were eventually beaten 3-0
in the final by Castleford and Allerton United.

The 1922-23 season had seen Frickley Colliery enter the Yorkshire
League with considerable success. They beat Fryston home and away
and ultimately finished in third spot behind the Bradford Park Avenue
and Halifax Town reserves teams. For Frickley's away match at Fryston,
Dick Foulkes was instrumental in getting his brother, Charlie (by then,
a Frickley reserve team player), a one-off game for Fryston. Frickley's
subsequent decision to fine Charlie ten shillings led to Dick falling out
with the committee and asking to be transferred back to Fryston. Both
brothers duly arrived back in time for the start of the following season.

The Return of Harry Millership

The Fryston defence was bolstered in preparation for the 1923-24
campaign by the acquisition of the erstwhile Altofts stalwarts, Bastow
and Bagnall. Dick Foulkes' value to the team was underlined by the
part he played in Fryston's opening league match, an encouraging
3-0 home win against Harrogate Town in which he scored with a
header and went close on several other occasions. However, Fryston
were unable to sustain this bright start to the season and finished a
disappointing fifteenth out of eighteen. They were also emphatically
beaten 8-2 by the Leeds-Bradford team, Rawdon, in the WRCC Cup.

In the English Cup first qualifying round tie against their Midland
League neighbours, Castleford Town, they faced a celebrated ex-
Fryston player who was making a nostalgic return home. Having left
Fryston for Blackpool in July 1912, Harry Millership had gone on to

play 31 league matches for the 'Seasiders' before his professional career was interrupted by World War I.[4] During the war, he guested for Leeds City, making his debut against Huddersfield Town in December 1917. Millership's team-mates included the great Clem Stephenson – who went on to captain Town's triple championship-winning side of 1924, 1925 and 1926 and eventually become Huddersfield's manager – and the free-scoring Leeds legend, Tommy McLeod. These were relatively successful days for Leeds, who became 'unofficial Champions of England' when they beat Stoke in a two-legged, inter-divisional play-off final in May 1918. Millership's goal-line clearance during Leeds' first-leg victory at Elland Road proved vital as Stoke could only claw one goal back in the return leg.

With the post-war resumption of league matches, Millership signed for Leeds, but he had only made eight appearances when the club was suddenly expelled from the league, having been found guilty of making illicit payments to wartime players. In a subsequent auctioning off of all Leeds' players, Millership was purchased by Second-Division Rotherham County for the club record fee of £1,000 (with only McLeod attracting a higher bid of £1,500).

It was during his time at Millmoor that Millership was capped six times for Wales. During the 1919-20 season, he played alongside the legendary 'Welsh Wizard' of the wing, Billy Meredith, in 1-1 draws against Ireland and Scotland, and a famous 2-1 win against an English side led by Charles Buchan at Highbury which confirmed Wales as Home International Champions. Wales fell just short of repeating their success a season later when Millership was again an ever-present in their campaign: a 2-1 defeat at Aberdeen, a goalless draw against England at Ninian Park (Cardiff), and a 2-1 victory over Ireland at the Vetch Field (Swansea).

By the end of the 1921-22 season, Millership had played in 81 league matches for the Millers and netted seven goals. He then joined Second Division Barnsley in September 1922 but only made five league appearances before moving on to Castleford Town in July 1923, by which time he had achieved the ripe old age of 33.

The Fryston team ready to take on Millership and his colleagues in this historic encounter was: Reynolds, Bastow, Bagnall, Blackburn, Charlie Foulkes, Westwood, Barnard, Dick Foulkes, Connor, Robins and Gelder. Given that Castleford Town's ground was situated a mere half-a-mile along Wheldon Road, it would have been difficult to consider a bigger and more prestigious local football match for The Colliers. Indeed, Dick Foulkes well recalled how Fryston had been promised a £1 per man win-bonus prior to the game: 'I remember Ernie Bagnall saying as we went out on t'field, "We'll kill the buggers for a bloody pound!"' This probably helps to explain why, according to the *Express*, 'Fryston were out to win, and they played very vigorously, and the methods of some of their players provoked the ire of the Castleford spectators.' With the exceptions of Millership and the England amateur international left-half, Prentice, Castleford were notably 'ill at ease against their aggressive opponents'.[5]

It was Castleford Town who attacked from the outset, with Haythorne missing from close range with the best chance of the first half. During a rare Fryston foray, 'Millership showed true artistry in the manner in which he robbed Barnard, and with a good kick he made the Fryston half the venue once more.'[6] High drama soon followed. Not long into the second half, a Town forward was brought down inside the area by Bagnall. Up stepped Millership for the resulting penalty but 'to the great disappointment of the Castleford supporters he sent the ball too high, and it went out of the field'.[7] He 'kicked it down bloody Duke Street', was how Dick Foulkes later recalled the incident. Whatever the actual scale of the miss, there is no doubt that it 'was certainly a stroke of good fortune for Fryston, and they became very aggressive for a time, but they usually found the defence of Millership was too much for them'.[8]

Castleford's resistance did not last. According to the *Express*:

> The best moment of the match followed a few minutes later. Robins put across a clever centre, which Reynolds, the Fryston goalie, fisted away to Patchett. He in turn passed to Charlesworth, who with an overhead kick sent the ball just over the bar. Play then went to the other end, where Connor took the ball to the line. It came back to Foulkes, who headed into the net. It was an easy and unexpected goal.[9]

Hard though they tried, Town could not penetrate a packed Fryston defence, and The Colliers were victorious. During the week, however, Town lodged an objection which resulted in Fryston being disqualified for fielding an unregistered player. 'It was Joe Westwood,' Dick Foulkes later recalled. 'Old Mickey [Leonard] fielded him. There were three on 'em from Maltby came and played. I think that Mickey went and told [the Castleford Town Manager] that we'd played a wrong 'un and we got kicked out. And the queer part about it was that, in the next round, Cas Town played Frickley!'

After retiring from the game, Harry Millership became landlord of the Castle Hotel in Castleford, before returning to Blackpool, where he worked as an attendant at the Winter Gardens and in the construction industry, before his eventual death in 1959. Dick Foulkes stayed at Fryston until the end of the season, when both he and his brother Charlie joined Second Division Bradford City at Mickey Leonard's instigation. Dick played a mere three matches for City's reserve team before making his first-team debut against Port Vale.

The Final Reckoning

The 1924-25 season proved one of the most memorable, yet controversial, in Fryston's entire history. After an opening 2-0 league win, at home to Monckton Athletic, The Colliers pushed the strong Midland League side, Wombwell, all the way in the preliminary round of the English Cup, losing a close-run replay 3-2 after the tie had initially been drawn 2-2. Successive league defeats followed (2-1 at Frickley, and 3-1 at home to Leeds City) before Fryston triggered a good run of form by soundly beating Harrogate Town 4-0 at home.

An old feud was resurrected in the course of Fryston's controversial 2-1 victory in mid-December at Goole. Fryston had taken the lead just before half time but Goole Town equalised on 60 minutes from a penalty. It was Fryston who eventually triumphed when, several minutes later, Grace 'shot through a forest of legs into the net, Marshall [the Goole goalkeeper] being evidently unsighted'.[10] At full time, however, the home crowd invaded the pitch and Fryston players were manhandled by spectators as they left the field under police escort. A stone was subsequently thrown through the window of the Fryston team bus as it left the ground. The referee's report emphasised that he 'had to caution Bagnall, one of the Fryston players, for ungentlemanly conduct during the first half, and at the close of the match, a section of the crowd made a slight demonstration against Bagnall'. He insisted, though, that, 'The game itself was played in a good spirit, and not more than six or seven free kicks had to be given except for offside.' The Goole club secretary was adamant, however, that Fryston's generally rough play had served to incite the crowd:

> 'In the first five minutes,' wrote Mr. Stephenson, 'The Fryston left full-back was warned for a foul on the Goole centre-forward, and cautioned for a foul on the Goole outside-right. Play continued [in this style], the main offenders being the Fryston left full-back, and in lesser degree one or two other Fryston players. During the second half the rough play continued, and the Goole outside-right, Hill, was deliberately kicked off his feet and sustained slight concussion, which, after treatment on the field, necessitated his removal to hospital. The Goole Committee had difficulty at this moment in restraining the crowd, and when several Goole players were in turn injured, it was obvious that every effort would be necessary to prevent trouble after the match. It is not thought that any player was hurt, and certainly the referee was not injured, but the spectators were unanimous in their condemnation of the play seen and the general neglect of the referee to adopt strict [intervention].'[11]

Notwithstanding a pre-Christmas defeat, 2-0 at Altofts, Fryston saw 1924 out as league leaders, their twenty points from fifteen games being superior to Castleford and Allerton's nineteen points from thirteen, and Brodsworth Main's seventeen from twelve. The Colliers' championship credentials were reaffirmed by an early January victory 1-0 at home to Brodsworth. However, a subsequent away defeat, 1-0 against the same opposition, followed by another against Castleford and Allerton United (3-0) left them with considerable ground to make up going into the end of the season, when, ironically, it was a 1-0 home setback against Goole that brought their campaign to rest. Fryston's final record of played 30, won 17, lost 10, drew 3 = 37 points left them in fourth place, behind Brodsworth (46 pts), Selby (40pts) and Castleford and Allerton United (38pts).

Fryston had narrowly prevailed 1-0 in their Embleton Cup semi-final against Wakefield (thanks to a hotly-disputed penalty by Soar) and came up against Altofts in the final. It was the latter who took a shock, two-minute lead through Hopson in a game watched by over 3,000 people at Wheldon Road. At one stage, proceedings were delayed due to fighting that developed in the stand. Generally, though, 'The game was fought out in an excellent spirit; there was no occasion for any player to be cautioned, and the game was well worth watching throughout.'[12] Jones hit the bar for Fryston, and Hunter the side-netting; and ultimately Fryston paid the price for not making the best of their many chances and lost out 1–0.

In the WRCC Cup campaign, Fryston progressed into the quarter-finals by easily beating Calverley 3–0 away from home. The Colliers took full advantage in the first half of the wind and slope that were both in their favour to establish a 3–0 lead (through Robins and Neate with two) after Calverley had missed an early penalty. Afterwards, 'Fryston continued to be very energetic and only a fine display of goal-keeping by Priestley prevented a big score being put up.'[13]

In the quarter-finals, Fryston had the satisfaction of beating their bugbears, Goole Town, 3–0 at home, to remain the only Castleford team left in the competition. Goole were roared on by an impressive away support, but it was Fryston who dominated throughout, with their centre-half, Leslie, in especially commanding form:

> So far as the game itself went Fryston were the better team and thoroughly deserved to win. Leslie opened the scoring in the first half after clever individual work. He trapped the ball when it was on the bounce and taking good aim he gave the Goole custodian practically no chance. This success encouraged the homesters, and they put themselves in a very strong position when Robins turned a centre from the wing into the net. Goole made occasional raids, but their attacks were broken up without much difficulty, and the interval arrived with Fryston two goals to the good. Goole opened the second half with one or two promising attacks, and once Ward got in an excellent shot, but the ball passed just over the bar. At the other end the visitors' goal had some narrow escapes, but eventually Neate put his side further ahead, Fryston thus winning by three clear goals.[14]

Fryston's semi-final encounter with Rawdon took place on the Leeds City ground at Harehills. Unusually for the time of year, play was badly affected by driving snow. The Colliers established a twelfth-minute lead when Jones finished off an elaborate passing movement from defence to attack. However, they surrendered this advantage just before half time when Baker in goal allowed a shot by Shaw to slip through his hands into the net. Fryston almost went behind immediately after the break when Rawdon spurned a good chance by shooting wide. Their luck held firm in the second half when, following Rawdon's loss of a player through injury, Neate scored what turned out to be the winning goal from a messy goalmouth scramble. Fryston would now play Harrogate Town in their first county cup final since World War I.

The final was played at Elland Road (Leeds) on 9 May before a crowd of 2,700. Rain fell throughout an entertaining match that Fryston initially looked destined to win:

> [Their] half-backs played a great game, with the result that the side always seemed to be masters of the situation. This lasted for 30 minutes, and then the game took an unexpected turn. Harrogate suddenly jumped into their best form and when they had taken the lead through Austick from a centre by E. Baines, they played with such confidence that they were then regarded as prospective winners. Fryston's play afterwards was disappointing. In midfield their work was good, but when it came to the crucial moments in front of goal they made bad mistakes which cost them dearly. Harrogate went further ahead, Smith netting from close range, and Harrogate crossed over with a most useful lead of two goals. Visions of Fryston pulling the game round came when Horton reduced the lead in the first few minutes of the second half, but very shortly afterwards Crowe clinched matters for Harrogate with a third goal, this being an end of the scoring.[15]

This was a bitter blow from which Fryston were very slow to recover. The 1925-26 season was a series of disapointments. In the first week of September, they were heavily defeated 7-0 by Mexborough in the preliminary round of the English Cup. In the league, a 1-0 home defeat by Monckton Athletic was their only loss in the first seven games. However, starting with a 2-0 home defeat by Brodsworth Main, they then experienced a long sequence of losses (including heavy 6-1 and 6-4 home defeats by York City Reserves and Altofts West Riding Colliery, respectively) which eventually saw them finish bottom of the league (played 28, won 4, drew 6, lost 18 = 14 points). The club's defeat in the first round of the WRCC Cup (2-1 at the hands of their old nemesis, Rawdon of Bradford) also meant that their attempt to succeed in the premier amateur county football competition continued to elude them and now seemed a more remote possibility than ever.

Introducing Jabie Foulkes

Having resigned from Yorkshire League, Fryston were now back in the Castleford and District League. Their first season outside the Yorkshire

League commenced just as the seven-month-long 1926 miners' strike was on the point of collapse.[16] The Colliers made a promising start to the season, beating Ferrybridge Power Station 5-0; and despite an inconsistency of form, they rose as high as second in the table at one point, before eventually finishing third behind unbeaten Brotherton Celtic and local rivals, Glass Houghton Welfare. However, a frightful 10-0 hammering suffered away to Denaby United in the preliminary round of the English Cup was a sobering reminder of how far they had now descended from the summit of county football. Fryston were a goal down after six minutes, and four in arrears by half time. Indeed, the Denaby goalkeeper only touched the ball twice in the whole match.

At the junior level of the game, a new star was entering the Foulkes footballing dynasty just as its oldest member was being forced into premature retirement. Dick Foulkes' two-year professional career was cut short when he sustained a cartilage injury playing against Wolves in the Central (reserve) League: 'Bradford put me on the transfer list for 250 quid while I was in bed in the hospital,' he complained. 'No one came in for me, though.' Foulkes found himself on the dole after the General Strike. Eventually, he secured a job as a bricklayer's mate, before returning to colliery life at Savile pit (Methley). It would be another two decades before Dick Foulkes resumed his footballing relationship with Fryston. In the meantime, though, his youngest brother was making the first steps towards forging an even greater reputation.

Born in 1913 in North Street, Fryston, Jabez (Jabie) Foulkes began his organised football career as the goal-scoring centre-forward and captain of the all-conquering Fryston school team of 1926-27:

I broke all records that year. I scored seven goals in each of two semi-finals. A teacher called Baxter took us, but old Rickaby was as keen as mustard. We won the Jackson Shield, League Championship and Sanders Cup. They were all good lads that year. I thought they'd all turn pro but, in the finish, there was only Freddie Astbury, who played for a Cheshire League team, other than me. (Jabez Foulkes)

Local newspaper reports indicate that Foulkes and his relative, Freddie Astbury, were the brightest stars in a universally talented Fryston team. During February 1927, Fryston braced themselves for a tough game against a strong Allerton Bywater side which had held them to a hard-fought draw, earlier that season, but a Foulkes hat-trick saw them to an emphatic 5-0 win. One week later, Foulkes and Astbury scored four goals each in a 10-0 home victory over Whitwood Mere, which took their goals total past 100 for the season. Having scored seven times in the semi-final of the Jackson Shield (a trophy competed for by teams from schools under the Knottingley District Education Sub-Committee), Foulkes added a hat-trick in the final, and Freddie Astbury scored two, as Fryston crushed Knottingley National 11-0.

Fryston secured a narrow 3-2 victory over Temple Street (with second-half goals by Matthews, Parrott and a Foulkes penalty) in the Sanders Cup quarter-final, before easily overcoming Pontefract Boys 9-0 in a semi-final in which Foulkes was in 'irresistible form', hitting two first-half goals, and a further five in the second. In the replayed final, Fryston beat Ashton Road 2-0, having drawn a closely contested initial encounter 2-2. Foulkes was on the mark with a penalty in the replay; and in the after-match reception he 'proved to be a speech maker as well as a footballer. He hoped Ashton Road would win next year if Fryston did not, and raised a broad smile from the assembled crowd when he informed them that he had a "good team".'[17]

On leaving school, Foulkes began working on Fryston pit top. He started his amateur football career, not at Fryston, but in the Leeds and District League with Whitwood Mere, where he had followed his brother Dick's advice by switching to outside-right on the grounds that he was far too small to be leading the attack. His entry into the professional ranks was certainly meteoric:

> I'd only played three matches when Huddersfield came in for me to play in their third team. After four matches with them, they put me in their second team and asked me to join their ground staff. My father went with me to sign on. I'd only been earning 12s 6d [63 pence] on Fryston pit top so, when [Huddersfield's manager] Clem Stephenson said, 'Will £4 10s [four pounds and fifty pence] be enough?' I felt like a millionaire! (Jabez Foulkes)

Jabie's older brother, Charlie, made his debut for Lincoln at the start of the 1927-28 season in the 4-1 home win against Wigan Borough in Division Three (North) on 29 August 1927. There are no records of Charlie having played prior to that point for the Bradford City first team; nor does he appear to have played for the Bournemouth first eleven following his move to the south coast. However, his Lincoln debut was to be the first of 64 appearances (chiefly at centre-half) for the club. In this, his first season, Lincoln were runners-up to Bradford Park Avenue and lost out 4-2 in a memorable third-round FA Cup tie to the eventual finalists, Huddersfield Town. Charlie ended his career at non-league Ashton United, where he made 112 appearances between October 1931 and May 1934.

Faded Promise

Fryston spent two seasons in the Leeds Amateur Senior League (1927-28 and 1928-29) but relevant information about them is frustratingly incomplete. The *Express* makes only two references in 1927-28, and most of the available detail is to be found in the *Leeds Mercury*. Fryston appear to have fared well in the league (for which the final positions are unavailable). Having beaten Pudsey Town 8-1 in their opening home fixture, they are only shown to have lost two subsequent games (though one of them was a 6-1 away thumping against Whitehall Printeries). An *Express* report provides an interesting account of The Colliers' 2-1 win at South Milford, and indicates the calibre of players on their books:

> The homesters forced a corner in the first fifteen minutes, and a good shot was sent in which Rotherforth, the visiting goalie, failed to save. Play was then end to end until five minutes before the interval, when Payne, the Fryston inside-left, sent in a fine drive and placed the visitors on level terms until the interval arrived… After fifteen minutes in the second half, Hunter, the visitors' left-wing, received the ball and scored with a hot shot, which gave Fryston the lead… R. Bury, the Fryston Colliery centre-forward, has signed as amateur for Bradford Park Avenue, and playing for them on Monday against Barnsley Reserves he created an excellent impression and scored three goals.[18]

Fryston also fared well in the Leeds Amateur Senior Cup. They progressed to the final on the strength of a 4-0 semi-final win over Whitehall Printeries. However, there are no further details of the final itself. In the WRCC Cup, The Colliers drew 1-1 away to the Halifax side, Southowram, and won 2-1 in the replay. Their second-round tie at Barnoldswick Town was abandoned without a goal being scored due to the heavy nature of the pitch. The elements failed to rescue Fryston from a 7-0 hiding in the replay.

The *Express* contains no details of Fryston's performance in the Leeds League during 1928-29. The *Leeds Mercury* records the outcomes of only three fixtures for the entire season (a 4-2 home win against Carlton Athletic; a 1-1 draw at Haw Mill; and a 5-4 setback at Beeston). The fact that Fryston are not included in the lists of results for all rounds of the WRCC Cup that season suggests that the club was either not entered or else failed to qualify.

The following season (1929-30) saw Fryston become runaway winners of the Castleford and District League. The Colliers won all but one of their games (the exception being a 3-2 defeat at Silkstone Rovers in November), including double-figure victories over Castleford YMCA (12-2) and Townville Recreation (11-0). Their five-point margin over second-placed Castleford PC was largely secured when they did the double over them in late February/early March, by winning 3-2 at home and even more decisively (4-0) away.

There are no mentions of The Colliers in *Express* reports for the next three seasons. We therefore pick up their story in the 1933-34 season, when they achieved a comfortable spot in the league and were engaged in a number of close encounters with the league and cup 'double' winners, Whitwood Mere. Having lost 4-1 at home to Whitwood in early October, Fryston were the first team to take a point off the eventual champions by drawing 2-2 in the return fixture at the end of the following February. The two sides then met in the semi-final of the Castleford and District FA League Cup, in which a Fryston team containing Astbury and Matthews from the all-conquering schoolboy side referred to previously were unlucky to incur a late equaliser, which slipped underneath the body of Rutherforth in goal, and the replay was won 2-1 by Whitwood.

It is known that Fryston competed for the next two seasons in the Castleford and District League. However, there are insufficient details to show how they actually fared. In August 1936, Fryston Colliery Welfare became one of six new clubs admitted to the Pontefract League for what was one of the strangest periods in their history. A spell of especially good form in October ensured that, at one stage, Fryston were riding as high as third in the table, behind Ferrybridge Amateurs and Pontefract United. However, their form soon became increasingly erratic, as exemplified by their two November matches against the previous season's champions, Pontefract United (formerly known as Tanshelf). In the first of these matches, Fryston registered a comprehensive 6-1 home league win. Two weeks later, however, United exacted full revenge, by hammering Fryston 8-0 in the Cas and District Cup. In their next league match, Fryston lost 7-3 at Purston to slip to eighth in the league (having played 10, won 5, lost 3 and drawn 2 = 12 points). They then lost 3-0 at home in the Pontefract and District Cup, before crashing 10-1 in what was to prove their final league outing at Brotherton United. There are no further match reports for Fryston for the remainder of that season, and henceforward they were absent from league tables up to and including 1941-42.

Jabie's Career – Which one was Stanley Matthews?

The footballing career of Jabie Foulkes had taken several twists and turns in the meantime. Foulkes had the undoubted misfortune to sign for Huddersfield Town in a period when they had a handful of international-class outside-rights, including Alec Jackson, and was given a free transfer to Stockport County in the summer of 1932. His arrival at Stockport coincided with that of the club's greatest-ever goal-scorer, Alf Lythgoe. Foulkes had played a mere three matches for the reserves when he was given his first team debut in the club's 5-1 Division Three (North) win against Darlington on 27 August 1932. Lythgoe had a more prolonged run of nineteen games in the reserves, scoring an impressive ten goals, before making his debut in County's 5-0 win against Walsall on Boxing Day.

> Funny thing, this Alf Lythgoe that got to be a crackerjack, at that time he was an outside-right, and I was an outside-right, but he couldn't get in t'team couldn't Lythgoe. And does tha know how he got in t'team? We were playing Walsall away and t'bloke who should have played centre-forward didn't turn up. He lived at Wolverhampton and his wife had had a youngster and he'd gone and hadn't got back, and Lythgoe played in his place and scored two goals and never looked back. (Jabez Foulkes)

That season, Lythgoe hit nineteen goals in twenty matches, and Foulkes seven goals in his 36 appearances as Stockport finished third in their division. Both players scored twice in County's remarkable 8-5 home league victory against Chester on 6 May 1933.

The following season (1933-34) was one of the most memorable in Stockport's entire history. Foulkes was ever-present, playing 42 games at his customary position of outside-right and contributing a healthy thirteen goals (while Lythgoe hit 46) as County ended up third again in the league. The Hatters also reached the final of the Third Division (North) Cup, narrowly losing out 4-3 to Darlington at Old Trafford. That season is best remembered, though, for Stockport's record-breaking 13-0 home win over Halifax Town, in their Third Division (North) fixture of 6 January 1934, which included eleven second-half goals. As Foulkes rightly maintains, 'It was *Guinness Book of Records* stuff! I only managed one of our goals but I laid on four others!'

Early in the 1934-35 season, Alf Lythgoe was snapped up by Huddersfield Town and, finding themselves deprived of his scoring potential, County finished only seventh in the league. However, that season Foulkes scored one of the most memorable and significant goals of his career – the equaliser, three minutes from time, in the 1-1 draw against West Ham in their FA Cup tie at Upton Park on 12 January 1935. In his final season at Stockport (1935-36), Foulkes made thirty league appearances and scored four times as the club finished fifth in the league.

Had it not been for the reoccurrence of a chronic shoulder injury just before his medical, Foulkes would almost certainly have signed for the Second Division champions-elect, Manchester United, in November 1936. The winger was eventually transferred instead for a fee of £2,000 to Second Division Bradford Park Avenue, where he completed two injury-ridden seasons. The undoubted highlight of his stay was Bradford's 2-1 home win in their 1936-37 FA Cup fourth-round replay against Stoke, which was watched by almost 31,000 people.

I played on the opposite touchline to Stanley Matthews. Next day, the *Daily Herald* said, 'Which one was Matthews?' Mind you, I did play a blinder that day. I never met him to talk to; just to shake hands on the pitch. Then we went off to Roker [Park] where Sunderland beat us one-nowt. Nineteen thirty-seven: Sunderland were cup-holders that year. (Jabez Foulkes)

74

Foulkes was at Avenue long enough to establish a brief relationship with arguably the greatest Bradford-born player of them all, the future Newcastle, Sunderland and England inside-forward, Len Shackleton:

> Shack was only a kid then. He used to come and train with us at Bradford. He would have been at Bradford Grammar School, I think. He went to Arsenal first off; then, according to form, he got homesick and returned home to Bradford. He had it, then – that touch of class – even when he was a kid. (Jabez Foulkes)

Foulkes moved on from Park Avenue to Halifax Town and played out the 1938-39 season at The Shay. He then played a mere three matches in the following season for Crewe Alexandra before his professional career was terminated by the outbreak of World War II.

The Fryston-born Foulkes saw his successful run in the game coincide with a drastic decline in the fortunes of his former village team. All of this had occurred in what were known, ironically, as the 'Great Depression' years of the 1930s. As the then Fryston Colliery under-manager, Jim Bullock explained in his celebrated memoirs, *Them and Us*, 'Cheap and cheaper coal was the order of the day in 1930 to 1938'; and it may have been significant that, unlike previous pit bosses like Soar and Purcell, who had been supportive of the colliery team, their successor of the 1930s exhibited a far less benevolent attitude: 'His attitude was different to mine, particularly his attitude to workpeople. He was a good pitman, he was a hard task-master, he was loyal to his owners and always maintained that that was where his only loyalty lay.'[19]

The club had been starved of any opportunity to bring home the WRCC Cup since its final against Harrogate Town in 1925. This was all about to change. The six-year wartime era was to see a remarkable resurrection of the Fryston Colliery team, a process in which relations between the pit's dynamic and more nurturing new manager, Jim Bullock, Dick and Jabie Foulkes, and the star players of Bradford Park Avenue were to prove extremely pivotal.

Chapter 4
War and Glory

Previous page: The Fryston Colliery team which won the 'grand slam' of local cups (Castleford and District FA Challenge Cup, Embleton Cup, Pontefract Infirmary Cup, Pontefract League Championship Shield and Cup) in the 1943-44 season. BACK ROW (left to right): Dick Foulkes (trainer), R. Hill, E. Knapton, P. Wycherley, W. Evans, F. Johnson and Jim Bullock (Colliery Manager). SEATED: T. Cawthorne, F. Astbury, S. Hunter and A. Roberts. FRONT: J. Hollyoak and J. Hay.

Early Inspiration

As the new Fryston pit manager, Jim Bullock did his utmost to ensure that wartime Fryston was a singularly vibrant village. Though subject to occasional 'black outs' and the type of austerity inevitably associated with times of conflict, Fryston was by no means the sober or depressing place one might have anticipated. Instead, as Bullock maintains in *Them and Us*, 'It was alive, teeming with activities every night.'[1] Bullock further explains in his book how he consciously applied his inherent sociability, capacity to talk and listen with genuine interest, and personal love of sports to his duties as pit manager:

> At Fryston we had a really good football team which won every possible trophy, captained by a young man named Fred Astbury, a member of the big family of Astburys... Fred Astbury is still with me. He was an ex-professional footballer who knew his job. As Colliery Manager and keen supporter of the team I travelled everywhere with them and at half time would go to the dressing room. They knew I was interested and they knew I expected them to win.[2]

It was an inspired move by Bullock which saw Dick Foulkes enlisted as team coach. During the 1930s, Foulkes had resumed his mining career, initially at Savile pit (Methley), and then at nearby Wheldale. Bullock persuaded the ex-pro to resume working at Fryston, where one of Foulkes' main 'duties' was to train up a side which had rejoined the Pontefract and District League for the start of the 1942-43 season.

Fryston were relatively successful that year. Runaway victories against teams like Brotherton (10-2), Baghill Rovers (3-0), Pontefract Forces (8-1), South Kirkby Old Mill (9-3) and, most spectacularly of all, Knottingley Forces (19-1). However, they were found wanting against the eventual champions, Milnsthorpe, losing 4-2 at home and 4-0 away. They were also knocked out in the early stages of the Cas and District Cup by Glass Houghton (4-1) but exacted revenge by beating the same opponents in the semi-final of the Embleton Cup. Anecdotal evidence suggests that Fryston went on to beat Snydale Road Athletic in the final, although there are no reports from which to officially confirm this.

Fryston's Bevin Boys

Fryston were fortunate at this time in being able to welcome fifteen professional footballers into the colliery workforce as 'Bevin Boys' – men who preferred entering reserved occupations like mining rather than joining the armed services.[3] No fewer than eight of these were internationals who, according to Jim Bullock, 'Coached my boys into one of the finest junior sides in the country.'[4] Most central to this activity was the cohort of players that arrived in dribs and drabs from Second Division Bradford Park Avenue. Three of the club's established stars, the Huddersfield-born full-back, Arthur Farrell, the Scottish international full-back, Jimmy Stephen, and – one of the greatest of them all – the English international inside-forward, Len Shackleton, arrived at the tail-end of the war, or just after hostilities had ceased. Two younger players, the Bradford-born left-winger, Geoff Walker, and the Scottish inside-forward, Johnny Downie, were both still in their late-teens, and by no means regulars in the Avenue line-up when they signed up to work at Fryston in the early 1940s.

The Lanark-born Downie made a particular impact on the people of Fryston, and is fondly remembered even to this day on account of his polite, congenial manner, and the degree to which he became integral to village life. Downie had arrived at Park Avenue as a seventeen-year-old in 1942, having been spotted by a scout while playing in the local youth league. He was immediately signed up to play for Avenue's Bradford-based 'nursery' side, East Bierley, in the West Riding Amateur League. 'I didn't get paid – not by them, anyway,' remembered Downie. 'They were a kind of finishing school. I lived in central Bradford, near to the ground, almost, at Lambert's farm, where they kept cows and chickens.'

Downie and his wife, Sheila, agreed that his landlady was an especially lovely woman, and they recalled how Mr Lambert acted as a kindly father figure for the Scot and other players in their care. It was Mr

Lambert's responsibility to ensure that all players observed a strict ten o'clock curfew or were duly punished for breaking it. Sheila's sister, Hilda (who was a policewoman at the time), was a good friend of Mrs Lambert's, and one night she was asked if she could sleep over and help keep an eye on the players while Mrs Lambert went off to visit London.

Mrs Lambert said to my sister, 'Oh, Hilda, do you think you could stay at my house? I want to go see my sisters.' And Hilda said, 'Oh yes.' She said, 'You do know that it will be looking after the footballers!' Hilda went over to my father and said, 'Mrs Lambert wants me to go and stay overnight while she goes to London, just for one night.' And he said, 'Well, you'll have to take Sheila.' I said that I didn't want to go, but she said, 'You'll like it! There's a footballer who's really funny, he's forever chasing the cats round!' And that's actually how I met Johnny. (Sheila Downie)

Downie's closest friend at this time was the Manningham-born winger, Derek Hawksworth, who signed for Avenue as a sixteen-year-old wartime amateur, making seventeen appearances between 1943 and 1946 – primarily, when on leave from serving in the Royal Air Force. Downie was also intent on joining the RAF, and had gone so far as to enquire about enlisting when the Avenue manager, Fred Emery, intervened and insisted that he enrol as a Bevin Boy, on the grounds that going down the mines would enable him to continue developing his footballing career. Indeed, Downie was to make steady progress while serving his time at Fryston. In 1942-43, the young Scot played in handful of matches for Avenue, including his debut in the 3-3 home draw against Sheffield Wednesday and home games against Leeds and Sunderland. He played only a couple of games in 1943-44, but seemed to make a breakthrough a year later in making over twenty appearances.

Downie arrived at Fryston in the company of Geoff Walker, a player described by the Bradford Park Avenue historians, Hartley and Clapham, as a 'tricky outside-left with a fierce shot'.[5] Downie concurred that Walker 'had a beautiful left foot: dribbling and taking people on – that was his game'. He also remembered how Walker's parents were greengrocers and that, 'Geoff did all the "brain work" – things involving writing and adding up – for them.' Walker was an Avenue regular from 1943-44 to 1945-46, before eventually joining First Division Middlesbrough for £6,000.

Having undergone initial training at the Pontefract Prince of Wales Colliery, Downie and Walker began working alongside each other on the trolleys. They initially commuted each day from Fryston to Bradford and back. As Downie subsequently related to Len Shackleton's biographer:

> They looked after us quite well there and allowed us to come home to Bradford. Each day I got the bus to Leeds, Leeds to Pontefract, Pontefract to the colliery; and it was very good. I wouldn't like to do it again, though: I wasn't happy down below. Up on top was all right, but we were a long way down below, most of us. I was at the loading end of the operation. When they got the coal out, we put it into trolleys. That was all the skill we had, really, for mining. To be fair, they couldn't allow us to be in a position where we could jeopardise others. So there was no working at the coalface, or anything like that.[6]

One day, Walker failed to take his underground responsibilities seriously enough – 'He was swinging on one of the trolleys like a kid trying to hitch a ride and he either fell right over or severely banged his leg' – and was forced to miss five Park Avenue matches as a consequence.

Eventually, Downie started lodging near the pit and only travelled to Bradford to train and play at weekends.

> I lived in the village. Couple of years I lived there. I don't know who it was. It was an old lady who lived with her husband. I do know that she left the teapot on the lip of the fire all night so that it was absolutely stewed for him! I used to train on the Wednesdays and go back to Fryston on the Thursday, Friday, and go back to Park Avenue on Saturday, then return to Fryston on Sunday night. I befriended a young woman called Edie Peat. I just liked her and wanted her to be my girlfriend but she wouldn't have had anything to do with me! I think she felt she could do a lot better somewhere else! (Johnny Downie)

Downie had difficulty recollecting the names of the men he may have worked, socialised or played football with in Fryston. However, Sheila Downie maintains how: 'We did have a photograph of Tommy Templeman and his wife, which suggests that he was friends with them.' This theory is borne out by a 1986 interview with Templeman, who recalled: 'He worked with me nearly three years did John. A right pal of mine was Johnny: grand bloke – a toff. He used to lodge with some people at t'bottom of Airedale – "Buzzer Bosworth's" aunt or somebody like that.'

Two Fryston stalwarts of the future, Jack Sharp and Harold 'Agga' Mattison vividly remember meeting Downie, even though they were only children. 'Oh, aye. I got right pally with Johnny even though I were just a kid,' recollects Sharp. 'He was a lovely fella – never spoke down at all to me and my mates when we got nattering about the game.' Mattison knows from talking to his older brothers that the influence of Downie and other Bevin Boys extended beyond formal coaching sessions to ad hoc football matches occurring on the 'stack' (an area of flattened wasteland on the periphery of the village). Mattison is also able to recollect how 'My brother played with Fryston and they played at Brotherton, Downie went to watch 'em; and they were one short were Fryston, so Downie played – in a Ponte league match, *in t'goals* for Fryston!'

Achieving the Grand Slam

The combined influence of Fryston's new coaching regime and the contingent of Bevin Boys paid immediate dividends. In 1943-44, Fryston fulfilled all the promise they had shown in the previous year. In the league, Fryston beat off the challenges of their principal rivals last time round, Milnsthorpe WMC and Hemsworth Rovers. Sid Hunter proved himself a prolific goal-scorer, while such mainstays of the side as Arthur 'Blood' Roberts, Freddie Astbury, Jackie Hollyoak, Jock Hay and Tabot 'Tabby' Cawthorne started to reach maturity.

The majority, though by no means all, of the players of this era worked at Fryston Colliery. Some were born and raised in Fryston, but others in nearby Brotherton. A minority had no connection either to the village or its mine:

> Sid Hunter and Oliver Kelsey, who was Fryston's first-choice 'keeper, were Fryston miners who lived over in Brotherton, and I think 'Tabby' Cawthorne did as well. Two or three of that team lived in Airedale: Jackie Hollyoak lived in Park Dale, and so did Jock Ayers, while Blood Roberts, he lived at t'bottom of Fryston Road. All three worked at t'pit. Freddie Astbury and 'Bunk' Evans both lived and worked in Fryston, but the likes of Hill and Reynolds didn't live or work round about here. (Ronnie Foulkes)

Having already beaten Hemsworth 3-2 in the Pontefract League Cup final, Fryston anticipated an equally close contest against Castleford Amateurs in the final of the Cas and District Cup, which was played before a large Easter Monday crowd at Glass Houghton:

This was the fourth consecutive appearance of the Amateurs in this competition, and as they are the only side to have beaten Fryston in a league game this season, a great struggle was expected. Both sides gave a splendid exhibition of football. Fryston were the more aggressive in the first half, and despite good goalkeeping by Worley, were leading by two goals to nil at half time, goals being scored by Astbury and Hay. On resuming the Amateurs attacked persistently, but found the Fryston defence very safe. Keeping up the pressure the Amateurs were awarded a penalty for a handling offence, and Hill scored with an unstoppable shot. Following this, Fryston took command of the game, and despite good defensive play by the Amateurs, for whom Tomlinson was outstanding, the Fryston team scored twice through Astbury and Hunter.[7]

Fryston repeated the dose by beating Amateurs 6-0 in the semi-final of the Pontefract Shield, and then overcoming Hemsworth 2-1 in the final. Hemsworth held Fryston to a 3-3 draw in the semi-final of the Pontefract Infirmary Cup, though The Colliers ultimately prevailed 2-1 in the replay. Thus, by the time that Jim Bullock had the pleasure of presenting the Fryston captain, Freddie Astbury, with the Pontefract Infirmary Trophy, following their 5-1 rout of Milnsthorpe, Fryston had achieved the unprecedented 'grand slam' of winning all five of the major local football competitions: namely the Cas and District Cup; Embleton Cup; Pontefract Infirmary Cup; and the Pontefract League Championship Shield and Cup.

Back in Pursuit

Not surprisingly, Fryston's application to re-join the more prestigious West Yorkshire League was instantly approved. Their chances of succeeding in this competition were significantly enhanced by the arrival of Jabie Foulkes, whose return, like that of his brother, Dick, owed much to the prompting of Jim Bullock. As Jabie's future son-in-law, Agga Mattison, explains:

My father-in-law used to play for Bradford Park Avenue; but during the war, he guested for a few local teams like Halifax Town. He was still in digs at Bradford when he met his wife in Yeadon and he started working for about eighteen months in the local mills; but he never grew to like it so he talked to Bullock about the possibility of getting a job at Fryston. At first, he used to catch three buses a day over from Yeadon. Then he got staying with relatives all week and going back to Yeadon at weekends. It was Bullock who eventually helped him get a house in Ferry Fryston. (Harold Mattison)

Foulkes' impact was incalculable, but such was the high quality of the side in general that his brother, Dick, felt justified in maintaining that, 'The way that team were playing, I'd have played them against any Third Division [equivalent to today's Division One] team that's playing now.'

In the league, Fryston quickly developed an air of invincibility. In early October, for example, a team comprising Wycherly, Hill, Evans, Hollyoak, Knapton, Roberts, Wright, Cawthorne, Hunter, Foulkes and Robinson earned a comprehensive home victory over Leeds United Reserves:

The score, 4-2, did not flatter the enterprising Colliery team who had easily three-quarters of the game in their favour; and it was only a fine display by Fearnley, the Leeds goalkeeper, that kept Fryston from increasing their total. Fryston attacked first, and after a series of good saves by Fearnley, Hunter opened the scoring after clever work by the forwards. He scored a second after fine work by Cawthorne, and Foulkes added a third before the interval. After some good work by Moule, the United right-winger, Donskin, netted for Leeds, after Wycherly had fumbled the ball. After some exciting end-to-end play Wright found the United goalkeeper out of position and scored with a well placed shot.[8]

In the fourth round of the WRCC Cup, Fryston visited Normanton St John's, whose field was ankle-deep in mud. The Fryston team on the day was Wycherley, Hill, Reynolds, Astbury, Roberts, Knapton, Hollyoak, Cawthorne, Hunter, Foulkes and Robinson. The Colliers set off to a flying start:

Normanton were soon forced back to the defence, and in the first few minutes a well placed free kick by Foulkes resulted in Cawthorne heading a neat goal. Fryston made a number of good movements, but offside play spoilt their efforts. St John's also made a series of dangerous moves, but the Colliery defence was solid. Foulkes put Fryston further ahead with a goal from a free kick, the ball hitting the upright and bouncing in the net. It was almost impossible to distinguish the players and many passes went astray. Foulkes hit the crossbar, and half time came with Fryston leading by two goals.[9]

The standard of football in the second half deteriorated as surface conditions grew worse. Normanton pulled a goal back but a Wycherley penalty save secured Fryston a 2-1 victory.

In the semi-final, played at Leeds University, Fryston faced a Leeds United Reserves team whom they had already beaten twice that season. Their pre-match confidence was reflected in their early dominance:

> After early exchanges, Foulkes struck the crossbar and the ball rebounded to Hunter, but Fearnley made a spectacular save, and then he tipped the ball over the bar from another shot by Foulkes, but from the corner kick by Bowery, Hunter opened the scoring. In the second half, Fryston soon increased their lead when Hay beat two men to send a perfect pass to Cawthorne, who made no mistake with his shot. Leeds were bewildered by the passing movements of the Colliery team, and were compelled to put all they knew into defence. Fryston forced a corner, and a Leeds player handled, and from the penalty, Hill struck the upright. A grand movement by Hay enabled him to score a third goal for the Colliery. Fryston made Leeds look like a third-rate team and much credit goes to them for their victory.[10]

In what was arguably the most important cup final to have occurred in the club's entire history, Fryston faced formidable opposition in none other than Johnny Downie's erstwhile club, East Bierley, a Bradford team which had joined the West Riding County Amateur League in 1935-36, and first won the league title in 1937-38. Though initially overshadowed by their great rivals, Bradford Rovers, who achieved the 'gram slam' of four trophies – the Bradford League, League Cup, WRCC Cup and Bradford and District Cup in 1938-39 – Bierley's fortunes took a dramatic turn for the better during World War II when, as we have already seen, they became a 'nursery' club for Bradford Park Avenue.

The club's big breakthrough came in 1942-43, when they met a strong Leeds United Reserves in the WRCC Cup final. The Leeds team was made up mostly of first-teamers and also included a pair of highly regarded guest players, Lowe of Aberdeen and Rutherford

(Rangers). Bierley reciprocated by including such players as Chick Farr in goals, Arthur Farrell (full-back) and Len Shackleton at inside-right. Shackleton scored twice as Bierley took the game 3-1. Soon afterwards, though, the match was declared 'void' following an inquiry which ruled that some of the participants in the match had been 'ineligible'.[11]

A year later, Bierley almost emulated Bradford Rovers' grand slam feat, winning three trophies (league and cup double and county cup), but losing out to Butterfield Sports in a replayed Bradford and District Cup third-round tie. However, they had another chance to one step better in 1944-45 and finally emulate Rovers' achievement:

> During the county cup run, Bierley took part in a classic tie against Huddersfield Town at Leeds Road. It was a game that lived for a long time in people's memories – experts called it one of the greatest games seen on the ground. Captaining Bierley that day was football veteran Jimmy Faulkner, who along with Bob (here, there and everywhere) Wood and young Geordie McTaff marshalled a Bierley defence that stood some tremendous pressure from Town. Bierley's Park Avenue protégé 18 year-old Clarke, from the Sheffield area, played a blinder and it was no fault of his that Town led 2-1 as the game went into the closing stages. Bierley's equaliser came when left-winger Dickens' persistence in chasing a seemingly lost ball led to a centre which Derek Hawksworth put away. In the dying moments Bierley's diminutive centre-forward Kendall hit his second and the winning goal.[12]

Sadly for Fryston, it was the irrepressible Kendall who also put paid to their hopes of winning the WRCC Cup by scoring another two goals in the final at Elland Road. There, a Bierley team including seven men currently registered with Bradford Park Avenue overcame The Colliers 3-1 in front of a crowd of some 5,000 people. Jack Sharp still remembers how:

> Fryston was practically empty on that day because we all took off on buses. I was only eight then. I can't remember much of the match, except for the general impression that we got beat comprehensively that day; but I do remember standing on a perimeter wall at Elland Road and cheering them along. They lost 3-1 to a very good side in East Bierley. In fact, I'm pretty sure they imported players in. Fryston definitely knew that they were up against part-time pros, while they were just pit lads, basically. But Fryston also had an exceptional side, mind, and to get to that final was a terrific achievement.

The *Bradford Telegraph and Argus* euphorically proclaimed how: 'The much-vaunted Fryston Colliery XI, including several professionals, must still be wondering how a purely amateur and partly boyish-looking side effortlessly romped home to victory.' The report maintained that Bierley's Park Avenue colts 'had the more experienced Fryston rearguard gasping and leg weary long before the whistle sounded to herald a 3-1 victory', and pointed out that 'the Bradford club's manager, Mr. Fred Emery, has a star in the making in McTaff but Bob Wood was outstanding on this occasion'.[13]

The *Express* was, perhaps not surprisingly, more generous in its appraisal of Fryston's performance, emphasising how they had been unlucky to lose one of their star players; that the game had been closer than the 3-1 score suggested, and that Foulkes had been prominent throughout:

> The early exchanges were very fast. They took the ball to the Bierley end, but after clever passing by the forwards, Robinson scraped over the bar. Fryston forced a corner, and Kay put across a lovely kick. Hunter had to pull the ball over his head, and was only just wide of the target. Fryston were on top at that stage, and Foulkes opened the scoring with a glorious goal from 25 yards out. Then Knapton was just wide with a first-time kick; and Foulkes again put in a long kick which deceived Clark, but dropped on top of the net. Bierley went through to the Fryston end, and Kendall scored the equaliser dead on half time. Fryston suffered on the resumption. Roberts, in heading a ball, was injured in the face and although he carried on, the effect was felt in the Fryston defence. A lapse by the Colliery defence, who appealed for offside, presented Bierley with a gift goal, and though individual efforts were made, Fryston lacked their usual combination. Bierley added a great goal immediately before the end.[14]

Having already won the West Riding Amateur League, Bierley went on to overcome Heckmondwike and Park View in the finals of the League Cup and Bradford and District Cup, respectively. The grand slam was now theirs, and on a par with the one achieved by their great rivals, Bradford Rovers.

Consolation and Charity

Having been deprived of the opportunity to achieve their own grand slam, Fryston had the consolation of still having a chance of winning the remaining three competitions in which they were entered. They had been required to work hard to reach the semi-finals of the West Yorkshire League Cup. In the first (home) leg of their second-round tie against Smith's Sports, they twice took the lead through Hunter and Cawthorne, only to be held to a 2-2 draw. Fryston's early pressure allowed them to establish a two-goal lead in the second leg with goals by Cawthorne and Bowery. Smith's then replied with a second-half penalty, but Robinson eased the away side's nerves by scoring from the rebound after Cawthorne had hit the upright. Thereafter, Fryston's 'stone wall' of a defence proved sufficiently impenetrable to ensure them a 3-1 win and 5-3 aggregate victory.

The Colliers' 3-1 first-leg semi-final victory over Ossett Rovers RASC would probably have been even more emphatic had Sid Hunter not been forced to leave the field, having sustained an injury while heading Fryston's equalising goal from a centre by Foulkes. The ten men of Fryston scored twice more through Robinson but were guilty of spurning a hatful of chances. In the away return leg, Ossett immediately reduced the aggregate arrears by scoring with less than a minute gone. However, Fryston gradually reasserted their superiority by scoring three times through an own goal, a Hill penalty and an opportunistic strike by Robinson. Ossett pulled one back but the outcome was never in doubt. Roberts, who had moved from centre-half to centre-forward to replace the injured Hunter, was unlucky not to extend Fryston's 3-2 victory on the day when he twice hit the crossbar.

Of arguably greater historical significance to followers of the professional game was Fryston's Embleton Cup semi-final against Snydale Road Athletic, which was played on the Castleford Amateurs ground. According to the *Express*, the Fryston team included 'a number of strange faces owing to work and injuries'.[15] Among those appearing for The Colliers were the Park Avenue Bevin Boys, Johnny Downie and Geoff Walker, and the Fryston-born full-back and York City captain, Sammy Gledhill. Following an even period of early play, the colliery team eventually ran out easy 6-3 winners, thanks in no small measure to the influence of their professionals:

Play was very even and entertaining for a good while, both goalkeepers being severely tested. Walker and Downey [sic] combined well on the left to give the first named his first goal of the game... Fryston opened the second half in fine style, Downey scoring without a Snydale player touching the ball from the kick-off. Snydale soon reduced the arrears when Rooker, who played a first-class game, headed past Kelsay [sic]. Kelsay, only a youth, gained the applause of both teams when he brought off a brilliant save from Jones. Rooker levelled the score with a neat goal. Fryston made headway and Whitham added to Fryston's score by hitting a dropping ball. Smith made a clever run on Snydale's right wing to centre the ball to Rooker, who completed his hat-trick. Play went down field again, this time to Walker, who gave Falaise his first goal. Whitham brought off a good save when Jowett 'fired' at point-blank range. Ellis was injured and went on the right wing. Walker showed his class in beating the Snydale goalie with a shot from a narrow angle. Ellis made a clever run and dribble to enable Falaise to close Fryston's scoring.[16]

Fryston then entered into a crucial series of matches. The first of these was the final of the West Yorkshire League Cup against Altofts Welfare, played before a large, enthusiastic crowd on the Castleford Rugby League ground on Wheldon Road. In a game marred by unusually heavy snowfalls for that time of year, Fryston built up a two-goal lead thanks to goals either side of half time by Sid Hunter. Colwood reduced Altofts' arrears, and Deakin and Webster each struck the Fryston woodwork as The Colliers hung on for a fortunate 2-1 victory.

After the match, the Fryston players returned to the village for a celebratory tea in the colliery canteen where they were given a marvellous reception by the pipe band of the Argyll and Sutherland Highlanders. Jim Bullock spoke warmly of his players as a 'grand set of lads' who, 'but for an accident to their centre-half the previous week, would have beaten Bierley at Leeds in the West Riding Cup final'. Fryston's Freddie Astbury was generous in his praise of East Bierley, maintaining that he and his team-mates had been beaten by 'the best side he had ever been up against'.[17] Astbury nonetheless remained confident that Fryston would succeed in lifting the two remaining cups they were playing for.

The skipper's optimism was vindicated on the following Monday evening when Fryston secured the Embleton Cup by beating Normanton St. John's 3-2 on the Castleford Amateurs' ground. Though Fryston took the lead through their centre-forward, Hill, they found themselves 2-1 down before the redoubtable Hunter grabbed an equaliser. Normanton were then unfortunate enough to have a goal disallowed for offside and, in a thrilling conclusion, Sammy Gledhill drove in a scorching 40-yard screamer to win the game for Fryston.

The following Saturday, Fryston returned to Elland Road to meet Huddersfield Town Reserves in the final of the West Yorkshire League Championship. The colliery eleven adapted themselves better to the greasy conditions brought on by continuous rain and entered the second half 2-0 up thanks to goals by Sid Hunter and Freddie Astbury. Huddersfield pulled a goal back from a direct free kick but, with Roberts outstanding at is heart, the Fryston defence looked impregnable. However, with the linesman trying hard to indicate to the referee that time was up, Wycherly was finally beaten with a cross-shot that brought the scores level, and a replay was required.

Fryston entered the replay without the talismanic Freddie Astbury who was absent through injury. Nevertheless, with their defence resolute as ever in containing early Huddersfield pressure, the tide soon turned in The Colliers' favour, thanks to sensational performances by Foulkes and Robinson:

A great run by Foulkes, whose shot slipped from the Huddersfield goalkeeper's grasp, opened the way for Hunter to score the first goal. From a run on the left Riddell headed a goal which was hotly disputed. Fryston swept down the field and for the rest of the half completely dominated the play. Foulkes again paved the way for Hunter's second goal, with a brilliant solo effort before parting with the ball. Robinson was a 'live wire' and must have tired the Huddersfield right-back with his twisting and turning runs. Robinson scored what was acclaimed as one of the finest goals seen on the ground. He received the ball from Knapton about 40 yards out, and after working his way past player after player, scored from two yards from the goal line and half-way from the corner flag.[18]

Fryston's growing superiority would have been reflected in a further score had Hollyoak not rammed his penalty kick against the crossbar. Theoretically at least, Huddersfield were given a lifeline when Batty scored from a penalty; but things were different in reality: 'Fryston ran Huddesfield to a standstill, and for the rest of the game they had to defend. Robinson twisted his way through in the last minute to make the score 4-2.'[19] It was a fitting end to another triumphant season for

Fryston – albeit one in which the coveted WRCC Cup continued to elude them.

In between playing the final against Huddersfield and the replay, Fryston staged the first in what would become a succession of charity matches involving the colliery's own players, their Bevin Boys and other star players from Bradford Park Avenue. Local miners had already contributed to a collection on behalf of the Merchant Navy, and it was anticipated that the gate from a match between Fryston and a Park Avenue XI, held on the Welfare ground in the first week of May, would greatly swell the coffers. Bradford's team on this occasion was: Farr, Stephen, Farrell, Stabb, Danskin, Elliott, Smith, Shackleton, Waterhouse, Naylor and Walker. There was no doubting who the majority of those present had come along to cheer.

Even at this early stage of his career, Len Shackleton had a nationwide reputation both for his consummate footballing skills and mischievous brand of on-field entertainment that earned him the nickname the 'Clown Prince of Soccer'. Rejected by Arsenal as a ground staff boy for allegedly being too small (he was only five-feet-two at the time), Shackleton returned north to sign for Park Avenue in August 1940. He quickly achieved star status, scoring no fewer than 167 goals in 210 games between making his debut and playing in his final match against West Ham United on 28 September 1946. According to his Bradford Park Avenue team-mate and future manager of West Ham and England, Ron Greenwood, Shackleton was blessed with 'lovely, almost unbelievable skills' and an unbreakable self-confidence. 'There was no one quite like our Len,' maintained Greenwood. 'He was a showman, a crowd-pleaser, a character who was larger than life.' In addition to playing 'one-twos' off opponents' legs or taunting them by sitting on the ball, Shackleton's speciality was that of cutting his foot under the ball 'so sharply that it would spin towards an opponent and then come back to him as if on a piece of string'.[20]

Those attending the game at Wheldon Road were suitably beguiled, and somewhat inevitably:

> Shackleton soon became a favourite with the crowd, and gave a faultless exhibition of forward play. On one occasion he dribbled his way from near the half-way line to score a fine goal. Fryston made one or two promising raids, but Stephen was up to his football international form. Smith scored a neat goal from Walker's corner, and Fryston came near to scoring through

Hunter, but Farr made a good save. Smith had to retire and Downie came on in his place. The Bradford half-back line took some breaking, with Danskin and Stabb doing good work in defence and attack, and it was a clever run by Stabb that enabled Naylor to score. Waterhouse scored a fourth goal after some clever forward play. The team were besieged by young Fryston football enthusiasts for autographs after the game.[21]

Anti-Climax: 1945-46

Fryston's hopes of going one better in 1945-46 by actually *winning* the WRCC Cup were soon dashed when they lost in the second round away to a very strong Selby Town Yorkshire League eleven, which included one player (Horsefield) who was currently on Arsenal's books. The Fryston team comprised: Kelsey, Rooker, Evans, Hay, Padgett, Astbury, Haxby, Cawthorne, Roberts, Foulkes and Templeman. It was they who made the early running:

> Fryston immediately attacked and Collins was tested with a great drive from Foulkes, who, throughout, was the spearhead of the visitors' attack... Fryston were by no means inferior to the Yorkshire League team, and drew first blood when Foulkes beat two players and scored with a fine ground shot.[22]

Selby soon hit their form and, shortly after Kelsey in the Fryston goal had brought off a pair of fine saves, the Yorkshire League side equalised in a movement involving every single one of their players. Hay hit the Selby upright with a header from a corner but it was the home side who went ahead, only for Roberts to equalise just before half time.

In the second half, Selby prospered from two controversial decisions in their favour. Firstly, Kelsey was barged over his own goal line without being in possession of the ball, leaving a Selby attacker to tap into an unguarded net. Then, 'A curious incident occurred when Fryston were awarded a penalty. Foulkes placed the ball on the spot, and, on the intervention of a Selby player, the referee ordered a bounce.'[23] Horsefield increased the Selby lead with a cleanly struck, long-range shot, and they could have gone even further ahead when a penalty kick was rammed against the bar. The 4-2 end result was certainly harsh on Fryston.

The Colliers remained the dominant force in the league, though. Their 10-1 away win against Normanton St John's in early December was the highlight of a season which saw them top the century of league goals as they finished as table-toppers for the second successive season (played 18, won 14, lost 3, drew 1 = 29 points). In second place were DP and E (Otley), who would be involved in run-ins with Fryston in both the Supplementary League and League Cup competitions.

Fryston's hopes of lifting the League Cup were raised when they came out on top in an epic second-round encounter, played over two legs, with Leeds United Reserves. With Foulkes absent through injury in both matches, Fryston did well to draw the away leg 2-2, with goals from Jowett and Cawthorne. The sides remained deadlocked at full time in the second leg with two more goals from Jowett and a third from Roberts earning The Colliers a 3-3 draw. The tie was eventually decided in the second period of extra time when Cawthorne latched onto a through-ball by Hay and slammed it into the top corner of the net, beyond the outstretched arms of the former Irish international Twoomey, to give Fryston an aggregate 6-5 win.

Foulkes was still absent for Fryston's semi-final first leg at home to DP and E. Despite this, they established a two-goal first-half lead through Jowett and Freddie Astbury. Fryston retained their advantage thanks to a penalty save by Kelsey; but in the second half, Cawthorne headed into his own net to leave them a mere one goal to the good on the final whistle. With Foulkes now restored to the attack, Fryston were still ahead on aggregate by half time in the second leg, with Cawthorne equalising DP and E's opening strike. In the second half, Foulkes hit the post from an acute angle before their opponents took the lead with a headed goal from a corner. It was not until the final minute that DP and E put the tie beyond Fryston's reach with their third goal of the match.

In the Supplementary League competition, Fryston overcame Rothwell 4-3 (home), Altofts 2-0 (away), and Normanton St John's 5-1 (home) for the right to meet DP and E again in the final, played at Altofts. Two first-half goals in the space of a minute gave DP and E a firm stranglehold on the match. Fryston hit the crossbar and had appeals for a penalty turned down but DP and E's overall superiority was underlined by a third goal early in the second half after Fryston had been pegged back by a succession of corners.

This left Fryston with only the Embleton Cup to play for. In the semi-final, they easily overcame Whitwood Mere 5-0 on Allerton

Bywater's ground (with goals from Cawthorne 2, Jackson, Astbury pen. and Jowett), despite fielding only ten men. The final against Altofts was played before a large crowd at Glass Houghton. The Fryston team comprised: Kelsey, Rooker, Reynolds, Hay, Fisher, Astbury, Jowett, Jackson, Roberts, Cawthorne and Childs. Fryston went two-up against the run of play, with goals by Cawthorne and Jowett, but strong Altofts pressure brought the sides level by early in the second half. From then on, it could really have been anyone's match. That was until:

> Hay placed a free kick perfectly for Cawthorne, who, along with Childs played a great game, to give Fryston the lead. Bennett, from a free kick, however, hit the crossbar and was given a goal. Altofts fought hard and Rooker had to kick off his own goal line to save a dangerous situation. The Fryston half-backs took play to the Altofts end and Astbury shot at Measham who didn't punch the ball far enough, for Jowett was waiting, and slammed home the winning goal.[24]

The curtain was brought down on another memorable season for Fryston by a second charity match between the colliery team and the Bradford Park Avenue first eleven, which not only contained the resident Bevin Boys, Jimmy Stephen and Johnny Downie, but also the future West Ham and England manager, Ron Greenwood. Avenue were confronted by a Fryston team comprising Swallow, Hay, Rooker, Roberts, Fisher, Astbury, Mosby, Jackson, Jowett, Moseley, and Hutchinson. As might have been expected, the colliery team was outclassed, with Johnny Downie playing a prominent part in their defeat:

> Bradford were a goal up in the first two minutes through Glasby, a second coming from Downie from a free kick well down the field. Horsman [crowned] a good forward movement for the next, and Gibbons [got] through for a fourth with a hard drive when the goalie was unsighted. And Fryston's response this half was a goal by Jackson, who cleverly turned the ball in after good approach work by his colleague... Horsman was responsible for Bradford's fifth goal and Downie rounded off their score with a sixth from a corner, giving the goalie no possible chance. Roberts brought the Fryston total to two, and a third with a header was very narrowly missed. Better positional play and being rather faster on the ball gave the visitors their victory by six goals to two.[25]

Afterwards, players on both sides and their guests were treated to dinner and a 'smoking concert' at the Grosvenor Café, Castleford. Jim

Bullock paid tribute to the Bradford club and jokingly mentioned that the colliery was indebted to the Minister of Labour and National Service, Ernest Bevin, for inventing the scheme that introduced such talented sportsmen to Fryston. Bullock was particularly grateful for the fact that the gate receipts had guaranteed that the club would stay on its feet for 'at least another season'. Although few could have credited it at the time, these words were soon to prove dismally and resoundingly ironic.

Chapter 5
Post-War Reconstruction

Return of the Bevin Boys

By the start of the 1946-47 season, Johnny Downie and Geoff Walker had been joined at Fryston Colliery by their fellow Bradford Park Avenue Bevin Boys, Arthur Farrell,[1] Jimmy Stephen and, most memorably of all, the great Len Shackleton.

Other than continuing to play for Park Avenue, Shackleton had spent the duration of the war making aircraft wirelesses for the General Electric Company (GEC). He had volunteered to join the RAF only to be turned down on the basis that his existing work was too vital to the war effort for him to abandon it. With the ending of hostilities, GEC decided to relocate to their former manufacturing base of Coventry, and though Shackleton had the option of going with them, there was no way that he was going to leave Park Avenue. It was not long before Shackleton was called up by the Army to undertake his National Service; but mindful of the effect that this might have on his playing career, he registered as a Bevin Boy. Unlike Johnny Downie and Geoff Walker, who chose to live in the vicinity of the pit, Shackleton opted to travel to and fro, and soon found himself making the daily 30-odd mile trip to Fryston in the company of Jimmy Stephen.

The Aberdeenshire-born James Findlay 'Jimmy' Stephen had signed schoolboy forms for Park Avenue as a sixteen-year-old in 1938, and turned professional the following year. Having made his debut in August 1939, he played consistently as right- or (primarily) left-back in wartime matches for Bradford, and also put in guest appearances for Halifax Town, Huddersfield Town and Middlesbrough. More significantly, he played in five wartime internationals for Scotland. He made his Scottish debut at left-back against England at Wembley, for whom Stanley Matthews was the opposing right-winger.

Fate had now brought the pair of them to Fryston, where Jim Bullock, not only assigned them to relatively undemanding roles in the pit-bottom joiners' shop, but also allowed them to work a special nine-to-five shift to compensate for the six-hour round trip they undertook each day. Jimmy Stephen recollects that this was an 'horrendous journey', given that both he and Shackleton lived on the outskirts of the city. 'We had to get a bus from home to the centre of Bradford,' he explained to Shackleton's biographer. 'Then we got a bus to Leeds, a bus from Leeds to Castleford and, finally, a bus from Castleford to Fryston.' This required the two men to leave their homes at 6am every day. Then there was the return journey. 'It was a dreadful way of life, really,' Stephen maintained.[2]

None of this took into account the harsh reality of life underground, for which Shackleton and Stephen were totally unprepared. The former spoke in his autobiography of the 'terrifying experience' involved in descending in the pit cage. The work itself was also more arduous than he could ever have imagined: 'One day at Fryston was sufficient to convince me I had made a real blunder by volunteering for mining, and I soon started investigating ways and means of "dodging the column" without being reprimanded for absenteeism. To be perfectly frank, I did not overwork myself.'[3] To his credit, though, Shackleton also spoke of his admiration for the Fryston miners (whom he rated 'among the most likeable and genuine people one could wish to meet').

By the time of his arrival at Fryston in mid-1946, 'Shack' had amassed a total of 167 goals in 210 wartime matches. His cavalier style of play was not to everyone's taste – reflected in the fact that he was occasionally barracked by sections of his home crowd. He cited this hostility as one of the contributing factors in his decision to accept a transfer to Newcastle United for a then British record fee of £13,000 in October 1946. Even by his own standards, he made a remarkable debut for Newcastle (on 5 October 1946), scoring six goals in their 13-0 win over Newport County, which represented a Second Division record: 'Three of them came in the space of 155 breathtaking seconds and, typically, he knocked in the last of the six with his backside.'[4] Shackleton maintained his good form in Newcastle's next two matches. However, by his own admission, he came crashing back down to earth in his fourth game for the club – away to Bradford Park Avenue.

'Shack' must already have known that his former club would be no pushovers. During the previous season, the nucleus of this side had created a sensation by beating a Manchester City side which included the great Frank Swift in goals over two legs in the FA Cup fourth round. Park Avenue had lost the first leg 3-1 at home, but triumphed in the return leg at Maine Road by the unbelievable score of 8-2. It therefore came as no surprise when Park Avenue rose to the occasion by beating Newcastle 2-1 with goals from Horsman and Downie. A crowd of 26,000 had the bonus of seeing Shackleton miss a penalty, which was saved by his old friend, Chick Farr, who chose which way to dive on the basis of the many hours he had spent facing up to his erstwhile colleague in training.

It was a mere two weeks after this game, and at the height of Shackleton's celebrity, that he joined forces with Jimmy Stephen to help pick a 'Fryston' team to play Frickley Colliery of the Midland League in a charity match at Castleford Rugby League football ground – an occasion arranged by Jim Bullock to raise funds to provide invalid motor chairs for disabled miners. To call the Fryston team 'star-studded' would constitute a gross understatement. Stephen himself had recently made his international debut as Scotland's captain in their first competitive match after the war (in fact, he put through his own goal in Scotland's 3–1 defeat in the British Home Championship by Wales). Among Fryston's other players were: Maddison (deputising for Chick Farr in goal), Farrell, Downie, Dix, Mordue and Smith (all Bradford Park Avenue), Walker (Middlesbrough), Shackleton (Newcastle United), Roberts and Gledhill (both York City). Other locally-based Fryston players were brought on as substitutes.

The occasion was slightly spoiled by a heavy rain which made conditions unpleasant for players and spectators alike. Nevertheless, a healthy attendance assured an £80 contribution to the charity, from a game in which the Fryston team won with predictable ease:

In the early stages both Shackleton and Walker netted with first-time drives, and Walker got a third goal before the change round. In the second half a grand movement from one end of the field to the other saw Shackleton thread his way through the opposition for a fourth goal. Just on time Lunn succeeded with a lovely goal to make the result a win for Fryston by 4 goals to 1. In spite of the clinging mud and greasy ball some skilful work was put in by both teams, and the match was thoroughly enjoyed. The Fryston team were provided with kit, except boots, by the Bradford Park Avenue club.[5]

Shackleton ceased working at Fryston pit subsequent to signing for Newcastle. In retaining his role as a Bevin Boy, he moved to

Gosforth pit where he worked with another legendary English player, the Newcastle centre-forward, Jackie Milburn. Shackleton's departure proved too much for Jimmy Stephen, whose chronic absenteeism led to his being drafted into National Service.

Stephen was subsequently transferred from Park Avenue to First Division Portsmouth in October 1949. Arthur Farrell played on at the club until Barnsley came in for him in 1951. Geoff Walker played eight more years for Middlesbrough before transferring to Doncaster Rovers in 1954. 'Shack' stayed for only two seasons with Newcastle before joining their north-east rivals, Sunderland, for a then British record fee of £20,000 in February 1948. This sum was only £2,000 more than the £18,000 paid out at roughly the same time by Manchester United to Bradford Park Avenue for the services of Johnny Downie, who became part of the Red Devils' 1952 league title-winning team, before reacquainting himself with Fryston Colliery Welfare more than a decade later.

A Rot Sets In

For reasons not altogether apparent from the meagre information available concerning Fryston's progress during the 1946-47 season (there are very few *Express* reports to speak of, for example), the team experienced a sudden decline of fortune. It is possible that the post-war return of service personnel may have neutralised any advantage accruing to from the fact that mining was a reserved occupation. There may also have been some relevance in Jim Bullock's rueful observation that the Nationalisation of the mines in January 1947 unexpectedly undermined the degree of autonomy previously accorded to pit managers like himself: 'Overnight, management status changed, we were no longer the king of our village, the number of officials above the Colliery Manager grew and grew. Instead of us running our pits as we used to, we found we couldn't make any important decisions.'[6] This situation is also liable to have applied, of course, to Bullock's investment in, and patronage of, the colliery football team.

Score-lines appearing in the *Yorkshire Post* and *Leeds Mercury* indicate an erratic start to the season: having drawn 4-4 at Pontefract United, and crashed 6-2 at home to Altofts, Fryston then meted out 8-0 and 11-1 thrashings to Wykebeck (away) and East End Park (home), respectively. An impressive 6-3 win at Newton was then sandwiched between home defeats against Smith's Sports (4-3) and Harehills Liberals (2-1), against whom Fryston had the misfortune to hit the woodwork six times.

Undeniable proof that Fryston Colliery Welfare had become a club in serious decline was provided when they were heavily beaten 8-0 at Harrogate Hotspurs. The West Yorkshire League table featured in the 13 December edition of the *Express* shows Altofts Welfare at the top (played 14, won 10, lost 3, drew 1 = 21 points) and the previously all-conquering Fryston a surprisingly poorly placed fourth from bottom (having played 14, won 4, lost 8, drawn 2 = 10 points). Disturbingly, The Colliers had played two more games than Newtown and East End Park (on ten and eight points, respectively), with Wykebeck Athletic totally cut adrift at the bottom on one point from thirteen games.

With their league form having deteriorated compared with that of previous seasons, at least Fryston could retrieve some satisfaction from a 3-1 home win over RAF Dishforth in the second round of the WRCC Cup; but following a remarkable 5-5 draw at Ravensthorpe in the third round, Fryston were emphatically beaten 9-1 in the home replay.

If these seemed perilous times for the club, they were nothing compared to what was to come in the second half of the season. Having lost their home league match 3-2 to the bottom club, Wykebeck Athletic, they were unceremoniously knocked out of the West Yorkshire League Cup, 9-4 at Newtown.

West Yorkshire Association Football League (WYAFL) minutes reinforce the impression that the club had begun floundering by January 1947, at which point they failed to turn up for their match at Harehills Liberals and ignored a summons to appear before the League Council in order to explain their absence. Things grew worse when the club also failed to attend their fixture at Rothwell Athletic on 26 April. The minutes show that the Rothwell secretary had written to request an explanation from Fryston but had not yet received a reply. The committee therefore fined Fryston £3 3s 0d (three pounds and fifteen pence), directed them to pay Rothwell's expenses of £1 5s 2d (one pound and twenty-six pence) and ordered the match to be re-arranged. The likelihood of this happening remained extremely doubtful: the Association's secretary read out a letter from Fryston, asking the committee to accept their resignation. He informed his fellow officials that he had already written back to Fryston, urging them to complete their fixtures, and the club had since responded that they would try their best to do so.[7]

The next meeting of the committee was attended by Fryston officials, who re-submitted their resignation on the grounds that the club was in 'a poor financial state'. They blamed this on the alleged failure of their recently-resigned club secretary to inform them of the club's perilous financial state of affairs. The Council agreed to accept Fryston's resignation without fine, but insisted that the club must relinquish its 'guarantee fee' of three pounds and fifteen pence.[8] Following this resignation, Fryston were now obliged to return to the Pontefract and District League, from which they had graduated a mere three years earlier; only this time, they would be starting in Division Two.

Rebuilding

Fryston's began their first season back in the Pontefract and District League in extremely promising style by winning their first four matches (including a 3-1 home win over the highly-rated Whitwood Mere), before finally dropping a point in a 2-2 home draw against Glass Houghton Welfare. With the ever-present Chunner Lister marshalling a tight defence and Jimmy Murtha proving an increasingly reliable source of goals, Fryston remained unbeaten until Christmas. However, in the New Year they became plagued by inconsistency, and the tide turned irreversibly against them in early February when they lost their top-of-the-table clash at Whitwood by the remarkable score of 7-5. By the end of the month, Whitwood had opened up a six-point lead which Fryston proved incapable of overturning.

As if to underline their potential, Fryston enjoyed a creditable run in that year's WRCC Cup competition, in which they were their league's only representatives. They beat Normanton St John's of the West Yorkshire League before narrowly losing a replayed tie against the much-fancied Bradford Rovers of the West Riding County Amateur League.

The next three seasons saw Fryston's progress falter. A record of three losses but only one win in their first eleven games of the 1948-49 season set a precedent for far too many draws (taken to extremes in The Colliers' 5-5 outcome at Pontefract United). In one such draw, at home to Hickson and Welch, one of the two opposition goals was scored by the young centre-forward, Fred Howard, whose prolific scoring feats that year could not prevent his side from finishing in the bottom four with Fryston. A year later, Fryston fared little better concluding the season fifth from bottom.

In the 1950-51 season, The Colliers performed better to eventually finish sixth. Fred Howard had continued to show his propensity for high scoring by hitting a sequence of hat-tricks for his new club, Glass Houghton Welfare, which included a 'seven' against Preston Athletic. Howard also scored a goal in each of Glass Houghton's two victories (2-0 home and 4-2 away) over Fryston, adding further evidence that he was on the way to becoming one of the Castleford area's greatest-ever goal-scorers. The same would eventually be said of Howard's slightly younger teammate in the Welfare side. Like Freddie Howard, J.C. 'Charlie' Barnett was about to figure prominently in the years leading up to Fryston's fabled encounter with Thackley.

Fred Howard and Charlie Barnett

Fred Howard and Charlie Barnett were both brought up in Glass Houghton, Castleford, where they eventually became inseparable teenage friends. Howard was born in March 1930 on the nearby Half Acres estate, which is situated on the edge of Castleford town centre. He and his older brother, Stan, were eight and twelve respectively when they moved with their parents to nearby Glass Houghton. Howard's father was a surface worker at Glass Houghton Colliery, and their mother a bottle washer at Lumbs' Glassworks, where, according to Stan: 'They used to have to smash ice in these troughs in t'winter, to wash 'em.' Stan remembers Freddie as 'a good lad, he were a good brother', who went to Temple Street primary school, followed by Ashton Road secondary, and then into a succession of jobs, starting with a period as a steel erector, working from mine to mine.

Stan Howard was an excellent junior Rugby League player, and played for the all-conquering Wheldale Under 19s, before starring at centre for the renowned Lock Lane thirteen. Stan knew his parents were proud of him, but he was equally aware of the fact that: 'My mam worshipped our Fred. He was all football, and he was the Golden Boy!'

Charlie Barnett was born in London in 1933; but following the death of his father in a motorcycle accident, he was adopted by Castleford-born parents and moved to Glass Houghton aged three, where he grew up in a house which overlooked the local cricket field. Barnett did his schooling at Glass Houghton primary, followed by the Castleford Boys' Modern. He was then employed in a number of temporary jobs before embarking on a 30-year career at Glass Houghton Colliery. He first got to know Fred Howard when the latter was a bigger lad of around twelve or thirteen and they used to go together to Glass Houghton Welfare for an impromptu game of football:

> There might've been fifteen-a-side giving it some welly, and our mothers used to come out and shout us in for us dinner, and then we'd go back again. It was that sort of game! And Freddie was always t'top player: we were average, but he was *outstanding*. I got to know Freddie right well, and he were a good mate to me all through my teenage years. (Charlie Barnett)

Luckily for Fred Howard, their street backed onto the home of Sammy Gledhill, who took him under his wing and arranged for him to have trials at York City. Being the shy, reserved person that he was, Howard turned for support to the younger Charlie Barnett:

> He says, 'Will you come with me?' and I says, 'Yeah.' York were in t'Football League then, of course, and they introduced us to their manager. Freddie were playing with the 'A' [reserve] team, but not at t'York City ground; it could've been Leeds or somewhere like that, and he got five goals did Freddie. I mean, bearing in mind that he'd never even played for 'em before! And not surprisingly, they signed him there and then, and after t'match, they fixed him up with a job in York. Well, it must've been about five or six weeks later, I dropped in on him, like, and says, 'How's it going Freddie?' and he says, 'Oh, I've packed it in with York.' I says, 'Never! Why on earth do that?' and he says, 'It were much too far to travel.' Well, you could catch a train from Cas to York in twenty minutes in them days; but that would have been too much like hard work for Freddie. He didn't like breaking sweat. But his footballing ability was outstanding; and if he'd got his back to the goal, that's when he was most dangerous, because he

could swivel, and – bang! – it were a goal. He wasn't what I'd call robust; he didn't get involved in tackles and all that, but, by God, could he put that ball away. And that's what made him my hero – now more so than then. (Charlie Barnett)

Having relinquished the chance to turn professional, Howard returned to Castleford and it was at this point that he began playing in the Pontefract and District League for Hickson and Welch. Rotherham United and Notts County both showed further interest but he was determined not to be uprooted.

Barnett's own football career started with his local Glass Houghton Youth Club; but as a thirteen-year-old he 'transferred' to the higher-ranking Townville Youth Club, where he stayed for a season and a half before being part of a 'player exchange' deal which saw Billy Smith go to Townville and Barnett move to Ferrybridge St Andrews. It was there that he befriended another Castleford goal-scoring legend, the future Ferrybridge Amateurs player, Stan Wright. Such was the quality of the St Andrews team that they eventually overtook the exceptionally gifted Whitwood Juniors as the dominant force in their league, and gained the league and cup 'double' in Barnett's final season with the club.

While at St Andrews, he was invited, along with Fryston's Joe Raftery, to play in a number of games with a Wolverhampton Wanderers 'nursery team', located at Wath-on-Dearne.

I played about eight games with them when I was fifteen or sixteen, and got eight or nine goals. Joe went with me. A good, tricky little footballer was Joe. The first match we played was against Leeds United, and their centre-half, Billy 'somebody', had played in t'first team, but I still got two goals that day. Things were okay for so long because we played in t'morning for Wolves Juniors, and in t'afternoon for St Andrews – two games in one day – but after one match, I said, 'Oh, I can't play next week 'cos I'm playing in a semi-final with t'lads.' I never heard owt else from 'em! (Charlie Barnett)

It was on turning eighteen that Barnett entered open-age football by joining Glass Houghton Welfare. As we shall soon see, this was the start of a memorable career in local football.

On the Road to Recovery

Jim Bullock recalls in *Them and Us* that it did not take long for National Coal Board officials to realise that the industry would be better served by returning managerial autonomy to pit bosses like himself: 'Everybody agreed that management at colliery level needed strengthening. Coal was got from the pits, not from London; and the strength or weakness of the industry is directly influenced by the management at colliery level.'[9] With his freedom to manoeuvre now restored, Bullock invested heavily in local welfare and leisure facilities. In 1951, he authorised the construction by Fryston miners both of a welfare hall and a sports arena on the outskirts of the village.[10] The old practices of allowing members of the sports team ('Bullock's Blue-Eyed Boys') time off or 'sympathetic shifts' to facilitate training or adequate recovery from matches were also reinstated.

It hardly seems coincidental, therefore, that Fryston hit championship form at last in the 1951-52 season. Chunner Lister was employed to great effect in an attacking role (scoring four goals, for example, in the 6-3 home win against Fairburn) as Fryston became far more ruthless and consistent. The four points they gained by doing the 'double' over their nearest rivals, Whitwood Mere, constituted the eventual difference between the two teams, with Fryston's final record being: played 14, won 11, drew 1, lost 2 = 23 points.

If Fryston had assumed they had nothing to fear from Fred Howard (who was now playing in the First Division with Glass Houghton), then they had not bargained for his appearances in cup competitions. It was a Howard hat-trick that set up Welfare's 6-2 quarter-final Cas and District Cup win over The Colliers. Fryston gained their revenge by beating Glass Houghton 2-0 in the semi-final of the Pontefract League Cup. They sustained this excellent end-of-season form in their Pontefract League Championship play-off against an Upton Arms Sports team who had held off the challenge of Blackie's and Glass Houghton Welfare to take the Division One Championship. The game was a close-run thing:

> A goal twenty seconds from the end of a splendid match robbed Fryston of victory, yet it was a goal good enough in itself to have won the match. F. Byron was the scorer from a free kick just outside the penalty box, and he sent the ball into the net through a group of players at terrific speed.

Bedford also scored for Upton, and Fryston's goals were by Cohen and Stockdale. The two teams agreed to 'share' the shield, and it was presented to Fryston, who will hold it for the first six months, by the President of the League [Mr. R.S. Millar].[11]

In an anti-climactic end to the season, Fryston lost out 3-2 to Bagleys' Recreation in the Pontefract League Cup final. The match was 'a hard, exciting tussle which made up in spirit for what it lacked in finesse'. Perry and D. Stockdale were the scorers for a Fryston team that 'did not go under to the Knottingley team without a struggle, but the winners always seemed to make ground more quickly'.[12]

Fryston's good form was maintained in their first year back in the First Division of the Pontefract and District League. By the time of their late-November top-of-the-table clash against Upton Social (formerly Upton Arms Sports), they shared with Upton the distinction of being the only two unbeaten teams in their league, with Fryston's record of nineteen points from eleven games being only one fewer than that of their rivals. The 1-1 draw produced a contest that was certainly 'worthy of leaders':

Fryston battled for the last twenty minutes without their goalkeeper, Portman, and right full-back, Wiltshire, who were both badly injured, in a vain attempt to prevent Upton's equalising goal. Portman sustained a badly bruised back, which necessitated treatment at the Pontefract General Infirmary, and Wiltshire received a cut nose, which required stitches. Templeman, the outside-left – one of four brothers in the team – went in goal, and centre-forward Lister became the emergency full-back. Despite the injuries, a grand spirit of sportsmanship prevailed throughout the match. Fryston scored after twenty minutes through Raftery, and there was little to choose between the teams until Fryston became handicapped. Even with only three forwards, Fryston caused anxiety to the home defence, but their own defence was the more frequently hard-pressed.[13]

In the next few weeks, Fryston started to lose matches they would normally have expected to win. Their 5-2 loss at lowly Fairburn involved the surrendering of an early 2-0 lead. Not long afterwards, they came up against fellow title challengers, Glass Houghton Athletic, for whom Freddie Howard and Charlie Barnett were on the team sheet.

Howard had actually started the season playing for Methley United in the West Yorkshire League First Division, having been transferred from Glass Houghton Welfare. Brought in ostensibly to replace the legendary United centre-forward, Tommy Ward, who had scored close on 200 goals in the past two seasons, Howard was an instant revelation, his nine goals in the first four games including five against Leeds United Union and a hat-trick against East End Park. Howard drew a blank in Methley's next game, a 1-0 win at Rothwell, but featured among the scorers in their following match, a 4-2 defeat at DP and E. Perhaps significantly, Howard had been shifted to outside-left in this match to make way at centre-forward for Tommy Ward, who had unexpectedly re-signed for the club. Things were never the same again, with Howard experiencing an unaccustomed goal drought that eventually saw him loaned out to Glass Houghton Athletic.

Charlie Barnett, meanwhile, had decided that he would be happier playing for Athletic ('who the majority of my mates played for'), rather than for Welfare. Barnett had announced his arrival from Welfare to Athletic by scoring seven of his club's eight goals in their Pontefract League match against Methley Junction Rovers. This was the prelude to a sensational spree of scoring by Barnett. In mid-December, his hat-trick in Athletic's 7-1 demolition of Resil Sports represented his sixth of the season (even discounting his seven goals against Methley). While Howard continued to accumulate his own fair share of goals (e.g. the hat-trick he scored in Athletic's 4-0 win at Fairburn), his exploits were frequently overshadowed by his centre-forward colleague, who went on to add another hat-trick in a win over Pontefract United Reserves to the four he snatched in the 9-2 return drubbing of Resil.

The two players created predictable havoc for Fryston, with Howard scoring twice and Barnett another in Athletic's 5-3 win. Fryston's cause was further undermined by the expulsion from the league (for non-payment of fines) of the Blackie's club. All the league matches in which Blackie's had so far participated were expunged from the records — a blow to Fryston, who had already recorded four points against them, compared to Upton's two. Upton consolidated their advantage by earning a 3-2 victory at Fryston that virtually secured the title. Playing with a strong wind at their backs, Fryston were two up at half time with goals from Raftery and Tommy Templeman. An own goal allowed Upton back into the game shortly after the restart and even a Jack Templeman save in the Fryston goals could not prevent defeat. Upton duly secured the title with a 5-0 victory over Pontefract

United before lapsing to their only league defeat of the season – a 4-2 home loss to Glass Houghton Athletic, for whom Charlie Barnett was once more on the score-sheet.

Fryston exacted revenge for Upton's championship success by beating them in the replayed final of the Pontefract League Cup competition. Both matches were played at Glass Houghton Welfare. In the first of them, two goalkeeping errors were instrumental in producing a 1-1 draw: 'The goals were scored by Websdale, Upton's right-back, whose long shot bounced over the Fryston goalkeeper's head, and by Stockdale, after the ball had been dropped in the Upton goalmouth.'[14] It was Stockdale's first-half goal which decided the replayed final in which 'there was little to choose between the two teams, and only some fine saves by Portman prevented Upton from drawing level in the final stages'.[15]

Frank Isles and Jack Sharp

That was not the only silverware entering the village that year. Fryston Youth Team's 7-0 win over Kippax in mid-April guaranteed them the Castleford and District Youth League Championship, while their 4-2 defeat of Hightown took them into the final of the Castleford FA Junior Cup competition for the third successive year. A subsequent victory over Westfield Wizards landed Fryston the celebrated 'double' and added to the impressive tally of trophies they had accumulated since the turn of the decade:

In the 1949-50 season they reached the semi-final of the Junior League Cup. The next season they were finalists in the Castleford and District Junior Challenge Cup competition and winners of the Normanton and District (Under 16) Cup and the Normanton and District Youth League Championship and Cup. In 1951 they reached the final of the Castleford and District Junior Challenge Cup and the Castleford and District Youth League, won the Castleford and District Youth League Cup, the 'Billy Empire' Cup (which was thereby won by a team outside Normanton for the first time in the eighteen years history of the competition), and the Normanton and District League Championship Cup and Under 16 Cup. In September of last year they were the only team to beat a team of German youths touring the West Riding.[16]

This last sentence alludes to Fryston's 5-2 victory over a touring team whose itinerary was arranged by the manager of Cadeby and Denaby Colliery. Fryston's scorers that day were Raymond 'Dobber' Sutcliffe, Frank Isles and John Sutton (the fifth was an own goal). These and other young players, like Geoff Eddy, Eric Lunn and Jack Sharp, were soon to be mainstays of the Fryston first team. Indeed, the likes of Sharp and Isles had already made their first-team debuts by now, the former being as young as fourteen when he first appeared on the sheet.

John ('Jack' or 'Jackie') Sharp and Frank Isles shared an impressive footballing pedigree. They were called after two great uncles, 'Frankie' and 'Johnny', both exceptionally gifted players, who were killed aged nineteen in the First World War. 'Whatever happened to them I don't know,' concedes Jack Sharp. 'One of them was reputed to be very, very good, indeed, but obviously the war broke out, and they both went and never came back. In fact I've still got their medals upstairs.'

The older of the two cousins, Frank Isles, was born in the 'Water Cottages', a small row of houses located just outside the village, adjacent to the sewage beds off Wheldon Road. His family moved into the village itself when Isles was only six-months-old, to occupy a house in the centrally located Smith Street. Isles attended Fryston School alongside such future Fryston team-mates as his fellow villager, Derek Stockdale, and John Sutton, who lived at the bottom of Fryston Road. Having progressed to Airedale Secondary Modern, Isles and other local football devotees enjoyed their first taste of organised football playing for the Fryston Juniors side, set up by an enthusiast called Harold Bosworth who lived at the bottom of Airedale.

It was through playing with the Juniors that Isles (even after he had begun working at the pit as an apprentice fitter) and three other Frystoners were selected, as part of a squad of thirteen, to represent the Castleford and District FA Minor team in the West Riding Minor Challenge Cup competition. In the third round, Castleford came up against a strong Leeds and District FA team which included Jack Charlton, the future centre-half in England's 1966 World Cup-winning team, at left-back:

He was already on the Leeds United books. He was about seventeen as well – there's actually only a month or so between us in age. It was icy conditions and, whether or not that had any bearing on it I don't know, but I had a right good game against him and we won 2-1. Pete Briers played in goal – he turned to rugby afterwards – and pulled some miraculous saves off, whether they hit him or not. But we won 2-1 and we got into the semi-final at Ripon where we played Harrogate. In the final, we played Wakefield and we won that one as well to take the trophy. We all got gold medals; and at that match, there were scouts from Bradford Park Avenue, who asked three of us from Cas and two from Wakefield to go to Bradford the season after. (Frank Isles)

Soon afterwards, therefore, Isles found himself playing regularly alongside Eric Lunn and Derek Stockdale for a Park Avenue minor side that was coached by Chick Farr. Typically, a group of youths from Normanton and Castleford would set out at eight o'clock each Saturday morning and catch the three buses required to get to Park Avenue. The youths would then turn out for their Northern Intermediate match on a practice field situated a mile away from the stadium, before returning afterwards to watch the first team's fixture for free. This continued until three-quarters of the way into the season, when Bradford's Juniors were supposed to be playing an away game at Newcastle.

Anyhow, we didn't get any message so I rang Derek Stockdale in Fryston and he said, 'I haven't got a card; they must have called it off.' Anyway, in t'Sunday paper it was 'Newcastle 8 Bradford Park Avenue 3' in t'Northern Intermediate League; and we got together and said, 'Well, if that's the trick they're pulling to save a bit of expense!' We all said, 'Bugger it!' and we never went no more. After that, I played for Fryston – well, I tried to: I trained and all that, but I didn't get in for the first couple of matches. They had this bloke called Pete Ward. He came from Whitwood. They had a fair side at that point. So I went to Airedale, 'cos I knew a few lads from Airedale, and played there for half a season before moving back to Fryston, who were then in a higher league than Airedale. So that's when I started out at outside-right, it would have been 1953 or '54. (Frank Isles)

Like his cousin, Frank, Jack Sharp was born just outside of the village, on Fryston Road. He was two-years-old when his parents moved into a little row of terraces 'right at the top end, in a little row of four cottages which were very nice – next to the "top chapel"'. Unusually for that time, he was born an only child. Even at junior school he excelled at all sports ('bar for swimming, for which they gave me extra lessons!'). Sharp can scarcely remember playing for Fryston Juniors, recalling that Bosworth was just in the process of winding down the team as he grew old enough to play for them. Even more to the point:

At school, at that time, I played more Rugby League than football. I played scrum-half for a combined Cas and Wakefield District side. They used to play such as Dewsbury and Hunslet down Wheldon Lane on Saturday afternoons. I first played when I was thirteen. The lad whose place I took was Don Fox, the Featherstone player from out Sharlston way who missed that vital kick from under the post at Wembley. I must have played, well, a dozen times at Wheldon Lane, and crowds would come and watch because it was only an hour before the senior match got started. You got changed at Wheldon Lane School – a matter of, what, a few hundred yards away from t'ground? You'd play the game, then go back to t'school for a sandwich. (Jack Sharp)

Though many good judges urged him to turn professional, Sharp's first priority was Association Football. By the time he was fifteen (and had already achieved his full adult size of five-foot-three or four), he was working in the company of grown men at the pit. He, too, had started out as an apprentice fitter, but confesses to being 'not mechanically minded'. In any case, 'All the lads I used to pal around with on the street corner and that were already underground. They were all down t'pit, and it was a couple of quid more than I was getting, so I said, I'd go and join 'em.' Already a 'man amongst boys', he walked into the Fryston team while scarcely in his teens, and having been selected for the English National Association of Boys' Clubs.

Frank Isles is in no doubt as to who was the most talented footballer in the club's entire history: 'We've had some great players for a village of this size,' says Isles, 'but I'll be surprised if there's been one any better than our Jack. I've never seen anybody fit to tie his laces.' It was the convergence of Sharp's career with that of another Fryston legend, their erstwhile nemesis, Freddie Howard, that would now prove the springboard for Fryston's continuing ascent as they prepared to enter the First Division of the Pontefract and District League.

Chapter 6
Freddie Howard's Heyday

Previous page: Fryston's goal-scorer extraordinaire, Freddie Howard, with one of the trophies he helped them win in the early- and mid-1950s.

Howard's Perfect Ten

Fryston renewed their strong rivalry with Upton Sports in the 1953-54 season, but also had strong pressure from Glass Houghton Athletic to contend with as all three clubs set their sights on the Pontefract and District League First Division title and gaining promotion to the West Yorkshire League. Fryston had stolen a march on their rivals by signing Freddie Howard, whose remarkable goal-scoring exploits for the club in this and subsequent seasons will form a major focus of discussion for the next three chapters.

The Colliers achieved a crucial breakthrough in their promotion push with a 2-1 home win against Upton in mid-September ('Young Fryston team shock champions'[1]), for which they had goals from Howard and the increasingly impressive Jack Sharp to thank. By mid-February, Howard had contributed a succession of hat-tricks, including 'fours' against Ackworth, Pontefract Collieries, and Darrington. The part he played in his team's demolition of lowly YEB Sports was remarkable, even by his own recent standards:

> Fryston created what is believed to be an all-time record in the PONTEFRACT LEAGUE when they scored twenty goals against YEB Sports, on Saturday. It is also believed that no player has ever matched the ten-goal scoring feat of Fryston's 23-year-old centre-forward, Fred Howard. All the Fryston forwards scored, and right-half Stockdale joined in and helped himself to a 'hat-trick'. In nineteen League and Cup games this season, Howard has scored 58 goals, and has contributed a major share to Fryston's remarkable record of 118 goals 'for' in eighteen league games, with only eighteen against.[2]

Fryston's next league match – a 9-0 win at Wilkinson's, which included a Howard hat-trick and a pair from Frankie Isles – underlined their championship credentials. A corresponding game in which second-placed Glass Houghton Athletic were overwhelmed 8-2 on their own ground by third-placed Upton Social, severely dented the former's chances, whilst re-galvanising the latter's bid to retain their title. At this stage, there was little to separate the three teams:

	P	W	L	D	Pts
Fryston Colliery Welfare	19	17	1	1	35
Upton Social	18	15	2	1	31
Glass Houghton Athletic	19	15	3	1	31

However, Athletic had more reason than their heavy defeat by Upton to feel pessimistic about. Hitherto, they had been able to rely on the goal-scoring heroics of their own star centre-forward, Charlie Barnett, which had included thirteen in two games against Pontefract Collieries. Now, though, Barnett had suddenly been poached by Yorkshire League team, Selby Town, and speculation inevitably focused on how well they might cope without him.

Athletic's back-to-back wins over Fryston shortly after Barnett's departure (a 2-1 home victory in the Infirmary Cup, and a repeat score in their away league match) suggested that they might not have too much cause for concern. In the first match, Fryston could point by way of excuse to the loss of Stockdale early in the game with a dislocated shoulder. Clearly, though, 'Athletic forgot all about their "loss-of-Barnett" complex, and were not upset by an early Fryston goal by Isles soon after Stockdale's departure.'[3] In the league game, a Fred Howard goal could not prevent Athletic from prevailing in a match in which they 'were well worth their victory, though the ball ran unkindly for Fryston'. This result had re-opened the race for the title. Athletic now trailed Fryston by two points, with both having two games to play. One of the Athletic's remaining games was at Upton – who, by taking six points from their final three games, could still tie with Fryston's maximum possible tally of 39 points.

Despite walloping Loscoe 13-0 in their next match, Fryston experienced a dramatic late-season loss of form, losing 8-3 at Methley in the Cas and District Cup (although Fred Howard at least had the satisfaction of scoring twice against his old club) and 3-2 in the Pontefract League Cup semi-final against Resil, when their goalkeeper, Jimmy Portman, was sent off. The Colliers rallied to achieve an easy 7-0 victory in their last league game against Glass Houghton Welfare, to record impressive final statistics of played 22, won 19, lost 2, drew 1 = 39 points. However, Upton's 4-2 win over Glass Houghton Athletic, and subsequent victories in their remaining two matches, meant that they were tied with Fryston and would have to play a deciding match. Upton entered the game having just beaten Resil in the final of the Pontefract Infirmary Cup; and in the subsequent championship play-off, 'Fryston won easily against a team which showed obvious signs of a very heavy programme in cup football. Isles and Howard each scored twice for the winners.'[4] Howard's two goals brought his end-of-season tally in all competitions to a remarkable 89.

A Sharp Career Move

Fryston began their return to the West Yorkshire League Division Two in some style. They had a solid goalkeeper in Portman; commanding half-backs in Battye, Lister and Winterbottom; great ball-players in the likes of Tommy Templeman, Dobber Sutcliffe and the emergent Jack Sharp; and of course, the firepower of Fred Howard, for whom 1954-55 would represent a prolonged master-class in the art of goal-scoring. Fryston's first four games produced a 100 per cent league record towards which Howard and Sharp had contributed at least a goal each in every game. In their next two games (both at home), the same two players continued their good form as Fryston first overcame Newton 7-0, with Howard hitting five, and Sharp and Sutcliffe the others; and then comfortably saw off Pontefract United 3-1 with goals by the same three scorers. Next up was an emphatic 8-2 victory over the previously unbeaten Robin Hood Athletic:

> In Howard, Fryston possessed a centre-forward who for a second time this season hit five goals in a match. It was an afternoon on which he seemed to be able to do all that was right. Sharpe [sic], the young outside-left, slipped in three goals to prove the value of a winger with a goal-scoring eye. Two players who were not among the goal-scorers – Sutcliffe (inside-right) and Lister (centre-half and captain) – also had much to do with the fine victory.[5]

Fryston (and Fred Howard in particular) maintained their form in the next two matches. First they overcame their closest rivals, Snydale Road Athletic, to record an impressive 3-2 away win, thanks to a

Howard hat-trick in the first fifteen minutes of the game, all from slender chances. Howard knocked in five more in Fryston's 6-2 home thrashing of Waddington's Sports. However, they then experienced their first setback of the season, in being overwhelmed 4-1 in their home WRCC Cup tie against the West Yorkshire League Division One team, Ossett Albion, to end their first such campaign for several seasons:

> The end of Fryston's notable record of having won all their matches this season was as much their own fault as the work of their opponents. Howard, who until Saturday had scored 22 goals, set the fashion by failing to score with two gilt-edged chances in the first half soon after having equalised a goal scored by the visitors early on. Portman fell from previous form and was three times at fault in the second half… Lister, at centre-half, tried desperately to stem Ossett's attack when his wing-halves were outplayed, but he could only delay the end. A compensating feature was the duel between Pepper (right-back) and a speedy Ossett winger, which ended all square, and then, of course, there was Howard's goal, which preserved his record of having scored in every match.[6]

The Colliers surrendered a 3-1 lead to draw 3-3 with Snydale in their next home league game, although, 'Howard in collecting Fryston's [first-half goal] celebrated his selection in the West Yorkshire League team, and kept his record of a goal in every match.'[7] The centre-forward followed up by scoring four in Fryston's 5-2 West Yorkshire League Division Two Cup match at home to Waddington's Sports, but was significantly absent (on duty for the league representative team) for their first league defeat of the season, 2-0 to Kippax Welfare. Restored to the side for their mid-December game at Farsley United, Howard made amends by scoring a hat-trick in an 8-2 victory which took his personal tally for the season so far to 31 out of the 52 goals scored by Fryston.

The Farsley game proved a pivotal moment in the career of Fryston's rising star, Jack Sharp. After the match, Sharp, his cousin Frank Isles, and their close friend, Dobber Sutcliffe, all returned to Jack's parents' house with the intention of having something to eat and then going out for the evening:

> I remember Dobber used to work Saturday mornings at the pit and he used to leave his bike at ours and go on the bus to wherever we went – to Farsley,

in this case. Then we'd come back and mum would give us something to eat and Dobber'd bugger off to Brotherton on his bike. What happened that particular day was that we came in and this bloke sat down at the table. He had one of those brown suede coats with fur on the collar. (Jack Sharp)

According to Frank Isles:

Me and Dobber said, 'What's this car doing here?' Our Jack didn't have a car back then. Dobber had to go in for his bike, so we all walked in. And at that time I lived at my Aunt Edie's because I lost my dad when I was twelve. My Uncle George was sat there and my Aunt Edie, and his dad says, 'This is Willie Watson from Halifax Town.'

The Willie Watson in question came from that rare breed of sportsmen, the 'double international',[8] who could claim the distinction of representing their country at both football and cricket. The likeable, quietly-spoken Yorkshireman had made his pre-war debut at wing-half for Huddersfield Town before playing seven post-war seasons with Sunderland. It was during his fourth season at Roker Park that Watson gained his first cap for England, in their 9-2 victory over Northern Ireland in 1949. In the meantime, he had also become a regular left-handed batsmen in the Yorkshire County Cricket team, having made his debut in 1939, and was by now one of the best-known (and best-loved) members of the England First XI.

The game that transformed Watson into a national hero was England's Lord's test match against Australia in 1953, when he and the Essex all-rounder, Trevor Bailey, spent a nerve-racking 345-minute fifth-wicket stand of 163 to save England from certain defeat. The Yorkshireman's innings of 109 was celebrated by the *Daily Sketch* headline of 'Wonderful Willie Watson'.[9] The resulting draw kept alive England's hopes of regaining the Ashes, which they subsequently managed to do with a victory at the Oval after four drawn games. Though still playing for Yorkshire and England at cricket, Watson had become player-manager of Halifax Town in 1954. All of this was lost on the youthful and relatively carefree Jack Sharp:

I didn't even know who he was, and I didn't even know that Halifax were interested; but we got talking and I soon realised what a smashing bloke he was – too nice to be a manager, to be fair. I didn't know him from Adam, and I certainly didn't know that he played for England back then. Obviously, somebody had been watching me on the sly, and I did find out later that it was a bloke called Higginbottom, and it was on his recommendation that they wanted to sign me. Obviously, I worked at the pit and he wanted me to go full time, but I thought, 'I've got all my mates in t'village.' I was one of the lads and there was a team of us, so I only ever went part-time. The good thing was that my dad, who was a deputy at Fryston pit, had a pact with the manager that I could have Tuesday and Thursday off and go train in Halifax. He was a sportsman was Jim [Bullock], so he tolerated me just working Mondays, Wednesdays and Fridays, and I'd go to Halifax on Tuesdays and Thursdays.

The Pimpernel of Forwards

Sharp continued to play in Fryston colours until the turn of the New Year. During that period, Fred Howard treated himself to another hat-trick in their 6-1 home win against Pontefract United. Both he (with two) and Sharp were among the scorer's in Fryston's 5-1 Christmas Day victory over neighbouring Townville and Airedale Athletic; and Howard grabbed the winning goal in a 2-1 Boxing Day win against the same club. As the 'old year' was brought to an end with a 2-0 home win over Woodlesford, the *Express* reflected on Howard's accomplishments thus far:

> Naming the outstanding local footballer of 1954 would not be easy, but high in any nomination list would be the name of Fred Howard, Fryston's centre-forward. Since September 11, when his club re-entered the West Yorkshire League, he has proved himself the Pimpernel of forwards – sought here and there by centre-halves: sometimes quietened, but never subdued. On Saturday, Woodlesford kept his name off the score sheet for a considerable time, but when it seemed he was tamed, he struck two goals in rapid succession and Woodlesford went home pointless. No side has prevented Howard from scoring this season, and his tally now reads: 2, 1, 5, 1, 5, 3, 5, 1, 1, 4, 2, 3, 3, 2, 1, 2: total 41.[10]

This 'Pimpernel of forwards' scored all four of Fryston's goals in their away draw at Newtown, a scoring feat he would subsequently repeat in his team's 5-0 Ramsden Cup victory at Woodlesford and 9-2 away win over Ackworth in the Pontefract Infirmary Cup. The Colliers were less successful in suffering a 3-1 setback against Kippax in the Ramsden Trophy semi-final. However, 'Just when it appeared that the Fryston centre-forward was going to lose his record of having scored in every match this season, he got the ball under Render's body and revived his side's hopes. But again the Kippax tactics prevailed.'[11]

A goal in each of Fryston's next two home victories (3-1 against Tadcaster Albion, and 4-0 against Farsley United) created inevitable speculation that, with only two league matches and an Infirmary Cup semi-final (and possible final) remaining, Howard might end the season having scored in every game in which he'd played. The striker maintained this possibility by scoring twice in a 2-2 draw at Robin Hood Athletic, which re-emphasised the value of a defensive mainstay to the side:

> A move by centre-half Lister brought a goal for Howard, and the centre-forward enabled Fryston to share the points by scoring again. The rally shook the home defence and the Welfare finished well on top. The defence, marshalled by Lister, was outstanding throughout.[12]

Fryston's final league match saw them losing away to Kippax (by the odd goal in seven) for the third time that season. Almost inevitably, though, it was Howard who stole the show, even in defeat:

> With the slope and wind in their favour, Fryston obtained the important first goal after only eight minutes, when Howard netted and achieved the feat of having scored in every League match this season. Kippax were not long behind, Voyce crossing for Booth to equalise after the ball had eluded several players. Booth added a second when Ogman paved the way; and early in the second half Voyce made the lead into two. An additional blow for Fryston was the loss of Sutcliffe, who pulled a muscle, but they fought back strongly and there were times when they looked worthy of the point which would have given them the championship. After another Howard goal, the woodwork rescued Kippax, and it was poor reward when Collinson swept past four defenders to restore the home team's two-goal lead. A penalty goal by Howard restored Fryston's hopes, but the task was just beyond them. Pepper (right-back) and Lister (centre-half) were outstanding for the losers.[13]

An element of anti-climax then followed. On the following Saturday, Fryston secured their league title without even kicking a ball when their nearest challengers, Snydale Road Athletic, succumbed 4-2 at Newtown and therefore could not overhaul Fryston's championship-winning total of 35 points from sixteen wins, three draws and three defeats. Howard was missing from Fryston's 8-2 Infirmary Cup semi-final win over Synthetic Chemicals, in which Frankie Isles ironically stole his thunder by hitting the net six times to register the best individual scoring feat of the season. The star forward was also absent for Fryston's victory in the final, against Depot Y and L regiment, in which a goal by his deputy, Geoff Eddy, and two by Dobber Sutcliffe earned Fryston a shaky 3-1 win. Nevertheless, there could be no denying that Howard's goal-scoring heroics in netting a total of 63 goals that season were the stuff from which legends are cast.

Ferry's Bridge Too Far

The end of the season saw Fryston's near neighbours, Ferrybridge Amateurs, come within touching distance of lifting the prestigious WRCC Cup for the first time in their history. Their opponents in the final were a crack Swillington Welfare team, which had not only beaten them 13-2 on the first day of the season, but had also thrashed them 5-0 at Ferrybridge in a mid-season West Yorkshire League Division One Cup game. Playing at centre-forward for Amateurs was Charlie Barnett, who had returned earlier in the season after enjoying a successful spell at Selby.

Barnett is not quite sure how or why Selby had first come in for him. 'Perhaps,' he reckons, 'they must have read the paper and seen I were scoring a few goals. They came down, enquiring if I would play with 'em, and I said, "Yeah, why not?"' Barnett remembers catching a bus to the ground, without really knowing anything about the club or even the town itself. His first game for Selby was an instant revelation. A future Fryston player, Geoff Garbett, was already playing with Selby as a part-time professional. It was during the course of Barnett's debut that Garbett offered him a small piece of crucial advice:

> I think the first match we played were at Scarborough, and we won 5-2. And I were centre-forward, and I were holding t'ball a bit like this and giving the defenders a bit of time to read me, and Geoff says, 'Don't hold it, hit it, just hit it first time!' So, when it came through next time, I hit it, and it went straight in t'back o' t'net. I got two, both similar, that day like. But it made me realise that I were in a different league and playing a different

game entirely. Anyway I got a couple of goals, and I finished up I scored 30-odd goals in my first season. (Charlie Barnett)

Barnett recalls that, as a fitter at Glass Houghton Colliery, he was required to start working on Saturday mornings and, therefore, had been forced to sacrifice his place at Selby. Though Methley United were one of several clubs eager to sign him, he opted instead for Ferrybridge Amateurs. The striker had made his debut for the club in their 3-2 late-October victory against Leeds UYML. According to the *Express*, Barnett could easily have opened the scoring with barely a minute gone were it not for 'alert goalkeeping', but was not to be denied when he opened the scoring ten minutes later. 'For the remainder of the game this former Glass Houghton player showed how well equipped he is for directing the ball with both head and foot. His colleagues were not always smart enough to take advantage of his work, and so the result remained in doubt until the final whistle.'[14] Barnett confirms that, 'When I came back from Selby to Amateurs, I were two moves in front of 'em, based on what I'd learned at Selby. I'd pass t'ball and be four yards offside by the time it had come back to me!'

Barnett's goals were instrumental in securing Ferry's passage into the quarter-finals of the WRCC Cup, where they played one of the leading Bradford Teams, Thackley of the West Yorkshire Amateur League. The Ferrybridge inside-right and captain (and scorer of four goals in earlier rounds), Roy Milner, was absent due to injury. Barnett's winning goal in the eighth minute settled a dour encounter. Thackley always did sufficient from there on in to 'keep the local supporters anxious'; but that said, 'Ferrybridge had the smarter look, with Barnett always on the alert, and twice he rapped in shots which only narrowly missed the mark.'[15] In the semi-final against Bradford Electricity, Ferry enjoyed a 4-0 success: 'Barnett scored all the Amateurs' goals and actually put the ball in the net six times. The former Glass Houghton leader has scored 10 of his side's 22 goals in the West Riding Cup.'[16]

It is possible that the torrential downpour an hour before Ferrybridge's WRCC Cup final against Swillington at Selby contributed to an extremely thrilling game. The sides were locked at two-all by the end of normal time, with Ferry's goals coming from two Roy Milner penalties (the first after Barnett had been pushed off the ball with the goal at his mercy). Swillington seized the initiative with two goals in the first period of extra time, before the Ferrybridge full-back, Melvyn Wright, 'took the ball half the length of the field, gave to, and received from L. Smith, and then squared the ball for Barnett to head the best goal of the match.'[17] However, in the second period of extra time, Swillington scored a fifth to deny the Amateurs an unprecedented club success.

Howard's Comings and Goings

The 1955-56 season opened with Freddie Howard having briefly left Fryston to play for their First Division rivals, Altofts Welfare. Ronnie Foulkes maintains that the move was related to one of the occasional differences that would occur between Howard and Dick Foulkes in which the latter invariably accused the star striker of being 'too nesh' (i.e. not physical enough). Howard's place at centre-forward was taken over by Geoff Eddy, who had the satisfaction of scoring in the club's 4-0 opening victory at home to Selby Town Reserves. Eddy's satisfaction was increased when he scored the game's only goal in Fryston's away fixture against Howard's new club.

The team was generally bolstered by the acquisition of two half-backs in Pearson and Lunn from Glass Houghton Welfare and Airedale Athletic, respectively. Soon afterwards, however, goals and wins became increasingly hard to come by for The Colliers. After incurring home defeats against Swillington and Altofts (2-1 and 4-1, respectively) and being held to a 1-1 home draw by Ossett Albion, Fryston then lost 2-0 at Rothwell Athletic, where 'Not even another rock-like display from Ronnie [Chunner] Lister, who is able to claim over 200 consecutive appearances for the club, could save Fryston from defeat... He and his defence, with goalkeeper Portman again outstanding, held the Athletic's forwards at bay until well into the second half, but they were always fighting a lost cause.'[18]

By October, Fred Howard had rejoined Fryston (firmly establishing a pattern of leaving and then quickly rejoining the club) and duly scored a goal in the first ten minutes of their match at DP and E, only to fall injured in the second half of a contest Fryston eventually lost 2-1. Fryston then recorded their first victory since 3 September by beating Farsley Celtic Reserves 3-1 at home in Howard's absence.

Although the centre-forward scored four times in Fryston's 6-0 Cas and District Cup victory against Whitwood Mere one week later, a combination of injury and poor form, which eventually saw him dropped from the side, resulted in a rare barren spell for this goal-scorer *par excellence*.

It was Ray Murfin, not Fred Howard, who proved to be Fryston's 'hat-trick hero' in the opening game of that season's WRCC Cup campaign, a 3-0 victory at Woodlesford. A week prior to the following round of matches, Fryston (then fifth from the bottom) took on the league leaders, Ferrybridge Amateurs, in an away match. Howard was out of luck in having two goals disallowed, but Charlie Barnett was on target for a game that an Amateurs team including the recently transferred Dobber Sutcliffe went on to win 2-1. A week later, Fryston went down to a 3-0 defeat at Bradford Rovers in the WRCC Cup, and this was followed by a 7-2 spanking in the league at Swillington. It was only after a goalless home draw and two back-to-back defeats against Yorkshire Amateurs Reserves (1-4 and 3-2) that Fryston next won a game, 3-2 away to Selby Town Reserves, thanks to a Ray Murfin hat-trick.

While Fryston's form remained erratic thereafter, the now-recalled Fred Howard's season started to turn for the better with Fryston's resounding 6-1 Greenwood Trophy victory over Carlton United:

> Five goals, from centre-forward Howard, who had lost his scoring touch and had been in the reserves until the match at Selby, might indicate a one-man victory, but that would be wrong, for there was some admirable team work. All Howard's goals were obtained as he ran on to through passes to push the ball round the oncoming goalkeeper.[19]

Howard was well contained in the next match, a 2-0 setback at Rothwell, in which he nonetheless struck a post in latching on to a through pass. It looked as though Fryston were heading to defeat at Methley one week later, when the home side established a 1-0 half-time lead, only for Fryston to earn a draw, thanks to fine displays by Isles and 'one of the best goals seen on the ground this season'[20] by Fred Howard. Howard's gradual return to form was rewarded by his selection for the West Yorkshire League in the last weekend of January, when Fryston went down 3-1 in his absence at Ossett Albion.

By mid-February, there were unmistakable signs that Howard was back to his inimitable best. The first such impression occurred in Fryston's 6-2 mauling by Ferrybridge in the semi-final of the Cas and District Cup. The following week's *Express* paid homage to Howard and his great friend and opposing centre-forward, Charlie Barnett:

The CASTLEFORD CUP semi-final, at Glass Houghton, on Saturday, might have been billed as 'starring those two prolific goal-scoring centre-forwards, Barnett, of Ferrybridge and Howard, of Fryston.' Both added to fine records – Barnett by scoring twice in the first 15 minutes and Howard, after shooting against the crossbar in the first half, by obtaining two goals in the opening 22 minutes of the second. But the centre-forwards faced a strong rival for individual honours in the well-built Ferrybridge outside-left, Millar, who scored three times, missed the easiest chance of the match, and had a goal, in the first minutes, disallowed.[21]

The next week's edition of the *Express* was even more eulogistic as it reported on an incident-packed Greenwood Cup second-round tie in which Fryston had lost out in a twelve-goal thriller at home to the mighty Swillington Welfare ('the post-war "wonders" of West Riding amateur football'). With Jimmy Portman below his best, Swillington raced into a 4-0 lead, which Howard reduced with a late first-half penalty. Then came a second-half rally by Fryston that shook the league leaders to their core:

Howard added three goals to level the scores and was on the point of putting Fryston ahead when brought down from behind. His penalty kick was finely saved, however, and off went Swillington to take the lead. Again Howard equalised and excitement grew as both teams became locked in the struggle for a semi-final place. But Swillington finished the match as they began it – with a late five-minute scoring spree of two goals.[22]

There was no stopping Howard now. One week later, he scored all the goals in Fryston's 5-0 thrashing of a hapless Harrogate DRA Reserves, prompting the admiring observation that 'There may be more skilful centre-forwards in junior football than Fred Howard of Fryston, but there can be few better marksmen. Fryston have scored 12 goals in their last three matches; Howard has obtained all of them. After a lean spell, he appears to have recovered the form of last season.'[23] Another followed in the 1-1 draw at Farsley Celtic Reserves, a game in which Howard also 'whipped in several snapshots which whistled past the posts'.[24] Howard's *pièce de résistance* was then witnessed in Fryston's home match against relegation rivals, Micklefield Welfare, who were put to the sword 9-2 with the centre-forward claiming no less than six of the goals scored:

> Friend and foe alike, including the league leaders, fail to push Howard, the Fryston centre-forward, out of the headlines. Having scored all his team's 13 goals in the last four matches… he obtained the first five of their nine on Saturday, before a colleague broke his sequence. But Howard, who has scored five or more goals in a match on three occasions since February 25 and reached 50 goals in this match, had the last word by scoring Fryston's ninth. Micklefield fielded a weakened team and Howard quickly placed them three goals behind. They rallied, however, and with the aid of a penalty kick were only a goal behind at half time. Without undue exertion, Fryston dominated the second half, Murfin and two reserves, Armitage and H. Astbury, taking the only chances allowed by Howard. Now, only a remarkable transformation can send Fryston back in the Second Division of the League.[25]

In the absence of Howard and Barnett (the former having been redeployed to score a hat-trick in a reserve team cup-tie), Fryston lost heavily (5-1) at home to Ferrybridge, before a drawn return match against Micklefield (4-4) saw Howard resume his astonishing first-team form by scoring another hat-trick. Howard was missing from Fryston's next match (a 1-0 home win against Harrogate Town), but scored in the return fixture, which Fryston lost heavily, 5-2. In the final league encounter, he scored twice in Fryston's 4-2 victory over Carlton United to leave the team fourth from bottom of the Division.

Howard was out of sorts in Fryston's last match of the season, a disappointing 4-2 setback against Moorthorpe Recreation in the Pontefract Infirmary Cup final, in which The Colliers' goals were scored by Rotherforth and Beaman. Fryston were handicapped by the fact that their 'keeper, Williams, was twice taken off injured, but this was not sufficient to excuse their defeat. 'The Moorthorpe forward line was always moving quickly, much to the discomfort of Fryston, who relied almost entirely on centre-forward Howard for their shooting. Howard struck the woodwork twice in the first half, but after working the ball cleverly, later failed with several chances.'[26]

As this last report emphasises, Freddie Howard's form had undoubtedly been less consistent than in previous seasons; but he had still nonetheless demonstrated that he remained one of the great goal-scoring exponents of the local football scene. Howard's two contemporaries, Jack Sharp and Frankie Isles, were in ideal positions to evaluate the centre-forward's ability and place in the local sporting pantheon. In both respects, Frank Isles is unequivocal:

> He was a great player, Freddie – undoubtedly the best out-and-out goal-getter we've ever witnessed in this area. He made goals out of nothing. I mean, Fryston'd be defending, they'd bump it up to Fred who'd take it on the turn and put you one-nil up! And that got your momentum going, see? He was at his most dangerous when he had his back to goal. You didn't know how to play him because it was sudden turn and shoot! Don't get me wrong, he got his goals from everywhere, but he was lethal when you couldn't see him to read him. He wasn't a Fryston lad – he was a Glass Houghton lad – but he gave us a great few years and we certainly got more goals out of him than anybody else. And don't forget, he had a good few lads around him, such as Joe Raf [Raftery] and Dobber Sutcliffe. He was a good inside-forward was Dobber – raw-boned and brave – while Joe was twinkle-toed and full of trickery. (Frank Isles)

Jack Sharp was equally complimentary at one level, regarding Howard as 'an instinctive player whose first touch was phenomenal. He was a classical finisher – good with his head and two great feet.' However, for Sharp, there was also a fatal flaw in Howard's make-up which could sometimes be exploited by those who were more aware of it than others: 'He was like lightning. Just let him settle down and play football and, sure as hell, he would destroy you. But if you had a word in his ear or muscled him around, things were likely to be different. I always felt he could be bullied out of a game by those who had his measure.'

The comments of Howard's daughter, Susan, are perhaps relevant to this argument. She maintains that her father was 'never a rowdy sort of bloke' and seldom drank or smoked. As for his home life:

> My mam and dad would argue like any married couple, but it was always very one-sided with him on the receiving end of it – and, if I'm honest, he were a bit *too* soft 'cos me mam was very hard on him. It's just that he were very quiet and sensitive: anybody wanted any help and he'd be there, and he'd take a car engine out and put it back with all the pieces – he could do anything like that. Remember, there were five on us, five girls, and he was a smashing dad. He used to get us up on a Sunday morning, on his one day off, pack up some corned beef sandwiches and whisk us off to t'seaside on a whim. We used to stop at Stamford Bridge, and get some chips and

eat 'em in the car. And then we'd come home, and, what's that song about 'Sitting in the back seat kissing and hugging with Fred'? We used to sing it to him all the way back home! (Susan Jackson)

This character assessment resonates with Frankie Isles' views on Howard's well-known propensity to move, back and forth between different clubs:

He never could settle, though, couldn't Fred. He tended to move about a bit. He wasn't the type of bloke to fall out with anybody. He was very laid back and sensitive. If things didn't go right, and he came under some criticism, he'd just move on without any argument. He was very quiet to be fair, but he was also easily led. If someone had come up and whispered in his ear, 'Come on and play for us,' he might have responded to 'em. He was like this was Freddie, he liked you to make a fuss on him. He was a smashing bloke, but if one of them from, say, Swillington had come and buttered him up, he'd have given 'em a go. (Frank Isles)

This is precisely what had occurred in relation to Howard's move to Altofts, and the pattern was about to be repeated as a new season began to dawn.

Chapter 7
Falling Apart at the Seams

Previous page: The Fryston team which played together in the early part of the 1960-61 season, the year that they were relegated into Division Two of the West Yorkshire League. Harold 'Agga' Mattison is standing on the extreme left of the photograph. Frank Isles is crouching (second from the left), with Freddie Howard (next right), followed by Terry Templeman.

Howard's Brief Adieu

At the risk of over-simplifying the matter, it is important to mention that Fryston's poor form occurred in the midst of a conflict-ridden period of industrial relations at the local mine, in which Jim Bullock's successor as manager, the Castleford-born Edgar Williams, was responding to an NCB directive to increase coal production or face the possibility of pit closure. Having succeeded Bullock towards the end of 1954, Williams spent the next four years of his eventual sixteen-year tenure as manager striving to make the colliery break even, and committed to eradicating what he perceived as worker indiscipline. It would be easy to overstate the impact of this 'purge'. Nevertheless, it was clearly inimical to the interests of the colliery football team:

> There was a nine o'clock shift coming on and I was wondering as to why they had such a hefty number. I was told that most of them were football players. There were people who ought to have been working underground that were working on the surface; and when I sent them down the mine, it pleased the other men considerably. There were other men working at the colliery just because they were important figures in the football team. They were soon found a proper job to do. (Edgar Williams)

Whatever the actual cause, Fryston's fortunes continued to decline. The 1956-57 season commenced with Freddie Howard having left the club once again, this time for a brief spell with Swillington Welfare, with Ray Murfin assuming the role of main striker by moving to centre-forward from inside-right. Murfin clearly relished his new role, scoring two hat-tricks and picking up a goal-a-game elsewhere in Fryston's first nine games. Following his three-goal haul in the 6-2 home win against Farsley Celtic, the *Express* made the point that, 'Such is the form of Murfin... that Fryston Colliery are not missing their former centre-forward, Fred Howard.'[1] Despite Murfin's exploits, this run yielded only five points. Fryston's results in this period included a remarkable 6-5 loss at DP and E, a 7-1 defeat at Methley and 3-0 home setback against Ferrybridge, prompting the prediction that, 'There is trouble ahead for Fryston unless they improve, for Saturday's result left them with only five points from a possible 18, though seven of the nine matches have been played at home.'[2]

Salt was rubbed into The Colliers' wounds in late November when Freddie Howard returned from a brief and unhappy spell at Swillington to make a guest appearance for Fryston in their 3-2 Cas and District Cup defeat at home to Wheldale, before signing on full-time for the latter a few weeks later. By this time, Ray Murfin had asked to be moved back to inside-forward or wing-half, where he felt he could be of more value to the side. He was replaced at centre-forward by Keith ('Banger') Langley, who scored two goals in Fryston's 4-3 win at Ferrybridge to help them record their first away win of the season. Although Langley continued to score regularly, a string of heavy defeats (e.g. 7-0 at East End Park and 8-1 at home to Swillington Welfare) saw Fryston slide down the table, where they finished second-bottom to Harrogate, having accumulated only seven wins from thirty matches, of which twenty were defeats. Cup success remained elusive in the meantime. In the WRCC Cup, they were comfortably beaten 3-1 in the first round by Methley, the same team who narrowly defeated them 3-2 after extra time in the final of the Embleton Cup.

Prodigal Son

Excitement clearly surrounded the prospect of a key player being restored to the Fryston team for the start of the 1957-58 season:

> A prominent player is returning to FRYSTON COLLIERY WELFARE in Fred Howard, a goal-scoring centre-forward, who needs little introduction. His 89 goals in a season put him in the shop window, and his return should increase Fryston's scoring potential. Early last season the club lost a number of matches by the odd goal, and finished second from the foot of the First Division table. Re-elected, they feel more confident also because Main, of Fairburn, has been secured to fill a long-standing goal-keeping vacancy, and Pepper, who missed all last season, will once more be available for a full-back position. The veteran, Lister, may also play at full-back this time. Rowlands, an outside-left from Normanton, has been signed, but Langley

and Haines, centre-forward and inside-left, respectively, have not re-signed. A stand, which will give cover for 200, is as yet incomplete.[3]

Howard lived up to pre-season expectations by scoring thirteen goals in Fryston's first nine games. He began by scoring Fryston's only goals in their opening two matches (3-1 and 4-1 home defeats to DP and E and his former club, Methley, respectively), and two more to cap an excellent team performance in their drawn away match against Methley. Half time came and went with Methley 1-0 up:

> Then Howard snatched a goal when he lobbed the ball over the head of the advancing Trehearne. More smooth working among the Methley forwards brought a second-half goal – another good one – for Heeley, but again Howard equalised, going through speedily when left unmarked and completing his run with a first-class shot. Methley seemed surprised by Fryston's survival, as no doubt other clubs will be if such fighting qualities are maintained.[4]

One of Howard's two goals in Fryston's next match, a 4–3 victory at home to Snydale, was an especially exciting affair in which he beat three defenders before sliding the ball past the goalkeeper. He then scored in Fryston's next match, a 2-1 defeat at Yorkshire Amateurs, though he and Langley (who had since re-signed for Fryston) were guilty of missing several chances that ultimately cost Fryston the game. Howard's two goals in Fryston's next home win (3-2 over Farsley Celtic Reserves) came after the visitors had established a half-time lead: 'Howard quickly threw a different light on things by scoring twice inside three minutes at the start of the second half. His first goal came immediately after the kick-off – the ball was re-passed to him and he cut down the middle – and the second when he got to a centre and turned it into the net from close in.'[5] Howard went one better by notching a hat-trick in Fryston's next fixture, an 8-1 triumph at Ossett Albion Reserves, only to be overshadowed by Rowlands, who struck four.

Fryston's defence was now starting to appear more solid, with the recently introduced nineteen-year-old centre-half, Harold 'Agga' Mattison, steadily maturing under the mentorship of Chunner Lister. The Fryston-born Mattison was the youngest of a family of four brothers and two sisters, although a fifth brother had died while only six-months-old. Mattison's second-oldest brother, Bill (who was nineteen years his senior), had played regularly for Fryston in the post-war period. Harold had actually played Rugby League up to leaving Airedale Secondary Modern. However, following a successful kick-about with a peer group which included Fryston players like Jack Sharp, he worked his way into the Fryston set-up: 'I started with Fryston's second team in t'Ponte league. I used to play right-half for 'em; a lad called David Bridges played centre-half in t'second team, Chunner were in t'first team, and then Dick Foulkes had an inspiration: he thought I'd make a good centre-half.'

Mattison had been fantastically impressed from the outset by the predatory goal-scoring capabilities of Freddie Howard: 'Freddie did everything at his own pace and wouldn't break sweat for anyone.'

Ironically, both Mattison and Howard were soon destined to leave Fryston. The former had only played a handful of first-team matches when he was spotted by a Halifax Town scout and was soon playing, albeit as an amateur, for their reserve team in the Yorkshire League, while Jack Sharp turned out for the first eleven. Meanwhile, it seems fair to say that Howard's goal for Fryston in the 4-3 setback at home to Harrogate Town Reserves in late September may have played a significant part in his transfer from the club. The home forwards, minus the injured Langley, had lacked firepower for most of the game but, according to the *Express*, 'It was the defence, without Mattison and Lister, which was chiefly to blame for defeat – the first at home since August 26.'[6]

Howard was not among the scorers in Fryston's next match, another costly affair (5-3) at Rothwell Athletic; and following a further defeat, 6-3 away to Selby Town, there was talk of his and other imminent departures from the club: 'Mattison (now on amateur forms with Halifax Town), Howard, who is being approached by Harrogate Town, and Pearson were absentees on Saturday. If Howard leaves Fryston once more, it will mean that the club has lost five of its best players to other teams this season.'[7]

Mattison was followed out of Fryston by Howard, who duly left for Harrogate. in departing from the club. With their defensive axis broken, Fryston began to concede alarming numbers of goals, as in their 7-2 and 7-0 defeats at Snydale and Ferrybridge Amateurs, respectively, and their 8-1 home thrashing by Altofts, which 'might have been more but for heroic display by Main in goal'.[8] A sequence of much narrower defeats, culminating in a spirited performance in the WRCC Cup, in which they lost their home tie to Snydale by the odd goal in five, raised speculation that, with Lister now back from injury, Fryston were getting their act back together. Such optimism proved short-lived, as Fryston went down 7-0 the following week to the reigning champions, Swillington Town. Despite occasional draws, Fryston continued to suffer heavy defeats – as in their home thrashings by Ossett Albion Reserves (5-0) and Selby Town Reserves (6-2), for whom the away centre-forward, Campbell, scored a double hat-trick. The latter game was also notable, however, for the surprise return to Fryston colours of Fred Howard, who typically marked the occasion with a goal.

Howard's fortunes fluctuated wildly during what was left of the season. In late February, the centre-forward scored a headed goal in Fryston's 1-1 home draw against St Michael's Old Boys. One week later, he was twice brought down with the goal beckoning in Fryston's 9-1 drubbing at Altofts; but within a fortnight he 'revealed all his old marksmanship'[9] by scoring four goals in Fryston's 7-3 win at Barwick and Scholes. Nothing went right for Howard and his team in their 5-0 home loss to Rothwell Athletic: 'Whatever it was, the only memories they made were three violent drives in the space of 10 minutes from between 20 to 25 yards by centre-forward Howard, the pace of which baffled the Rothwell goalkeeper completely. On each occasion, before he was quite sure what happened, the ball was rebounding from the woodwork.'[10] Finally, in the first minute of Fryston's Embleton Cup tie against Ferrybridge (which they eventually lost 2-1), Howard sustained a head injury in a duel with the opposing centre-half, Pete Sands, and was immediately taken to hospital.

Fryston's last four games of the season constituted a roller-coaster ride. Having first beaten St Michael's Old Boys away 3-0 (with two goals by Murphy and one by Langley), The Colliers were annihilated 10-0 at Farsley Celtic. Bizarrely, they then proceeded to end Swillington's hopes of a successive championship by heavily defeating them 5-1, thanks partly to an outstanding display by Fred Howard – who occupied the role of makeshift goalkeeper! A final away defeat (4-2) at Harrogate Town Reserves gave Fryston a fourth-from-bottom finish, having played 30, won 7, drawn 5 and lost 18, for a total of 19 points. The 115 goals conceded by the club represented the worst defensive record in Division One.

Howard's Full Circle

In one of the major ironies of the late 1950s, Fred Howard moved to Glass Houghton Welfare (for whom he would score prolifically all season in the West Yorkshire League Second Division), while his old friend Charlie Barnett moved via the same team from Ferrybridge to Fryston, where he enjoyed a brief Indian summer:

> I mean I were about 29 or maybe 30 then, knocking on. I left and I played a bit at Glass Houghton Welfare, but I didn't get on and all that, and then I went up to Fryston and I played with them. I were talking to the likes of Tommy Owen and John Pearson. They were all Glass Houghton lads who were up at Fryston at the time; so just as I were on about packing in, they all says, 'Nay, come down to Fryston with us lot.' So I went down and played a couple or three good seasons with them. (Charlie Barnett)

Fryston also welcomed back a disillusioned Agga Mattison, whose brief career with Halifax had concluded on a sour note earlier that summer when the club decided not to renew his services: 'I ended t'season and they paid me up what they owed me in train fare and bus fare and one thing and another, they give me it all in change, no pound notes.'

With these two players on board, Fryston made a bright start to the 1958-59 campaign, during which they enjoyed a good 5-3 away win at Altofts (thanks chiefly to a Barnett hat-trick) and a 4-1 home win over Snydale (with Owen scoring all four). However, a 5-2 thumping at Methley then heralded an inconsistent spell in which two home wins were followed by a terrible 10-3 mauling at DP and E, despite a Charlie Barnett hat-trick.

> That's right [laughs] because, I remember, we went into t'pub after, and we sat down and this old chap's sat there with his pipe and pint, like. He says, 'Nah then, where've you lot been? Playing football?' I says, 'Aye, we've been playing down at DP and E, Otley.' He says, 'Oh aye, well how did you get on?' So I says 'Don't ask!' He says, 'Why not, for heaven's sake?' I says, 'We lost 10-3!' He says, 'Don't thee worry thissen about it, lad, they're a bloody good rugby side is Otley.' (Charlie Barnett)

For all that, Fryston briefly topped the league in mid-October, after destroying Ferrybridge 6-1, but were soon displaced by the eventual champions, Swillington Town, who savaged them 5-1 at home. Fryston's faint hopes of winning the championship started to fade with a 1-0 defeat at Ferrybridge in late January. Heavy defeats against Snydale (7-3) and Farsley Celtic Reserves (8-0) underlined that they had been mere pretenders to the title. Nevertheless, their final placement of fifth (played 26, won 15, drew 1, lost 10 = 31 points) represented a welcome improvement on previous seasons' performances.

Fryston's corresponding cup campaigns were plagued by inconsistency. In the WRCC Cup The Colliers beat their deadliest foe, Ferrybridge Amateurs, in the second round. The game finished 3-1 to Fryston, with goals by Owen (2) and Garbett, despite the fact that they were outplayed by the Amateurs. In the next round, they registered a thumping 7-1 win against a Hatfield Main side which had conceded 40 goals in their last four matches. They should also have won in the next round at home to Bradford Rovers, when they twice led before going down 3-2 in extra time.

In the Greenwood Trophy, Fryston came heavily unstuck at Altofts, who were 7-0 up at half-time and eventually won 8-3. In the Cas and District Cup final, they once again faced Ferrybridge Amateurs, but this time Fryston were convincingly beaten 5-1. They exacted revenge for this defeat by beating the same opponents 4-0 in the Embleton Cup semi-final, before overcoming Knottingley 3-2 in the final after the sides had originally drawn two-each.

On their way to the Cas and District Cup final, The Colliers had beaten Glass Houghton Welfare in a replayed semi-final. The first match had ended in a 2-2 draw, with Fred Howard inevitably scoring both of the Glass Houghton goals against his former club. However, he was then carried off having sustained a serious leg injury. It was initially feared that this calamity might force him to retire from the game.

New Blood and Old

The *Express* preview of the 1959-60 season was optimistic about Fryston's chances of success. Basing its assessment on the previous season's performance, the *Express* recalled how, 'Fryston's team building brought a marked improvement and, for a period, the side was running well with the leaders. To be nine points behind the champions in the final table was something quite unexpected after the disappointments of past seasons and the record would have been better but for some unaccountable lapses.[11] Agga Mattison had just signed on as a semi-professional for Frickley Colliery, prompting Charlie Barnett to switch from centre-forward to centre-half in a bid to bolster the defence.

The season did not start half as well as expected, with Fryston's injury-hit side (often lacking six or seven first-teamers) only winning one of their first half-dozen matches. The absence of first-team regulars at least provided them with an opportunity to 'blood' younger players, notably the locally-born David Rotherforth, who scored on a difficult debut in which Fryston were clobbered 6-2 at home by East End Park.

Rotherforth was born in July 1940 in North Street, Fryston. His father was a ripper at Fryston pit. Rotherforth went to Fryston School, followed by Airedale Secondary Modern. However, rather than following his father down the pit, he started out working as an apprentice fitter at Pollards Bearings, Ferrybridge. Since entering his teens, Rotherforth had competed as a sprinter:

> I was a member of the Pontefract and Castleford Athletic Club in my youth. I played for the school, and a few of us Fryston Juniors at that time had a team at Fryston youth club. There were no leagues and we couldn't get matches, there were just friendlies here and there We were all around fifteen, sixteen, seventeen, so we joined the Pontefract and District League, open-age. There was Brian Wood and Archie Ward for sure, and I've a feeling that Terry Templeman might also have played. I was working in Ferrybridge; and because I got to know a lot of locals, my first senior team was Ferrybridge Amateurs. I eventually got into the first team alongside such worthies as Stan Wright, Roy Milner and Dobber Sutcliffe, who'd played with Fryston years before. I played centre-forward alongside Stan. In fact, Stan was in the RAF and he couldn't get every week and I think that's how I got in initially. I think it might have been that I wasn't getting into the first team as much – and when you're twenty, you think you ought to have an automatic place – but there were a lot of excellent, mature players at Ferry. I was aggrieved that they were old and past it, but looking back, they were only 26, 27, and just approaching their prime. I went straight in Fryston's first team. (David Rotherforth)

Fryston's league form was not about to improve. They sustained further heavy defeats – 7-2 at Guiseley and 8-2 at lowly East End Park.

The Colliers put up a better fight in that year's WRCC Cup, coming from two goals down to win by the odd goal in five at Bradford Rovers, before narrowly losing 2-1 in the next round at Tadcaster Albion.

Back in the league, however, an old friend was about to make a return to first-team action. The injury Freddie Howard sustained whilst playing against Fryston for Glass Houghton Welfare didn't force his retirement after all. In fact, before the year was out, Howard had resumed his Fryston career, albeit as centre-forward for the reserves, where he joined the likes of Chunner Lister and the youthful Terry Templeman in the West Yorkshire League Division Three. Having appeared only sporadically so far that season, Howard's hat-trick in Fryston Reserves' 8-1 home win over Pontefract Collieries Reserves earned him a place in the first team against Ferrybridge Amateurs.

Even with a returning Freddie, Fryston were subjected to a 7-1 drubbing by the Amateurs. Only two goal-line clearances by Charlie Barnett saved them from an even worse humiliation. Needless to say, it was Howard who scored the only Fryston goal, although it stood poor comparison alongside the three and four goal hauls for the opposition by Wright and Millar, respectively. The veteran striker nonetheless came into his own in Fryston's next home game, in which they earned a 4-2 victory over Farsley Celtic Reserves:

An early goal scored by Isles seemed to restore confidence in the side. It was not disturbed either by a quickly taken indirect free kick from which Farsley crashed home an equalising goal before the home defenders had assessed the situation, for Howard revealed his old scoring touch when he raced on to a splendidly-placed through pass to restore the lead. There was a further test for Fryston's nerve when they three times blocked Farsley shots only to prevent a second equaliser. But that was the last they thought of defeat as Howard went on to complete a 'hat-trick'. The margin might have been widened had the centre-forward been aware on other occasions of well-positioned colleagues.[12]

However, this was not to be the prelude of some great escape by Fryston. Shortly thereafter, they experienced further humiliating defeats (7-0 and 9-3 away to Snydale and Ferrybridge, respectively). Howard's two goals in Fryston's 5-3 home win against DP and E and a stunning hat-trick in the first ten minutes of Fryston's final home game (a 4-3 victory against Robin Hood Athletic) showed that he was still capable of producing devastating spells of goal-scoring, but age and injury were ensuring that it no longer occurred with the chilling consistency of yesteryear. The Colliers' poor return of six wins out of 26 matches put them third-bottom of a league in which the 98 goals they had conceded constituted the second-worst defensive record of the season. Only the veto saved them from being relegated back into Division Two.

Chapter 8
Like Pieces of a Jigsaw

Previous page: Shepherds Welfare – runaway champions of the Pontefract and District League Division One in the 1960-61 season. The following year, Johnny Appleyard (standing, extreme left), Brian Wood (standing, extreme right) and Peter Waddington (crouching with the ball) all turned out for Fryston. Terry Templeman (crouching to Waddington's left) had a highly successful 1961-62 season in the West Yorkshire League First Division with Ferrybridge Amateurs, before also signing for Fryston a year later.

Cobbo Robinson

It is highly conceivable that the variable form displayed by Fryston at the outset of the 1960-61 season was the cause of renewed concern for their players, officials and supporters. However, there were sufficient indications to suggest that the club still had the capacity to reconsolidate their position in the West Yorkshire League First Division. Their record of two wins and two defeats from the first four games included heavy losses at home to Guiseley (5-2) and away to Methley (4-2); but as the *Express* report for the Methley game somewhat reassuringly emphasised, at least Fryston could still point to the goal-scoring touch of an apparently rejuvenated Freddie Howard as a redoubtable standby in times of trouble:

> Two centre-forwards who have proved elusive to centre-halves in most parts of the West Riding indicated quite clearly in this WEST YORKSHIRE LEAGUE match that, though time may have taken away some of the polish, it has not dimmed their boots too much. All except one of the six goals came from Hall and Howard, the former now having achieved a 'hat-trick' in each of Methley's three opening matches. For Fryston, Howard has seven goals from four appearances, having scored two goals on each of three occasions. There was never a great deal of difference between the teams – praise for Fryston considering that Methley's previous two matches yielded them 16 goals.[1]

There was further cause for local optimism in the fact that Agga Mattison had recently returned from his spell with Frickley, and in the increasingly impressive form being displayed by the teenage right-winger, Barry 'Cobbo' Robinson, who had joined them in the close season.

Robinson was born just outside of Fryston village, along Wheldon Road, and later moved with his parents via Airedale to Ferry Fryston. Having joined Fryston Colliery aged fourteen, he soon started working alongside Chunner Lister in the 'wagon shop' (repairing and servicing railway vehicles). He was a regular Leeds United supporter, catching the train from Castleford to Beeston for home games. John Charles was the local favourite, but Robinson 'had a thing about Stanley Matthews and Tom Finney. I modelled myself on great wingers – wizards of the dribble – though my favourite goal was when Jackie Milburn nutted that one into the top corner at Wembley.' Standing little more than five-feet-four, Fryston's new 'wizard of the dribble' had made a spirited debut in the team's 1-0 home win against Farsley Celtic Reserves in late September.

Robinson now formed part of a Fryston side whose form appeared to be improving in the build-up to their first-round WRCC Cup tie at home to the equally in-form Shepherds Welfare, leaders of the Pontefract and District League First Division. Prior to the Shepherds tie, The Colliers had secured three wins and only one defeat (a 2-1 setback against Altofts) out of four consecutive home games. Included among these victories was a 6-0 thrashing of Robin Hood Athletic, which constituted Fryston's best display of the season. This good form was maintained a week before the Shepherds match with a 3-1 win against Harrogate Town.

Shepherds Welfare

Fryston's opponents in the first round of the WRCC Cup, Shepherds Welfare, comprised a team of talented and relatively youthful players all hailing from the Fryston/Airedale area. By this stage of the season, Shepherds (whose name derived from a new National Coal Board housing estate, recently established in nearby Townville) had dropped a mere three points, surrendering two of them in a dramatic 7-4 drubbing away to their old Castleford Youth League rivals, Fairburn Welfare. Captained by the old Fryston stalwart, George Battye, Shepherds contained a nucleus of key players – some with prior experience of having played with Fryston – who would soon join (or re-join) The Colliers.

One of these was the slightly built but famously acrobatic goalkeeper, Harold 'Archie' Ward, who was born and raised on Park Dale, a cul-de-sac just off Fryston Road. Having attended Fryston Juniors and

Airedale Secondary Modern, Ward began work at the Fryston coal-face: 'I worked all the while down the pit: nine yards long and a yard in every day with a pick and a shovel. No wonder my hands are hard!' Even as a schoolboy, Ward had harboured ambitions of being a goalkeeper:

> I always used to go and watch Fryston play and I'd stand behind the goals. Jimmy Portman was a great goalkeeper and I guess he was my early inspiration. I'd go get the ball for him every time it went dead. I'd started out with Fairburn but a Fryston official called Alf Atack saw me playing one day and asked me to sign for Fryston. That was when I was about sixteen or seventeen. I had a brief spell with them, but it was Shepherds that guaranteed me a regular slot. (Harold Ward)

It was the prospect of a secure team place that also lured the teak-hard defender, Brian Wood, from Fryston to Shepherds. The popular 'Woody' was a war baby – born in Fryston village in 1939. One of a family of six girls and three boys, his older brother was seriously injured in a rockfall down the mine. Like most new recruits at Fryston Colliery, he started out 'sizing' coal on the screens. Six months later, he transferred to the Lamp Room. It was at this point that he was called on to do his National Service. The only way for him to avoid this was to start working underground. Once there, he eventually became captain of the First Aid Team. From an early age, football was an important feature of Wood's social existence:

> The individual I looked up to was Chunner Lister. He was quite a bit older than me but he gave me a lot of encouragement. I first started playing when Fryston Youth Club entered a side in t'Ponte League, open-age. In fact, we played against Fryston themselves. We were all young 'uns, of course, and we were getting hammered all t'time – if we lost 2-0, we used to go get drunk because we nearly won! But the bulk of us moved up to Fryston then. I started in t'second team. I can't remember whether I was sixteen or seventeen, but I got in t' first team twice that year. There weren't that many of 'em playing then who actually worked at Fryston pit. I can remember my first match, it was at Farsley Celtic, and it was knee-deep in mud, and I couldn't kick the ball ten yards I tell thee! This inside-left who I was marking, I think he scored four that day. I couldn't get anywhere near him! (Brian Wood)

The Shepherds star striker, Pete Waddington was born half-a-mile outside of Fryston village, just up the hill at 199, Fryston Road. His father, Tommy, a Wheldale miner, had been a tough-tackling full-back for Castleford Town and Fryston in the 1920s. Waddington junior started his football career as a fourteen-year-old inside-forward for YEB Sports ('I think they used to share their ground with Townville and, being local, I got a game with them'). A year later, the Airedale PE teacher, Stan Clayton, organised for him to have trials with Huddersfield Town, which involved taking part in weekly training sessions with the full-time professionals:

> Bearing in mind I'd just turned fifteen, I was over the bloody moon! I used to catch a bus from Airedale to Castleford, from Castleford to Wakefield, from there to Dewsbury, and then on to Beck Lane. They used to give me tea and supper money and travelling expenses. I went there while Andy Beattie was manager. I went about five or six times; saw all the big noises – Glazzard, Metcalfe, etc. – and I couldn't believe I was rubbing shoulders with England internationals. I was only fifteen, sixteen, but I could talk to them as easily as speaking to my closest mates. But there was a notice-board outside the changing rooms and we'd heard on the grapevine that Andy Beattie and Huddersfield were parting company over some disagreement or other. We got told that they were keeping all their registered professionals, but that all part-timers and amateurs – including me – were to be released without further notice. (Peter Waddington)

His dream now over, Waddington returned to play for Townville and Airedale (winning an Embleton Cup winner's medal with them in 1954-55), and thereafter for Airedale Athletic. Like Fred Howard before him, Waddington had reason to be grateful to Sammy Gledhill, who had now moved from Glass Houghton to live just round the corner on Royd's Avenue: 'He was a bit of a mentor for me during my youth, and I like to think that I listened carefully because he certainly gave me lots of good advice.' Waddington was originally employed at Lumbs' glassworks before making studs for sports shoes for a firm called Blakey's in Leeds. Having married a Fryston woman, Mary Holmes, he began working at Fryston pit and lived with his in-laws on Brook Street, before being granted a pit house on the newly-built Shepherds Estate. It was not long before he started playing at centre-forward for Shepherds Welfare – with immediate success:

> Well, we hardly lost a match! In fact, I won a pair of 'Stanley Matthews' football boots through being featured in the 'Green 'Un'. I netted something like twelve goals in two matches and that's how I got 'em. I reckon I played

all the matches and hardly a game went by without me scoring – head, both feet, back of my arse, anyway I could. (Peter Waddington)

Not surprisingly, therefore, Fryston's county cup tie with Shepherds was an eagerly-awaited contest, but the match itself turned out to be disappointingly one-sided. The game was effectively won for Fryston in the first nine minutes, with goals by Cobbo Robinson (playing on the left wing) and Brian Lane at centre-forward. Shortly before half time, Howard (at inside-right) made the game safe with a headed third goal. The visitors would have felt especially disappointed by their performance:

Possessing several former Fryston players, Shepherds were keen to do well, but their lone goal was delayed until the latter stages of the match, when Waddington diverted the ball after Gale had shouted to a colleague to let it run through. That goal apart, Shepherds were rarely dangerous.[2]

This brief setback turned out to be the only blip in an otherwise hugely successful season for Shepherds. Quickly putting their county cup exit behind them, the Townville team bore down inexorably on the Pontefract League title, with two more newly-recruited ex-Fryston players, in Johnny Appleyard and Terry Templeman, making further contributions to their success.

The tall, village-born Appleyard, was a skilful and physically imposing regular right-half in the Fryston reserves who, like Templeman, was now pushing to establish a secure first-team place. The son of a Fryston miner (Jack Appleyard) and his wife, Mary Jane (or 'Jinny'), Appleyard worked as a bricklayer's labourer at the pit. His future wife, Carol, was also born in Fryston. Her father, Harry Townsley, was a professional Rugby League player for Castleford. Carol and Johnny first started seeing each other as part of a group of local youths who used to congregate at the top of one of the village streets:

About sixteen on us. I'd have been about sixteen then and he were one year older. He was already six-foot-two and ginger-haired – strong, silent type: he was always very popular but ever so quiet. He didn't say a deal. He had a lot of mates, all footballers, and he tended to like his beer. I don't remember him getting into any trouble generally speaking, but he had that sort of reputation, as a real hard case, on t'football field! (Carol Woolley)

The prodigiously talented and tireless inside-forward, Terry Templeman, was the youngest of a family of eight village-born children (six boys and two girls). Templeman was born in the same Smith Street as Agga Mattison and their mothers regularly attended church together. Like most young men of his generation, Templeman initially worked on the pit top in the stores before going underground at eighteen to work on the coal belts. All bar one of his brothers played local football. Three of them (Dennis, Freddie and Tommy) played in outfield positions for Fryston. A fourth brother, Jack, used to play in goals before turning his hand to refereeing. Terry began his football career by playing for Fryston Youth Club alongside David Rotherforth. Brief spells in the Fryston first and second teams were followed by a move to Shepherds in November 1960, which produced immediate dividends.

Such was Shepherds' dominance in the league that they had already won the title with four matches still to play. The *Express* report of Shepherds' 4-1 home victory over second-placed Monk Fryston United, maintains that, 'Shepherds were particularly well served by their centre-half and captain, Battye, and by [Terry] Templeman, the former Fryston player who was making his debut and who scored a great goal from 30 yards out.'[3] The club's 4-2 victory over previously unbeaten Moorthorpe Recreation included two goals by the free-scoring Pete Waddington in a generally good all-round team performance in which 'Aitken and Wood, in the defence, and [he] were the stars of a very capable side'.[4] It was also two first-half goals by Waddington which enabled Shepherds to avenge their only defeat so far that season, by beating their 'bogey team', Fairburn, 2-0.

Decline and Fall

Fryston emerged from their first-round WRCC Cup victory over Shepherds to suffer an inexplicable loss of form. Their next fixture, against the previous year's champions, Snydale Road Athletic, saw The Colliers thrashed 6-1. Further setbacks then followed (1-0 and 4-1 away to Ferrybridge Amateurs and Robin Hood Athletic, respectively). In the encounter with Ferrybridge, up-and-coming Cobbo Robinson had been brought into direct conflict with the future Leeds and England left-winger, turned full-back, Terry Cooper, who had also begun working at Fryston, as a fitter in the 'loco' (locomotive) shed. Earlier that season, the two youngsters had played together in the Castleford and District FA Minor team:

Terry had played for the district side the previous year when they won it. This following year [1960-61] we got licked 7-2 by Barkston Ash. Cooper scored from a penalty. Then somebody took a free kick on t'edge of t'box. It came to me, I pulled it down and slotted it, sidefoot, into t'net. Most of the Barkston Ash Team were from Great Preston. They were far too good for us. I was playing inside-forward and Cooper was centre-forward, even though we were both wingers. Terry already had this reputation, and people like 'Tadger' Rotherforth told us that he was already outstanding at fifteen. I remember that game I played against him for Fryston. I remember him coming back and tackling me! He was a good dribbler and had a pretty good shot but he used to somehow hit it with his toe-end, rather than his instep! (Barry Robinson)

It was on the back of this poor run that Fryston entered their second-round WRCC Cup match against Robin Hood Athletic, against whom they enjoyed a brief rejuvenation:

Both teams overcame the conditions to a large extent and after some pleasing play, Howard, beating three defenders, placed Fryston ahead. Bridges, at centre-half, and Lister, at right-back, stemmed the flow of Robin Hood attacks and Mattison, at left-half, played as a captain should. Having thrown the home team back, Fryston scored again through the 17-year-old Robinson, who received the ball from Howard, after a pass by Lane. Robinson often had the Robin Hood defence in trouble in the second half, but it was the home team who scored, Gale having no chance. Howard got another goal and then the Fryston defence packed tightly to ensure a safe passage into the next round.[5]

While Fryston's league form continued to give grave cause for concern, they could count themselves unlucky to lose their third-round WRCC Cup tie at home to Harehills Amateurs. Murfin and Howard scored for Fryston, but both the latter and Cobbo Robinson were guilty of missing easy chances in a game that Fryston should have won, but ultimately lost 3-2 after extra time. On the same day, Ferrybridge Amateurs were on the receiving end of a 6-1 trouncing by DP and E, provoking the *Express* to bemoan the fact that not since Castleford and Allerton United lifted the trophy in 1926, had the WRCC been won by a local side.[6]

Fryston's 3-1 home league defeat in their return match against Snydale marked the continuation of an unproductive period in which the acquisition of only a single point had seen them slide to fourth-bottom of the table (played 14, won 5, drawn 1, lost 8 = 11 points). Worse still, Fryston's luck appeared to be deserting them – exemplified by their 6-1 defeat against fellow strugglers Farsley Celtic Reserves in which Chunner Lister was carried off with a seriously injured knee, making him the third Fryston centre-half to have recently been put out of action.

When Fryston's elusive next victory was eventually achieved (in the form of a 3-0 win at Knottingley Albion), it came either side of catastrophic defeats at Ferrybridge Amateurs (7-2) and Guiseley (6-1). The latter game saw Guiseley clinch the First Division Championship by a single point from Snydale. Their position was in stark contrast to the one now experienced by Fryston:

> Fryston, whose doom at the other end of the table is now sealed – unless the veto saves them as last year – kept the new champions anxious until the last 15 minutes. They took the lead after 10 minutes when Mattinson [sic], playing at centre-forward on this occasion, forced the way through and gave the goalkeeper no chance... With 25 minutes of the second half gone, Fryston were still level, but then a disputed penalty enabled Guiseley to grab the lead. A breakaway by Howard almost brought Fryston an equaliser, the goalkeeper making a fine save. Then, in the last 15 minutes, the resolute Fryston defence collapsed and Guiseley's championship hopes were assured.[7]

Fryston were unable to draw any consolation in the Cas and District Cup. The Colliers reached the final thanks to a Fred Howard winner in Fryston's 2-1 victory over his old club, Glass Houghton Welfare, in a replayed semi-final, but lost 2-0 to Ferrybridge Amateurs in the final. Ferrybridge's triumph was the eighth successive occasion on which they had lifted the trophy. It was hardly any comfort to Fryston that:

> For a side so badly off in the West Yorkshire League, [they] played admirably at times, especially in the second half, when their short and precise passing, varied with an occasional long through ball, was superior to anything Ferrybridge produced.[8]

As if to underline what a woeful season they had experienced, Fryston were hammered 5-0 in their final league match at Harrogate – a result which meant that they had won only one league match since defeating the same opponents on 29 October 1960, and that they were so firmly anchored to the bottom of the First Division (played 26, won 4, drawn 5, lost 17 = 13 points) that even the veto could not rescue them this time.

Sharp's Return

Fryston started the 1961-62 season without Fred Howard, who had moved to Airedale Athletic, but with several familiar faces back in their ranks. These included the Shepherds contingent of Archie Ward, Johnny Appleyard, Pete Waddington and Brian Wood, but not Terry Templeman, who had been lured to Ferrybridge Amateurs. Even more excitement greeted the news that Jack Sharp was also re-entering the Fryston team – and would undoubtedly be bringing all those years of experience as a professional back with him.

In the 1956-57 season, for example, Sharp had played for Halifax against Leeds United at Elland Road in the annual West Riding County Senior Cup knock-out competition, which featured all the professional teams of the area. Halifax lost 3-1 to a team which included the legendary Leeds and Welsh international, John Charles:

> It was raining and we had the old, heavy balls back then with the protruding laces in. And I'll always remember, we had a lad called Arthur Johnson in goal, who used to live right near to Liverpool race track at Aintree. That particular night, John Charles hit a ball on the volley, just before half time, and with it being wet, Arthur had these gloves on and he managed to punch the ball, and it went off over there. Good save! Well, they blew up for half time, and after we'd gone in, he couldn't take his gloves off; and when he eventually did, every knuckle had the skin taken off. Charles was the big man of that day but I only played against him that once and was lucky enough to score our goal. It was a cross-cum-shot and I think it just deceived the 'keeper, whether I intended it to or not! (Jack Sharp)

Sharp's spell at Halifax coincided with the formation of Football League Divisions Three and Four: the top halves of the Third Division

(North) and Third Division (South) were placed in to Division Three, while the bottom halves of each of the old divisions were located in Division Four. Thus, in the 1958-59 season, Sharp found himself travelling to places like Reading, Plymouth and Norwich:

> I especially remember playing Norwich because they went on to the semi-final of the FA Cup from the Third Division. The season before, they doubled our 'win bonus' as an incentive to get in t'top half of t'table, I used to get fourteen quid and four quid winning pay; but that year they gave us eight quid bonus and I'm glad to say it worked. (Jack Sharp)

The wingman departed Halifax for Goole having sustained a major injury. 'I broke my ankle at one stage,' he recollects. 'It was training actually – it wasn't even in a game. They used to make us run out of town up onto some playing fields, and that's when I did it.' His brief spell in the Midland League with Goole hardly improved his fitness. 'I know I didn't train like I should of done,' he readily confesses. However, according to Agga Mattison, there was something about Sharp's return to Fryston that proved instantly transformative:

> Well, Frickley were after him before he went to Goole, but after Goole there wasn't much local interest. I think he played one match for Ferrybridge [Amateurs]. Charlie Harrison [their manager] bought him a pair of boots, but he left Ferry straight away to come to Fryston. And once he'd come back, he became a fitness fanatic, and went from being a winger, to full-back. (Harold Mattison)

Sharp was unable to play in Fryston's opening two matches – both 1-1 draws, away to Glass Houghton and Britannia Works (Huddersfield) – but already speculation was rife as to what impact his return might have on The Colliers' chances: 'It remains to be seen whether Jack Sharp, the former Halifax Town and Goole forward who has been signed, can do the trick with his powerful shooting, when he recovers from an injury sustained in training.'[9] Fryston lost the first but won the second of their next two league games, at which point Sharp made his return debut – fittingly enough in Fryston's home game against Halifax Town Reserves. Although Fryston were heavily beaten 6-2, Sharp joined Frankie Isles on the score sheet. The diminutive ex-professional earned plaudits in Fryston's next game, a 3-1 win at Hightown, in which Agga Mattison scored twice: 'The ex-Halifax Town inside-forward was a source of trouble which Hightown were unable to fathom,' reported the *Express*. 'His fine ball distribution should have led to some tall scoring.'[10]

Fryston continued to perform erratically in league and cup competitions alike. In the course of a remarkable first-round Cas and District Cup match, The Colliers recovered from being 5-1 down to win 8-5 at Fairburn (with David Rotherforth grabbing a hat-trick and Pete Waddington two), thanks largely to a 'Trojan like' performance' by Sharp.[11] However, they were eliminated in the following round by Glass Houghton Welfare. Fryston did not last long in the Watson Cup, losing 3-2 at Airedale Athletic, for whom Fred Howard predictably registered a hat-trick. That year's WRCC Cup campaign was also short-lived, with Fryston suffering an 8-3 thrashing, away to Firth Sports:

> Fryston Colliery Welfare did not know what to expect next in the mud at Brighouse. There were three goals in the opening seven minutes, the first when Fryston's Lee trickled the ball back to his goalkeeper, who could not free himself from the mud. Firth Sports got another 'fluke' to lead three-one at half time and then Fryston were favoured when the home goalkeeper threw the ball and it struck Pete Waddington in the face and rebounded into the net. Waddington, who got Fryston's first goal, might have had a hat-trick but failed from the penalty spot.[12]

By now, Agga Mattison had begun playing regularly for Stockport County Reserves after his father-in-law, Jabie Foulkes, had arranged trials on his behalf. Jack Sharp was also invited to play the occasional match for Stockport. With Fryston having to re-shuffle their team in the absence of both players, their organisation was apt to break down – a tendency exemplified by their 8-0 hammering at Britannia Works:

> Now without Jackie Sharp to guide them, Fryston looked a poor side... There was a sharp contrast in spirit and application in a game which the home team clearly deserved to win.[13]

Fryston's woeful form also resulted in a 5-2 home defeat against champions-elect, Glass Houghton Welfare, a game in which Pete Waddington, playing at centre-half, was carried off, having been kicked in the head. Having won only three, lost five and drawn four of their first twelve matches, Fryston welcomed the return from Airedale of the old warhorse, Fred Howard. The veteran goal-scorer's first two games were spent badly out of position, although he did score in the third, a 2-2 away draw at Halifax:

> Roaming Fred Howard, who rejoined Fryston from Airedale and appeared as goalkeeper in the last 2 matches, marked his return to centre-forward by putting his side into a two-one second-half lead after having two of his old-style shots brilliantly saved… Fryston owed a lot to right-half, Appleyard, though he tended to spoil things at times by being too robust.[14]

In Fryston's next match (a 3-1 home defeat to Airedale Athletic), Howard reputedly spurned five good chances against his erstwhile team-mates. However, Fryston struck gold the following week, when the strongest team they had fielded for some time succeeded in beating Wheldale Colliery Welfare, 6-3 away, thanks largely to three goals from David Rotherforth, to claim their first victory since 10 October. With Pete Waddington increasingly deployed at half-back, it fell to Howard and Rotherforth to score the team's goals, something which they did with reasonable success. For example, Howard scored a hat-trick in Fryston's 4-3 return win over Wheldale, while Rotherforth struck three in a 4-1 victory over second-placed Yorkshire Copper Works.

A 5-2 home defeat by Farsley United in their penultimate league match suggested that Fryston were still not ready to challenge for promotion back into the First Division. Nevertheless, a 1-0 win over Knottingley Albion (with Waddington the scorer) brought the curtain down on a season in which Fryston had steadily improved on their early indifferent form. Within Castleford and district, The Colliers were living in the shadow of Glass Houghton (the Second Division [South] champions) and, especially, their great rivals, Ferrybridge Amateurs.

The Final Pieces

The Amateurs had succeeded not only in securing the First Division championship, but also in becoming the first local team for 36 years to lift the prestigious WRCC Cup. With twenty minutes remaining of their final at East End Park, 'Ferry' found themselves 2-0 down to Rothwell Athletic. However, they then struck back with goals by Berry (70 minutes), the inside-right and captain, Roy Milner (80 minutes), and a winner four minutes from time by inside-left, Terry Walsh. The victory was especially satisfying for Milner, who had scored two of his side's goals when they were beaten in the 1955 final by Swillington Town.

Ferrybridge owed a great deal to Terry Templeman. That season, 'Temp' had also played two games for Stockport County Reserves, and believes that he would have stood more chance of being signed on permanently had they not played him out of position on the left wing. The young Frystoner was also played out of position – only this time on the right flank – in Ferrybridge's WRCC final against Rothwell.

We were losing 2-0 at half time. I'd never played on t'right wing in my life, but that day they put me on t'right wing. When I played at inside-forward I'd always got t'ball, doing something with it, whereas in t'final I weren't doing owt. So I just says to Roy Milner, t'captain, 'Get thissen over here and let me go there!' I shifted to inside-right and, though I say it meself, I'm certain I made a big difference – in fact, I think I won t'match for 'em, if I'm totally honest about it. Well, anyway, we came back and licked 'em, 3-2. (Terry Templeman)

During the close season, Templeman took stock of the fact that the recent exodus of his former Shepherds colleagues and the signing of Jack Sharp was being consolidated by the arrival of other exciting signings, and decided to risk his future by returning to Fryston:

So I wrote Tabby Cawthorne [at Ferrybridge] a letter telling him I were going to Fryston. Anyway, I was in our house, carding with some of t'Fryston lads, including Sharpie, and this knock comes on t'door. It's Charlie Harrison and Roy Milner. Well, I didn't say, 'Come in,' 'cos t'lads were already in, like! Charlie Harrison says, 'What's this about thee going to Fryston? Tha knows Sharpie's well past it now, for one!' I don't know whether Jackie heard him or what, but I didn't let 'em get in t'house. Anyway, he says, 'Just think about it: tha knows tha'll be better off with us,' but I thought, 'No, I've made my mind up. I'm going back to Fryston.' (Terry Templeman)

Prior to the start of the 1962-63 season, the Fryston committee decided that the team were to start playing in the maroon strip with pale blue arms that was synonymous with teams like Aston Villa and West Ham United. Ron Foulkes attributes this change of colours to an influx of Fryston youth club players in the close season, who stated a preference to continue playing in the type of strip they had been wearing up to joining the seniors.

> That year, Fryston youth team came up to Fryston and that's how they took over that maroon strip from 'em. Tha'd got Cliff Braund and a kid called Charlie Sykes who were both inside-forwards; another kid called Wright at half-back, and Trevor Ward at outside-left. They all came from t'youth team and they brought them shirts with 'em. (Ronnie Foulkes)

Of the players mentioned, it was Braund and Ward who would go on to establish themselves as successful first-team players. Both were the sons of Wheldale miners, and they were born within days of each other: Ward on 9 September 1944, and Braund eleven days later. Although Braund lived on Fryston Road and Ward above Airedale in nearby Redhill, they both joined Airedale infant school on precisely the same day, and struck an immediate friendship in the process. The two boys were briefly parted when Braund's family moved to a different part of Airedale and he was relocated to a separate school for eighteen months. However, they were soon reunited when they both passed the eleven plus and started attending Castleford Grammar School.

Ward had initially embarked on a Rugby Union career, turning out at full-back for Castleford RUFC for eighteen months before a good roughing up by opposition forwards persuaded him to turn to Association Football instead. He initially spent a full season as a fifteen-year-old with the prestigious Great Preston Juniors, who were based close to the Kippax area of Castleford.

That season, Cliff Braund had begun playing with the Fryston Youth Club team and was already forging a considerable local reputation:

> I got picked for the Leeds and District Boys Under 16s, then I got picked for the West Riding side and was heading towards the North of England trials. I played for the West Riding against the East Riding at Oakwell [Barnsley] and I scored twice in the first fifteen minutes, but this centre-half took a dislike to me and kicked the shit out of my leg. So I got carried off after fifteen minutes and never made the trials! But I also played for Fryston Youth Club. My favourite ground at that stage was the old quarry at Fryston. You could play on that pitch and look up at the surrounding rock faces and imagine they were stands, just like Wembley. We used to let our imaginations run riot! (Cliff Braund)

A panoramic view of Fryston village and the pit yard, taken in the 1960s.

A view of Fryston Colliery, shot in the 1950s.

A team photo of Leeds City in the 1917-18 season, containing a rare glimpse of the Fryston, Blackpool, Leeds, Rotherham County, Castleford Town and Welsh international full-back, Harry Millership (crouching, front left). To Millership's immediate left is the great Huddersfield Town player and manager, Clem Stephenson. On the back row (extreme right) is the legendary Huddersfield and Arsenal manager, Herbert Chapman.

The Fryston Colliery Junior team of 1919-20 which won the Castleford and District FA Junior Challenge Cup. Centrally seated in the middle row is the future Bradford City player, Dick Foulkes, who was trainer of the Fryston teams appearing in the 1945 and 1963 West Riding County FA Challenge Cup finals.

A rare photograph of the all-conquering Fryston School team of 1926-27. Holding the ball is the Fryston star-player and captain, Jabie Foulkes.

Foulkes (extreme right) is pictured with his Stockport County colleagues with whom he appeared in the club's record-breaking 13-0 home win over Halifax Town on 6 January 1934.

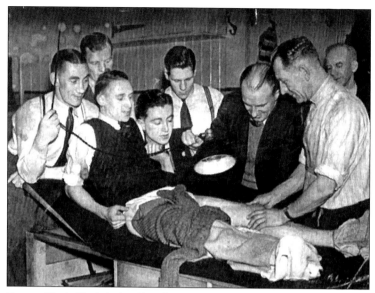

Fryston 'Bevin Boy', Arthur Farrell, receives treatment from the Bradford Park Avenue physiotherapist. Just on his shoulder are his Fryston co-workers and Park Avenue team-mates, Johnny Downie and (to the rear of Downie) the great Len Shackleton. On the extreme left of the photograph is Avenue's legendary Scottish-born goalkeeper, 'Chick' Farr.

The Bradford Park Avenue side that played Fryston in a charity match at Wheldon Road in May 1946. Johnny Downie is on the extreme right of the photograph. Positioned immediately behind him is the future West Ham and England manager, Ron Greenwood.

A youthful Jack Sharp (right), pictured in the early 1950s with two other emerging local talents, Billy Haines (centre) and Ken Hopkins (left).

Fryston's Colliery Manager of the 1940s and early 1950s, Jim Bullock, signs his name in concrete to commemorate the opening of the Fryston Miners' Welfare, which was built from start to finish by local miners.

The Fryston team that went on to win the 1954-55 West Yorkshire Second Division championship. BACK ROW (left to right): G. Battye, R. Lister (captain), J. Portman (goalkeeper), A. Smith and F. Howard. FRONT ROW: C. Pepper, F. Isles, R. Sutcliffe, R. Astbury, J. Raftery and J. Sharp.

Agga Mattison (left) and Brian Wood (right) look on as Archie Ward shows a safe pair of hands.

Terry Templeman shoots past the opposition goalkeeper as Phil Monks looks set to pounce on any possible rebound.

Thackley's wingman, Ray Cole (centre), gets an uplifting experience, courtesy of his centre-half and captain, David Waddington (left), and goalkeeper, Ken Hill (right).

'Grinning like a wolf!' Fryston's skipper, Pete Waddington, is pictured at a close-season presentation evening in 1963. The West Riding County FA Challenge Cup is second in from the right. On the left is the Snydale Road Athletic captain, Nicky Atkinson, whose side lost out to Thackley in the 1963 WRCC Cup semi-final.

Fryston Colliery Welfare circa 1980, when they lost 3-1 in the final of the West Riding County Cup to the Bradford team, Guiseley. Standing on the extreme left of the photograph is the long-serving Fryston player and team manager, Trevor Winter.

The last stage of a long journey? Fryston's charismatic goalkeeper, the late Archie Ward, pictured in his adoptive Australia.

Braund persuaded Ward to join him down at Fryston. The two of them were among the cohort of players invited to train pre-season with the Fryston first team:

> We were lowly placed in the league that year but I didn't go to Fryston thinking that I was going to win a hatful of medals. I went into the first team on the recommendation of the young-ish fella who used to run the youth team. He was also an ex-Grammar School lad, albeit a few years older than me and Cliff. To be truthful, I think I stepped into the boots of Tommy Templeman, who was their left-winger. We played about four pre-season friendlies and, I always remember, Cliff scored this fabulously spectacular goal from a scissors-kick, where he must have been five foot off the floor on the edge of the area. It put down a marker and we were pretty well-established by the end of the season. (Trevor Ward)

The two players were among those selected for Fryston's first league fixture of the 1962-63 season. By this stage, Ward had begun work as a trainee mining surveyor, based at Allerton Bywater, while Braund was continuing his studies as a sixth-former at Castleford Grammar. Word had somehow reached Ward that he had been included in the first-team line up but Cliff Braund had naively made his way down to Fryston's home ground keeping his fingers crossed that he might be lucky enough to be selected for the second eleven.

> But this guy came up – I can't remember his name – and said, 'Oh, you're with the first team, Cliff,' which I knew nothing about because I didn't work at the pit. So I had to run back up to the Magnet and board the first bus that went anywhere remotely near Whitwood, where Fryston were playing Whitwood Mere. Despite getting off at the wrong stop, I got there just before the kick-off. They put me at inside-forward. Terry Templeman was one and I was the other. I'd never played in that position before in my life. At school, they played me on the wing or at centre-forward. My forte was scoring goals. Fryston won 2-1 but I was *crap*, and that was putting it kindly! (Cliff Braund)

A slightly late starter that season for Fryston was Cobbo Robinson. Some weeks after the Castleford FA Minor team's defeat against Barkston Ash FA, Robinson had been invited to play for the successful Great Preston Juniors. Virtually invincible, Preston won the West Riding Minor Cup as well as every other competition they entered, with Robinson starring on the wing. He especially remembers playing

Huddersfield ICI at Swillington in one of the later rounds of the county cup:

> I think the score was 7-3 or 8-3 and they cancelled the game ten minutes before time! In that first game, I scored the first three goals in twenty minutes. Jimmy Scoular [the Bradford Park Avenue player-manager] was watching the match and someone said, 'What about him, then?' and he said 'Too small.' In the replay, I scored again inside ten minutes and we beat 'em 4-1 this time. Towards the end of that season, somebody at Kippax said, 'Come play with us and I'll get thee trials with Scunthorpe United,' but nowt came of it and, after a couple of matches, I went back to Fryston. (Barry Robinson)

Robinson found to his instant satisfaction that the team he was now joining 'had somehow come together ready formed. We were like the pieces of a jigsaw,' he ventured, 'that snapped beautifully into place.' Notably absent from the resulting picture was a certain Freddie Howard, whose days as a Fryston first-team regular seemed to be well and truly over.

Chapter 9
Just Like a Family

Previous page: One permutation of the Fryston Colliery Welfare team which contested the 1962-63 West Yorkshire League Division Two (South) championship.

Brothers in Arms

Fryston entered the 1962-63 season with a new-found sense of togetherness. Brian Wood said that, 'Although we weren't a right good side to begin with on leaving Shepherds, it wasn't too long before we all gelled together like one.' Agga Mattison attributes the powerful team ethic that served Fryston so well to the strong sense of local identity and egalitarian ethos that pervaded the entire team. In his view, the team was 'just like a family':

> Well, the best thing about it, the majority of 'em were Fryston lads – they were born, worked or lived in Fryston, and for most on us it was all three! And such as Pete, we already knew him from school; and in any case, even he was *half* a Frystoner – he married a Fryston lass! Braundy and Wardy, they lived in Airedale and hadn't come from miles away. I tell thee, they were all *local lads*, and there weren't any so-called stars among us. I should say Jack were t'biggest star we'd got, and even he were a Frystoner, just like the rest on us. We weren't playing for the colliery as such, but we *were* playing for the village. (Harold Mattison)

Trevor Ward asserts that it was the 'almost magical, alchemic fusion' of the complementary personalities and talents of the team that made it greater than the sum of its parts. Ward is therefore only partly inclined to agree with Mattison's assessment:

> *Partly* but not entirely, because the nucleus came from Fryston but they'd all gone away in order to come back home, and it really felt like we'd all blown in on a wind of change and that something exciting was happening. We were a confident team because we knitted together straight away. (Trevor Ward)

It is therefore pertinent to consider at this point what precisely it was, in terms both of the individual characteristics of each player and the values and ethos of the team as a whole, which made them 'gel' so well and complement each other.

The goalkeeper, Archie Ward, was obviously aware both of his strengths and limitations: 'I guess I was instinctive as a 'keeper,' he maintained. 'I relied on my born reactions in the main. I was a weak bugger on the ground – whoops, straight between the legs sometimes! I don't want to piss in my own pocket but one or two used to call me "the cat" in deference to Peter Bonetti, though Gordon Banks was my goalkeeping hero, first and foremost.' Brian Wood would not dispute the 'keeper's assessment of his own abilities:

> Archie was a cracking goalie but he was a bit bloody doolally! He could pull off the most stupid and brilliant stunts all in the space of the same match. I remember one match at Snydale where their centre-forward broke through, and Archie grabbed hold of his leg, so that he was dragging Archie, while we're all shouting, 'Let him go! Let him go!' because we knew the ref was about to give a penalty. (Brian Wood)

Wood himself was one of Fryston's most versatile players. Depending on the circumstances, he was capable of acting as a redoubtable right full-back, 'stopper' centre-half or, even, standby goalkeeper. Wood was deceptively frail in appearance, and what he may have lacked in natural talent, he more than made up for in toughness and determination. He was 'as hard as stone', according to Terry Templeman. 'He'd tackle owt and do it for a full 90 minutes at a time – a great club man, arguably the best.' 'Putting it simply,' explained Trevor Ward, 'I've always said he was the greatest trier to ever set foot on a football field. He wasn't a brilliant player, and that's not to say he was a poor one by any means, but he always tried 150 per cent, every time.' For a large part of the 1962–63 season, Wood occupied the centre-half berth, with one or the other of two fellow Frystoners, Keith Mattison or Frankie Isles, settling in at right-back.

The lesser-known of the two Mattisons in the Fryston team was Agga's cousin, Keith, who was popularly known as 'Genie'. Jack Sharp recalls how this particular member of the Mattison family came into football relatively late on in life:

> I could never remember him kicking a football in his teens, but then he suddenly started playing. He was another big, tall lad. They got him playing one or two games in t'second team and then he came on a treat. He was a quick, strong player, and it was soon a case of him being one of the first names on the sheet. Him and Agga are cousins – their fathers were brothers.

He's never altered: he's a big, raw-boned lad and extremely pleasant with it. (Jack Sharp)

By the early 1960s, Frank Isles had become something of a utility player for Fryston, sometimes occupying his preferred position on the wing, but increasingly slotting in at full-back. Few people had ever shown more dedication to the club:

I was a trier. I held my own. I was good enough to get picked, and there were some really good players down the years but I always seemed to get a game. I was mainly a layer-on. In them early days with the big balls, I always struggled to hoof 'em some distance, whereas our Jack was strong enough to hit 'em where he liked. I was a right-winger but I didn't take corners because I didn't have the strength to land it in. I used to be a good reader of a game and I used to help others. And when you were in a good team, you couldn't help but tap the odd one or two of 'em in. (Frank Isles)

One player in the Fryston team was, by common consent, 'a class apart' from the rest. Asked which player was the best he had ever played alongside *or* against, Pete Waddington's response was spontaneously unequivocal:

Sharpie! Jack Sharp was *absolutely brilliant!* He went from winger to half-back to full-back and he fitted each position like a glove. That's a professional footballer for thee. He could just as easily lick a defender on the outside and cross it as mark the opposition winger out of the game. Tremendous skill and attitude — best I've ever seen in a local footballer. The way he held himself on a pitch — his supreme authority and confidence — was inspirational; but he also had that sense of responsibility for his team-mates and he was always looking out for you — helping and encouraging, and giving you the occasional kick up the backside if necessary. We always expected a lot of him and he nearly always delivered. (Peter Waddington)

The ex-Halifax player's relationship with Waddington was certainly based on a powerful mutual respect: 'He was arguably our main play-maker,' is Sharp's assessment of his skipper, 'and he had the right brain, skills and charisma for the job. He was good enough to get into any local side, was Pete.' Cliff Braund places an equivalent value on Waddington's importance to Fryston:

He was the heartbeat of the team, the driving force. I can see him now gritting his teeth and clenching his fists: 'Come on, we can have this lot for breakfast!' He was a fabulous player: skilful, fierce tackler and strong in the air. He wasn't fast but he was very, very strong; a good passer and naturally two-footed. He was a proper joker in the pack as well. He had this irresistible smile – beautiful, like a wolf! (Cliff Braund)

However, Braund also clearly regards Waddington as having exemplified Fryston's determination to show no quarter in an era in which patterns of physical intimidation and gamesmanship were the norm:

I once saw Pete clatter into this guy and put him down hurt. The referee gives a free kick and is about to call him over for a booking, but Pete trots over, ruffles the guy's hair, pats him on the shoulder and kisses him on the cheek. The referee grins and forgets all about the booking and, 60 seconds later, Pete clatters him again!

A similar assessment could be made of Fryston's other wing-half, Johnny Appleyard, who was, in Trevor Ward's estimation:

The best stopper ever to have graced a football field. You could rely on him for anything. In all the time I played with him, I can't recall him ever making a mistake. In those days there were a lot of players used to leave their foot in, because referees were more lenient then, and Johnny wasn't the type to forgive them their trespasses! (Trevor Ward)

Pete Waddington concurs that 'Johnny was a law unto himself. You could tell him in his ear, "That so-and-so is giving our right-winger some stick. What's tha gonna do about it?" and he'd say, "Just leave it with me, Pete."'

At centre-half for Fryston was the commanding figure of Agga Mattison, whose game was imbued with an attitude and finesse imported from his various flirtations with the professional game. Along with Jack Sharp, he formed an experienced core at the heart of the Fryston team. 'He and Jackie Sharp were the old pros,' explained Cliff Braund. 'They'd been around the block and brought the skills, the know-how and balance to the defence and midfield.' For Archie Ward, Mattison was 'Dependable – a colossus at the back'; and as Trevor Ward explained:

Nobody got any change out of him in the air. He was six-foot-two, but the point was he made himself six-foot-five! He was a gentle giant. He wasn't a clogger by nature. Mind you, if he had to sort somebody out, he'd do it on the sly. He wasn't brilliant with his feet but he was a class apart with his head and he could tackle anything that moved. (Trevor Ward)

Image, size, personality and skill were all inseparable components of Barry Robinson's football make up: 'A cheeky little lad,' was how Cliff Braund chose to describe him. 'Well-dressed, flashing smile – he was a little Beatle to look at.' Several colleagues concur with Pete Waddington's view that the diminutive winger 'could definitely have made the grade if only he'd been a bit bigger'. They also agree that his small stature never detracted from his determination:

> The thing about Barry was that he never gave up. He was one of those that, whenever he lost the ball, he'd chase back for it. We were that type of team to be honest. But he was the George Best of the team – fantastic little dribbler and beautiful crosser of the ball. (Trevor Ward)

'Mr Perpetual Motion' was the term used by Archie Ward to characterise the youthful Terry Templeman. 'All heart he was,' asserted Ward. 'He was a midfield fetcher-and-carrier, who kept running all day for the sake of the team.' As Brian Wood explained, 'Inside-forwards at that time had to drop back, get the ball, and feed it to the centre-forward and wingers, and Terry was very adept at that.' Trevor Ward maintains that the comparison with Eusebio was well-justified: 'He had a cannonball shot for one – he couldn't half hit a ball! You couldn't take a free kick off him. If Terry was within 35 yards of a free kick being given it was "Come here, give us that ball!" and nobody had a chance of getting it off him.' Templeman's overall importance to Fryston was emphasised by Cobbo Robinson: 'I'd say that Terry was the hub of the team. He was here, there and everywhere, always making himself available and showing endless stamina.' Equally crucial, though, was the virtually telepathic relationship that developed between the upfield trio of Templeman, Trevor Ward and Cliff Braund.

Cliff Braund and Trevor Ward's Castleford Grammar School background earned them the collective nickname of Fryston's 'posh lads'. In Jack Sharp's opinion, they proved to be 'a pair of nuggets' for Fryston. According to Archie Ward, '"Brawny" was a bloody good player – quick, skilful, and a tough nut, too. He'd run till he bloody dropped. He had a great shot on him, especially on the volley.' By his own admission, he was notorious for his short-temper and, according to Trevor Ward, was often petulant in his reaction to being tackled heavily. Ward remembers the infamous occasion when, during a match against Methley, Braund retaliated to an incident in which he had been raked down the back of the leg by turning round and slapping his opponent across the face. 'But,' as Braund self-mockingly protests, 'it was a far more physical game back then':

> The full-backs I came across always kicked you in the first five minutes, so I used to get my retaliation in first. I was a real pain in the arse! I was immature. Part of the problem was that I was playing with these tough, physical guys like Johnny, Pete and Sharpie, while I was this young, relatively puny slip of a kid, and I didn't want to show them that I was scared. If somebody kicked me, I gave them it back straight away. Pete would laugh at me: 'You're doing it all wrong. You make a note of his number, don't say anything to him, don't warn him – nothing. Wait until your turn arrives, then you get in there and do him.' Pete, Terry and the rest of 'em, they made me grow up, and grow up fast. (Cliff Braund)

Trevor Ward was a six-footer who was as adept at crossing the ball out on the left as heading in a Terry Templeman or Cobbo Robinson centre from the opposite touchline. Ward has a staunch advocate in Agga Mattison who maintained that, 'If I'd have been picking the team, Trevor Ward would've been the first man in every time.' Frank Isles was another of Ward's many admirers:

> He'd a very good left foot had Wardy, natural left-footer. He was six foot, quick and very well-balanced. He could come in off the left wing and score goals, but he could score with his head as well. He did move to centre-forward later in his career but he was naturally left-sided and there weren't very many about. He could beat a man easily and get a cross in, no problem. (Frank Isles)

In Cliff Braund's opinion, the value of his partnership with Trevor Ward lay especially in the instinctive understanding they shared of each other's tactical awareness and positional play:

> I just knew which area to put the ball in for Trev. Thread it just behind the centre-back and nine out of ten times he'd score. And he knew which one I'd do the dummy on and step over for him to tap it in. He wouldn't need to call because we'd already done it a hundred times before. (Cliff Braund)

It was generally considered by the Fryston players that, whilst David Rotherforth was not a 'natural' footballer, his capacity as a 'born sprinter' was a fantastic asset for the team. As Jack Sharp explains, 'David was very sharp – a trained athlete. If you hit a ball over the top, he was onto it like lightning.' Rotherforth is apt to agree that his speed was his principal asset:

> Obviously, my biggest strength was that I was pretty quick. I used to think I could play a bit as well. It was no good being quick if you didn't have the ball control as well. Heading the ball wasn't one of my strong points. It was more about latching onto the end of a good through ball. (David Rotherforth)

There was a common feeling among Rotherforth's Fryston colleagues that his dedication to the game of football might have been compromised by his competing focus on athletics:

> We were pretty good mates because we played up front together. But I never got the impression that he was playing football because he *loved* the game with all his heart and soul like the rest of us. In fact, if we hadn't had such a good season, I think he'd have packed in playing much earlier than he did. (Trevor Ward)

Leaders and Followers

Trevor Ward is lavishly sincere in his praise of what he calls the 'backroom team' which helped not only to ensure the effectiveness and viability of Fryston Colliery Welfare as a team, but also as a football club.

> The main ones I remember are Benny Binks, who spent hours upon hours looking after Fryston with disregard for any other aspect of his life, and his missus was the same. Chunner Lister, Ronnie, never missed a game. He was always there and whatever you wanted, he could get it. Alf Atack – whenever you turned round he was there, reliable as ever, carrying the bag, putting the goalposts up – thankless tasks that we just took for granted. Then there was Frank [Isles] who eventually became involved in the committee, Fryston through and through. He took his boots with him everywhere just in case we were a player or two short. That's what you call devotion. But I'll reserve a special mention for Billy Bridges, who came from a really long-established Fryston family. Well, he was the main fund-raiser. He used to have a little

box like that and he had all the names of the football teams on it. You used to pay ten pence, it might even have been a shilling in those days, and you picked a team. And when he'd sold them all, he used to reveal a team on the other side of the box, and the winning person used to win a certain amount and the balance went into the club coffers. Sometimes, he might run three or four of them, depending on demand, and that was regardless of whether we were playing home or away. He was never a footballer, but like all the others, he lived for the sake of Fryston. (Trevor Ward)

Closest of all to the actual team were its manager, Dick Foulkes, and his 'right-hand man', Chunner Lister. According to Jack Sharp, the former was 'a down-to-earth man and Fryston through and through. He was a comical bugger, and he'd love to come out with t'lads.' The weekly process of selecting the team was ostensibly a matter for the club committee. However, it was Foulkes who always had the final say:

Everybody would be arguing about who should play left-back and whether this or that player was on form or should be left out. And this would go on for an hour. We'd all reach a consensus, but then Dick would say, 'No. Put that player back in and take that bugger out.' We'd go so far as to have a vote, but if Dick didn't like the outcome, we'd re-open the discussion again! We had a committee of eight and Dick wasn't the manager but he effectively ran the team. He always had t'final word. (Frank Isles)

Being closer to the players in age and modern sensibility, Chunner Lister was regarded by many of them more as a friend and confidant. To the youthful Cobbo Robinson, Lister 'was like a second father'. The fact that the two men worked together on the wagons made it possible for the older man to keep a paternal eye on his teenage protégé. 'Owt that went wrong,' insists Robinson, 'he sorted out for me. I had this dicky car that kept breaking down due to a faulty petrol pump at t'back, I kept taking it back to t'garage but they weren't fixing it right, so Chunner says, "Hang on, I'm coming with thee this time." It was right as rain after that.'

There was nothing scientific or systematic about the training and coaching regimes implemented by the Fryston management. The Fryston players unanimously agree that they were chiefly reliant on 'natural skill' and a 'spirit of togetherness'. Thus, Cliff Braund vividly remembers how training consisted of 'a few stretching exercises, a couple of laps, some shots in, and then five- or seven-a-side, depending on how many of us showed up'. Occasionally, a senior member of the team, like Frank Isles, might suggest a planned move for the following Saturday; otherwise, as Braund maintains, there was no additional emphasis on advance preparation for the game ahead: 'Dick and Chunner used to show up on match day and do a lot of talking and encouraging; but I don't recall them playing a big part in terms of tactics and organisation – that was left to Sharpie, Agga and Pete.' Pete Waddington confirms that Lister's and Foulkes' input stopped short of being tactical: 'I suppose their contribution was in knowing the mentality of opposition players: "Watch that centre-forward, he's likely to take a tumble in the area"; "Get onto that goalkeeper – he's frail and he doesn't want to know."'

There is no doubt at all that Waddington's leadership style, personality and tactical acumen had a powerful bearing on the side. In Trevor Ward's opinion, 'You couldn't have picked anybody else to be captain of that team. He was a leader in that way. He never mentored anybody or explained how to do things like Jackie did, but he had that authority when he played.' As a naturally two-footed player, Waddington had the versatility to slot into any role for the sake of the team and could empathise with those in any position. His extrovert and entertaining nature, and instinctive capacity to 'read the opposition', were visible hallmarks of his captaincy:

> I suppose I had a knack of lifting the players and getting that bit more effort out of them whenever I could sense that morale was sagging or complacency was setting in. I could also analyse what was happening inside individual encounters, so I'd come straight out and say: 'Come on Brian or Johnny, you're giving that player too much space. Get tighter on him and let him know you're there!' It was all about reading the game and motivating players. (Peter Waddington)

Brian Wood is more than half-serious in maintaining that 'Pete was a very good footballer, but he was even better at telling jokes – keeping the spirits up and leading by example'; while Agga Mattison is adamant that every good team has a Pete Waddington in it, 'acting about and things', to help keep things calm, 'especially in a corner'. According to Frank Isles, Fryston's own 'clown prince of football' used to monopolise the back five seats of the team coach:

He never stopped telling jokes, and he always had new material somehow. He had an aura about him. He was compulsive listening for, I don't care who you were, you couldn't help but like him. (Frank Isles)

Cobbo Robinson and Brian Wood each alluded to the shared abilities of Pete Waddington and Jack Sharp to employ subtle psychological ploys that were designed to get the best out of their colleagues. Thus, as Robinson maintains, 'Pete and Sharpie used to get that bit of "kidology" going – make you feel you'd done something amazing to keep your confidence up.' Brian Wood also relates how the two colleagues used to 'play on our individual psyches a bit – and maybe touch a nerve if ever t'situation demanded it'. He recalls a vital away match in the 1962-63 season as a primary example:

And all the way on t'bus, Jackie kept whispering in my ear, 'He plays for bloody Tranmere does their centre-forward. I can't see thee coping with him.' He must have said it a dozen times until I got sick to the back teeth with it. But anyway, by the time we got to Keighley, bloody steam was coming out of my nostrils and there was no way I was gonna let the little bugger get past me. (Brian Wood)

The strong collective ethic pervading the Fryston team was both reflected in and reinforced by the inevitable post-match social gatherings:

It was a very inclusive ethos. After a game with Fryston, we all used to go down to the club: get dressed up, maybe have an hour in town and then get down to Fryston where they put a table aside, at the right-hand side near the stage, for the players. From there, we used to move on to the Fryston Hotel, where the same turn, a local singer and comedian, used to put a turn on for us after he'd been out on his paying gigs. We're talking about twelve midnight. (Trevor Ward)

Ward's wife, Carol, has a fond recollection of such nights and the 'brilliant atmosphere' that surrounded them. 'I went along with Cliff's wife, Elaine,' she recalls. 'We used to go out with them two and Terry and Sheila Templeman.' Matches were also attended by a regular group of supporters: 'Benny Binks and his wife and daughter, for example; Cliff's parents and Elaine. It was a fabulous family club.'

The essence of what made Fryston such a satisfying and cohesive team to play for is nicely encapsulated by Cliff Braund:

They were all strong but affable people who didn't complain about life. They just got on with it. They'd do a double shift down the pit and then come along and run their guts out on the field: live hard, work hard, play hard. (Cliff Braund)

No wonder, then, that Pete Waddington should refer to Fryston as 'the best team I've ever played with. I wouldn't alter any of the players; I wouldn't change a thing.' It was this cohesive group of personnel which entered the 1962-63 season with an eye on the West Yorkshire League Division Two (South) championship and still considering they might have an outside chance of lifting the coveted, but so far unattainable, WRCC Cup.

Chapter 10
Bound for Glory?

Previous page: 'Just like Eusebio!' Terry Templeman follows up to score in one of Fryston's matches.

Early-Season Promise

As we saw in chapter 8, the 1962-63 season started with a 2-1 victory for Fryston over Whitwood, a result which provided a good springboard for a season in which The Colliers took eleven points from their first six matches to share the joint leadership with East Ardsley. A 1-1 home draw against Knottingley Albion was the only blemish on an otherwise perfect record. Among initial highlights were a 5-0 home thrashing of local rivals, Airedale Athletic, and a scintillating 4-1 away win against East End Park (until recently a Yorkshire League side), in which David Rotherforth scored a hat-trick. Arguably the toughest game so far was their home match against Britannia Works (Huddersfield), when Trevor Ward wrong-footed the home right-back to fire home the winner with twenty minutes left.

It was this good form and newly-acquired winning habit that Fryston took into their first-round away tie of the WRCC Cup against Goole United, the previous season's winners of the Scunthorpe League. This was a far more difficult encounter than the 4-2 scoreline in Fryston's favour might suggest. Goole took an early lead, which they deservedly maintained until close on half time. It was at this point that crude steps were taken to stifle the opposition 'midfield general':

> I know they were running us ragged, and they'd got this one player who was running rings round us. I remember Pete [Waddington] saying to one or two others, 'We've got to do summat about him – quick!' And I don't know whether it were him or Appy [Johnny Appleyard], but they kicked him up in t'air and I'm nearly sure he got carted off to hospital. (Barry Robinson)

Almost immediately Fryston equalised through Braund to enter half time undeservedly level. The ten-man opposition regained the lead early in the second half, but Fryston registered two quick replies, from

Rotherforth and Robinson, before Lane wrapped things up twenty minutes from time.

Fryston's momentum was maintained in subsequent league and cup competitions. While one of their closest league rivals, Keighley Central, were suffering their first defeat of the season, 2-0 away to Castleford Town, Fryston were recording a 3-2 win at Pontefract Collieries, where they had to withstand a stirring fight-back by the home side after a Trevor Ward hat-trick had established an apparently unassailable lead.

> I remember playing that game because all three were headers – and they needed to be because the pitch wasn't fit for football. I would say that half the goals I scored that season were with headers somewhere between the edge of the six-yard box and the penalty spot as I came in from the left-hand side, and the crosses were provided either by Terry Temp or Cobbo. With Terry Temp it was virtually telepathic. We were in a practice game when he first did it but it was Jack Sharp who instilled in me the importance of getting in there just in case the ball arrived. (Trevor Ward)

This victory was followed by an easy 5-0 win in the Cas and District Cup against the Castleford youth team, Hundhill United, and a 2-0 defeat of Allerton in the Watson Cup (otherwise known as the West Yorkshire League Division Two Cup).

The second round of the WRCC Cup saw all local teams bar Fryston and holders, Ferrybridge Amateurs, eliminated. Glass Houghton Welfare were beaten 4-2 at home by Kirkheaton Rovers and Methley United 2-1 on their home ground by Bradford Rovers. Heavy defeats were inflicted on Allerton, who lost 9-2 at Brook Sports, and Whitwood Mere, who were trounced 8-1 by the impressive looking Bradford side, Thackley, who by all accounts should have registered an even higher score:

> Jimmy Dickinson's early goal for Whitwood Mere United against Thackley, who have won all their [West Riding] County Amateur League games so far, did not have the happy sequel hoped for. It was not long before a home shot hit United's right-back Dove on the thigh and flew into goal and then there was only one team in it. If an element of luck existed about several of Thackley's seven later goals, other efforts might have succeeded but for the splendid goalkeeping of Pick.[1]

Ferrybridge won comfortably 4-1 at home to the lowly West Riding County Amateur League team, International Harvesters. Fryston's 5-1 thrashing of Scholemoor Amateurs was achieved with encouraging aplomb:

> Fryston's young left-wing pair, Trevor Ward and Cliff Braund, each got two goals in the defeat of Scholemoor Amateurs, in a match in which the visitors displayed little more than a never-say-die spirit. This was no lop-sided victory, however, for there was the usual balance about the Fryston team. It is this new blend which is behind the side's transformation. They have now gone 11 cup and league games without defeat with only Knottingley Albion preventing them from winning.[2]

Keeping the Momentum Going

David Rotherforth's importance to Fryston was underlined by a fine individual performance in the team's crucial mid-November clash away to the hitherto unbeaten league leaders, Ardsley Celtic. Despite an early Rotherforth goal, Fryston found themselves 2-1 down with a mere ten minutes played. Things looked even more unpromising for Fryston when Brian Wood was sent off for 'dissent' and Pete Waddington was forced to abandon his role as play-making wing-half to fill in at centre-half. However, with Terry Templeman playing his heart out, Fryston took control and scored five goals in a row (three of them by Rotherforth) to lead 6-2 midway through the second half. A late rally by Ardsley reduced the final deficit to two goals, but Fryston's well-merited victory ensured that they now remained the only unbeaten team in their division.

It was not a distinction they were able to enjoy for long. Archie Ward was absent with a thigh injury from the Fryston team which suffered their first loss of the season, 1-0 away to Ferrybridge Amateurs Reserves. The vital headed goal for 'Ferry' was scored in the last ten minutes by their right-winger, Whitaker. On the day in question, Fryston's reserve team drew their Division Three (South) match against Yorkshire Copper Works Reserves. The most notable feature of this otherwise unremarkable game was that it marked the return to Fryston (from Sunday league football) of Freddie Howard, albeit for a prolonged spell in the second eleven.

In the following week's WRCC Cup third round, Ferrybridge Amateurs left it late before coming from a goal down to beat Harehills Amateurs (Leeds) by the odd goal in three. Fryston had 'plenty to spare', though, in overcoming Glass Houghton Welfare's conquerors, Kirkheaton, 4-1 away.

In a thoroughly entertaining match, Fryston gave a first-half grip which gave them an interval lead of two goals and then clinched a place in the fourth round with a goal in the last 15 minutes. Rotherforth, who scored two fine goals from acute angles, put Fryston into a fairly early lead but it was held for seconds only against this smart Kirkheaton side which knocked Glass Houghton Welfare out in the second round. Before half time, however, Trevor Ward, at outside-left, supplied his scoring touch once more and Rotherforth added his second. Ward notched the second-half goal. Though Fryston's success was very much a team effort, Templeman, at inside-forward, stood out in a 'fetch and carry' role and Isles played strongly at left-back. In goal, Andy Comer, again deputising for Harold Ward, made some good saves.[3]

The Colliers' form proved less decisive in other cup competitions. First, they let slip a two-goal lead to draw with East End Park in the Watson Cup. They then incurred a 3-1 home defeat by Glass Houghton Welfare in the quarter-finals of the Cas and District Cup. The club was rescued from what might otherwise have proved a fatal dip in form by the 'Big Freeze' of December 1962 to early March 1963, which caused the almost total suspension of the sporting calendar.

Mud. Glorious Mud

Following the spring thaw, Fryston secured a nervous 1-0 victory over Turnbridge WMC in the WRCC Cup fourth round. The team's controversial winner was scored by Barry Robinson who resumed where he left off, pre-freeze, by scoring his third in as many games:

A disputed goal in the first 10 minutes by their young winger Robinson carried Fryston through to the quarter-final. Robinson, who had gone inside, ran on to a pass from the wing and steered the ball wide of the visitors' goalkeeper. Strong protests by the Turnbridge defenders that Robinson was offside were ignored by the referee. After half an hour both sides wilted. Although the going was quite good, Turnbridge, however, missed an excellent opportunity when one of their inside-forwards fired over the bar from a few yards' range. Earlier, home goalkeeper Ward turned a fine shot on to the bar, and at the other end, Robinson sent a shot against the foot of a post. In a match in which defences dominated, Fryston right-back Isles was outstanding.[4]

Fryston's victory set up a quarter-final tie against Earby, while Ferrybridge's 5-1 win over Gilderstone Athletic also guaranteed the holders a place in the next round.

The muddy grounds resulting from the thaw did not prove unduly disadvantageous to the young Fryston team, who followed up their county cup win by beating Allerton 6-0 at home (with Ward and Robinson each scoring twice), and Knottingley Albion 2-0 away with goals by David Rotherforth. A week earlier, Albion had done Fryston a huge favour by beating the latter's closest rivals, Keighley Central, 2-0 away. The club's long-term prospects of winning the league and WRCC Cup were not helped, however, by a 3-3 draw (after extra time) in their replayed Watson Cup quarter-final against East End Park, an outcome which added yet another game to an already congested calendar. However, things continued to look healthy when, at the end of March, Fryston avenged their only league defeat of the season by beating Ferrybridge Amateurs Reserves 3-1 with goals by Braund (2) and Ward.

On the eve of Fryston's WRCC Cup quarter-final tie with Earby, a club located high in the Pennines at the Yorkshire-Lancashire border, the *Express* reported that The Colliers were planning to incorporate a 'night out' into their long return journey.[5] The fixture was subject to a pre-match inspection by a West Riding County FA official, following complaints by Earby's previous Challenge Cup opponents, East End Park, that they had been forced to get changed on their coach and share three buckets of water in getting washed afterwards. Not surprisingly, this turned out to be one of the strangest and more unforgettable trips of the season.

Trevor Ward can still vividly recall how the two chartered coaches transporting the Fryston players, their partners and supporters to the game had 'got lost three times' before following the small road sign marked 'Earby' up a narrow country lane flanked by stone walls for as far as the eye could see:

We'd seen the arrow for Earby village and the bus driver pulls up and scratches his head: 'Well, I'm sure that this is it!' And it was just *desolate*, there wasn't a soul about. You could see it was a football field because it had all the familiar makings, but there was a path running right the way across it from one goal to the other! And there were four houses where this path led to; and when you looked at it, you thought, 'This *can't* be a football club!'

Suddenly, however, two young men came trotting out of one of the houses in their football gear. They quickly emerged from a ramshackle garden shed with goalposts and corner flags which they immediately started to set up. Then, six more players appeared from a neighbouring house and proceeded to re-mark the pitch with lines of sawdust. The field and its surrounding area resembled nothing more than a bog, and it was therefore with considerable trepidation that the smartly dressed Fryston party began to step down from their coaches. However, as Trevor Ward explains:

There wasn't a dry spot anywhere. So when you stopped off the bus, your foot planted straight into a puddle. And you can imagine what the women felt like! My wife still reminds me of it after all these years. She had a bright yellow coat on and white stiletto-type shoes. We, the players, all got off the bus in our suits, carrying bags with our gear in, and this bloke came across: 'Oh, I see you've got here, then!' We says, 'Aye, it were a bit of a struggle but can you tell us where t'dressing rooms are?' 'Dressing rooms?' he says. 'Didn't you come changed for playing football?' So we says, 'No, we're planning on travelling on to Bradford after, like.' And he gives it, 'Oh, we haven't got no changing rooms but there's a bit on a hen hut over there and we can lay on some buckets of water!' So all the women climbed off the buses and had to re-gather in one of 'em while we all got changed in the other. Eventually, when everybody bucked up the courage to make it to the touchline, there were 80-odd of our spectators compared with only three of theirs! The referee turned up with only ten minutes to spare and, as we all lined up for t'kick-off, this woman walked straight across the field with two dogs! *Unbelievable* it were!

Given such difficult and unconventional surroundings, Fryston went on to win the game with unexpected ease. With the first-half wind behind them, The Colliers struck the woodwork twice and had two goal-bound efforts cleared off the line. Two fine saves by the Earby goalkeeper further ensured that the game remained goalless at the interval. However, this all changed on the resumption when, now playing into the wind, 'Fryston controlled the half better and when left-winger, Trevor Ward, crossed the ball, outside-right Robinson, having moved inside, snapped up the chance. Not long afterwards inside-left Braund scored a second goal after Terry Templeman had driven the ball into the goalmouth. Such was Fryston's superiority that goalkeeper Archie Ward had only one serious shot to save.'[6]

At full time, the Earby officials produced a solitary tin bath for the benefit of the Fryston players. Brian Wood recollects how the water was bitterly cold: 'I can remember me and Johnny Appleyard fighting to get in it first! After t'first half a dozen had washed t'mud off their legs, it was like a big bowl of Oxo.' True to plan, the Fryston party set off afterwards for nearby Craven for a typical night out:

> We all spilled out into this club kind of thing. They'd got a turn on, like, and this bloke called Andy, who was t'bus driver and well-known for his George-Formby-style impersonation, decided to get up on t'stage, and he started playing t'piano – 'Mule Train'! One of t'members of t'Fryston committee, a bloke called Horace, had this little gun that fired caps, and as this waiter were coming round, and Andy's singing away, Horace fired this bloody gun, and t'waiter dropped this tray of beer. Anyway, a bit later on, this waiter comes to t'table where Pete Waddington's sitting, and Pete orders this round and tells t'waiter he was sorry what had happened and to get one for hissen as compensation for his trauma. So, t'waiter eventually came back with t'drinks and asked Pete for t'money. And Pete says, 'I think tha's overcharged me', and t'waiter says, 'But tha told me to get one for missen.' And Pete says, 'Aye, that's reight enough, cock, but I expected *thee* to pay for it!' (Ronnie Foulkes)

Fryston returned home in the early hours of Sunday morning to discover that Ferrybridge Amateurs had surrendered their title by losing 2-1 at home to DP and E, thus making The Colliers the only surviving Castleford club in that year's competition.

From Dream to Nightmare?

Fryston kept their sights firmly set on achieving the 'triple' (Second Division [South] championship, Watson Cup and West Riding County FA Challenge Cup) by securing six successive home wins in mid- to late-April, including vital victories against their two closest rivals, Keighley Central (1-0) and Ardsley Celtic (4-0). Fryston were especially indebted for their success to Trevor Ward, whose total of eight goals included at least one in every match. According to the *Express*, 'These key points against Keighley Central and Ardsley Celtic have put the title on the Fryston road from Glass Houghton, last year's winners.' The paper added that 'Only a serious lapse can turn it back.'[7]

Such confidence was premature. In the build-up to their WRCC Cup semi-final against DP and E at East End Park, Fryston suffered their worst spell of the season. A Tuesday night fixture saw them beaten by the only goal in their vital match at Keighley. There were less than ten minutes remaining when an Appleyard back-pass failed to reach Archie Ward and allowed an opponent to nip in and squeeze the ball inside the post. Two evenings later, only an opposition penalty miss prevented Fryston from going down at Britannia Works, where a goal from Rotherforth earned a fortunate one-all draw. The following Saturday's match against Halifax Town Reserves proved chastening for The Colliers. The *Express* reports that Fryston 'were run off their feet'[8] by a side containing four players with Football League experience. At one stage, the visitors were down to eight men, having lost Trevor Ward and Keith Mattison through injury, and Johnny Appleyard to a sending-off twenty minutes from time. It was an occasion that Cliff Braund is sure he will never forget:

> The best team I felt we ever played against was Halifax Town Reserves. We beat them 2-0 in the league at our place. They didn't like that very much. Some of them were young pros, while others were first-teamers coming back from injury. When we played them away, it was chucking it down at night under the floodlights, and we lost heavily 4-0 and we were lucky to get nil. They absolutely took us to pieces in what were alien conditions for us. It didn't matter what we did, they always got the better of us. I remember running my balls off while they passed it around in their little triangles. I was a bit depressed but Trevor laughed it off afterwards. He said, 'Come on, there wasn't anything we could have done against that sort of class.'

A further setback occurred the following Tuesday night when Fryston lost their second replay in the Watson Cup against East End Park. Fryston had tried to have the match postponed because they were due to play their WRCC Cup semi-final an evening later. However, they were ordered to play or risk incurring a £20 fine, so they opted to field a team comprising five reserves and three regulars playing out of position. To make matters worse, Frank Isles was injured with only five minutes gone and failed to return for the second half. These handicaps proved insurmountable and Fryston lost 2-0.

Semi-Final Marathon

The Colliers entered their WRCC Cup semi-final against DP and E at East End Park with their confidence slightly shaken. This was reflected in a diffident performance, during which an uncharacteristic defensive error by Brian Wood enabled Otley to take a seventh-minute lead. Cliff Braund equalised from a spot-kick eight minutes later; but in the tense affair that followed, neither side succeeded in adding to their score. Wood believes that he should not be judged too harshly for having made the mistake which led to Otley's goal:

> That centre-forward who I played against was an ex-pro. It was towards the back end of his career, so he didn't do a lot of running; but give him half a chance and he was deadly. In the first of them drawn games, I only gave him half-a-yard and he scored. (Brian Wood)

The replay, which took place one week later on the same ground, was mostly dominated by Fryston, who took a fourteenth-minute lead when Trevor Ward shot past the advancing Otley goalkeeper. A subsequent Ward effort was then headed off the line with the 'keeper out of position in what proved the first of a series of narrow escapes for DP and E. However, nine minutes from half time, another unfortunate slip-up by Brian Wood allowed the opposition to equalise, only for Cliff Braund to restore Fryston's lead six minutes later with a headed goal from a cross by Trevor Ward. The Colliers' composed second-half display then took them to the brink of their first county cup final appearance since 1945. However, a splendidly taken direct free kick, eight minutes from the end of normal time, thwarted their ambitions. The extra time period saw both teams come close to winning the match: only two minutes into it, Archie Ward made a crucial diving save at the feet of an opposition forward; while at the other end, Cobbo Robinson struck the crossbar from only six yards out. With the scores still level at 2-2 after 150 minutes, another replay was required.

The second replay between the two sides (played at Yorkshire Amateurs' Bracken Edge ground) was rendered controversial by a pre-match incident involving David Rotherforth, who had apparently left Fryston officials in some doubt as to whether he would be working that night and therefore be unable to play:

> When it came to the third match against Otley, I went straight from work fully expecting to play, but Benny Binks pulled me to one side and he said to me, 'Oh, we didn't think you were coming tonight, 'cos you were working.' I said, 'Well, I've been working in Leeds but I'm here now, aren't I?' He said, 'Ah, but we've already picked the team,' and I thought, 'Well, fair enough, if that's it,' and left the changing room in order to watch the match. There were a lot of lads who played in the second team outside, and looking at them, I couldn't figure out who'd taken my place. And when the Fryston team came out, they'd two wrong 'uns in their line-up: they'd two Glass Houghton Welfare players in their team, and that's what got to me. I thought, 'Fair enough, he's come out with a statement that he didn't know whether I was coming or not, but I should have been replaced by one of the lads who were playing in the second team, not someone from Glass Houghton Welfare.' I never had anything to do with Fryston after that. I could have said something that night, and Fryston would never have won that cup. Another thing that upset me was that, of all the lads that I'd played with that season, not one of them piped up. I think if I'd have been in their position, I'd have said, 'Oh, wait on a minute! We've come this far together; we can't be doing all this.' I didn't stay for the match and I didn't take it up afterwards. Saying that, I think I watched the first five minutes before slinging my hook back home. (David Rotherforth)

Rotherforth's view of events is firmly contradicted by his colleagues. For example, Brian Wood is unconvinced of the accuracy of his story: 'No. *They* (DP and E) had a couple by all accounts, but we didn't have any ringers in, I'll tell you that for nothing. I'm pretty sure it was our usual side.' Pete Waddington believes there is a good chance that Rotherforth may have deceived himself into thinking that Glass Houghton players attending the match as supporters of the Fryston team had been brought in as replacements: 'Bear in mind that some of the lads worked and played Sunday football with any number of Castleford players,' said Waddington. 'I can easily see how he might have made the mistake of thinking how one of 'em was stepping into his boots. No, I can't blame him for that.'

The game itself was also full of drama. In yet another match that was destined to go into extra time, Fryston were the slightly more dangerous of the two teams during the scheduled 90 minutes. Terry

Templeman struck the crossbar and Pete Waddington turned a cross by the same player onto a post. However, Otley also had their chances – most notably when one of their forwards smashed the ball straight at Archie Ward from point blank range. Extra time began with a flurry of near misses by Fryston, with Ward, Waddington and Robinson all going close, before Cobbo went past a defender and scored from twelve yards out.

> That set the rot in, but it was a lucky goal, actually! I broke through and it just happened to travel onto my left foot and I thought, 'I'm just going to hit it and hope.' The goalie dived where I intended to hit it, which was in the bottom corner; but because I didn't catch it right, it deceived him by going straight. I remember leaping up in the air and hugging Tempy. I just clung on tight in all the excitement. He must have thought I was never going to let go of him! (Barry Robinson)

With Fryston still leading going into the second period of extra time, DP and E inexplicably imploded, handing Fryston what the *Express* reporter described as 'two needlessly conceded penalties' (one converted by Sharp and the other by Mattison), and committing a defensive error which allowed Trevor Ward to run through and score unopposed from six yards out. According to Brian Wood, 'I know that, in that 4-0 win over 'em, they just packed in after that first goal – it knocked the stuffing out of 'em. You could see it in their faces.' Fryston's regular penalty taker, Cliff Braund, was in no shape to take the penalty kicks on this occasion, having sustained concussion when a goalkeeping clearance hit him flush on the head. The *Express* was generous in its post-match appraisal of the Fryston defensive performance, emphasising how: 'Ex-Halifax Town professional Jack Sharp has played some great football at full-back in the 330 minutes' play since May 3 and on this occasion the whole Fryston defence rarely put a foot wrong.'[9]

Fryston had therefore made it to the WRCC Cup final for the first time in eighteen years, where they would need to overcome the much-fancied Bradford team, Thackley, to win the trophy for the first time in their history. As if this did not constitute enough pressure in itself for them to have to contend with, Fryston were also now aware that it would be necessary for them to win their last five league games (all in an eight-day period) to be certain of winning the West Yorkshire

League Division Two (South) title. The fact that Keighley Central had wound up their league programme with a 3-0 win over Halifax Town Reserves meant that the former had now accumulated 43 points from 26 games, compared with Ardsley Celtic's 38 from 26, and Fryston's 34 from 21. Fryston therefore needed five points to make sure of the second promotion place. While four wins and a draw might be sufficient to make them outright champions – as long as they achieved a superior goal average (the old system of dividing the total goals scored by the total goals conceded) in the process – only five straight wins would absolutely *guarantee them* the title. It was clearly going to take a superhuman effort to win *either* the league *or* the cherished county cup. The possibility of *winning them both* to secure the 'double' was surely beyond their capabilities. Or was it?

Chapter 11
Sharp's Triumph

Previous page: Fryston's inspirational full-back, the ex-Halifax Town professional, Jack Sharp (pictured right), in celebratory mood with his team-mate, 'Mr Versatile' Brian Wood.

Thackley: Pride of Bradford

The team now preparing to ruin Fryston's dream of a first-ever WRCC Cup victory was, by common consensus, the finest amateur side in Bradford. Thackley AFC was founded in 1930 by local church-goers and they initially entered the Mutual Sunday League under the name of Thackley Wesleyans. Following a brief spell in the Bradford Amateur League, they joined the West Yorkshire Amateur League shortly after the outbreak of World War II (in 1939), having lifted the Bradford and District Cup for the first time the previous season. The club won its first WYAL title in 1947-48, and superseded this feat a year later by landing the league and cup double. For much of the following decade, Thackley were overshadowed by their great rivals, Salts (Saltaire), for whom the goal-scoring exploits of Don Glover were legendary. It was not until 1958-59 that Thackley next won the league title, though they did gain the distinction, meanwhile, of being the first team ever to win the Bradford and District Cup in three successive seasons (1958, 1959 and 1960). In 1961-62, they were serious contenders for the WRCC Cup, before surrendering a 1-0 lead and missing a penalty in their 2-1 quarter-final setback against Keighley Central.

By the start of the 1962-63 season, Thackley enjoyed such an unrivalled stature in the Bradford area that, as their goalkeeper of the time, Ken Hill, points out, 'If you wanted to play amateur football at the best level then you had to play for Thackley. But they came for you; you didn't go to Thackley, Thackley *came to you*. The scouts would pick you out.' Notwithstanding Hill's insistence that 'We were never paid a penny; the most we ever got was a Kit Kat apiece after a match we played in Sheffield,' the club had developed a distinctly professional ethos by now, which owed much to the arrival of the youthful Peter Glover, an ex-Bradford City professional. Glover had briefly captained Thackley in the late 1950s before embarking on what seemed like a promising career for Bradford City. He made his first-team debut in the drawn final of the West Riding County Senior Cup against Leeds United at Valley Parade on 25 November 1957.

Big Jack [Charlton] was playing, and so were Chris Crowe, and Jackie Overfield. In fact, Chris Crowe went past me on the inside. I turned and chased him and, just as he was bearing down on the penalty area, I thought, 'Go on, do him!' and [claps] down he went, but the free kick was cleared, much to my relief. So off I goes, running up the field, but I feels a little tug on the arm and there, alongside me, not looking me in the face, is Arthur Ellis, World Cup referee, who says: 'Listen son, I know it's your debut, and I know that there's eight or nine thousand here, and most of 'em have come to see you, 'cos you're the local lad, but if you do that again, you'll soon be sat with 'em. Understood?' (Peter Glover)

Glover made his league debut a mere five days later but this was to be his one and only senior appearance due to the development of a debilitating shoulder injury. He briefly turned to refereeing but had only officiated three games before Thackley invited him to return as first-team coach. Glover quickly amassed an impressive collection of coaching qualifications and began introducing training methods and standards of preparation that would have put many of the smaller Football League clubs to shame.

Another key contributing factor to the club ethos was the professional experience already accumulated by key players in the Thackley side. The seasoned wing-half, Jack Walker, had turned out in reserve games for Bradford Park Avenue before settling into Yorkshire League football with Farsley Celtic, where he briefly played alongside a Leeds United legend in the making:

I played with Paul Madeley. It would've been 1959 or thereabouts – I can't remember precisely. In fact, Madeley only played five months for Farsley, and then he went to Leeds. He were seventeen and I were about 22, 23. And he just had time, when he got the ball he just had time; nothing moved him at all. He was solid – quiet and gentle but totally unflappable. (Jack Walker)

A second player boasting professional experience with Bradford Park Avenue was the six-foot-three centre-half and captain, David Waddington. Although a life-long Bradford City supporter, the Undercliffe-born Waddington had joined Avenue as a sixteen-year-old junior and had progressed to playing in occasional reserve matches before a blood clot resulting from a kick on the calf sidelined him for a year and dampened his enthusiasm for the professional game. Shortly after resuming with Bolton Methodists in the Bradford League, Waddington (by now aged eighteen) was spotted by a Thackley committee member and invited down for trials. Such was the esteem in which he was held that, long after becoming a Thackley regular, he used to turn out in occasional midweek matches for Bradford City.

The final refugee from the professional game was the talented midfielder, John Gunnell, who could claim the distinction of having scored a hat-trick in a televised five-a-side youth football competition, sponsored by the *News of the World*. Gunnell spent a full season as a regular in Bradford Park Avenue Reserves before a serious illness threatened to permanently curtail his career. The Avenue player-manager at the time was the famous Scot, Jimmy Scoular, and Gunnell trained each day alongside such Avenue legends as the strikers 'Jock' Buchanan, Bobby Ham and the club's record goal-scorer, Kevin Hector.

Hector were in t'junior team, as I were playing for the second team. While I reckon they pushed me forward too quickly, they brought him on much steadier, which was clearly to his benefit. But that illness knocked me down, and I knew I couldn't play like I used to be able to play, so it put me off playing altogether. You know, if you're only playing at 80 per cent... I still had a chance of turning pro but I decided I wanted to play with my mates at Thackley, instead. (John Gunnell)

Twice-weekly training sessions (each Tuesday and Thursday) were often followed by tactical discussions involving blackboard and chalk. Generally speaking, Thackley's playing approach was predicated on a system in which each player was aware of his specific role and an accent on team work was paramount. As David Waddington explained, 'It was mainly about keeping to agreed tactics, such as everybody falling back once we lost the ball; and sticking to the exact role you were supposed to be carrying out.' Thus, according to Jack Walker, 'The main thing to me was that, when you got the ball you didn't have to look where the person was. Peter's training methods ensured that your support player was automatically available.'

This enviable combination of mature local scouting structures, unrivalled reputation and professional ethos were the factors which helped make Thackley such a formidable adversary.

Having said that, we all lived within a five-mile radius – within a quarter-of-an-hour of one another – and we used to see each other socially for parties and things like that. And bear in mind, we'd got the best facilities available: beautiful wide field to play on, no slopes, no hidden things, good football surface – always had grass on it, always flat and even. But the thing was that anything we wanted for, we had. I mean we had a coach to take us virtually everywhere we went; we had our boots cleaned for us, and when you got in t'dressing room, all your tackle were already laid out for you, and when you'd finished, you'd just throw it in a pile. (Ken Hill)

Height and sheer physical strength were key factors in ensuring that Thackley's defence was seldom penetrated. Tallest of all was the six-foot-five Hill, who was also a number four batsman in the Bradford League, and considered good enough to have attended trials with Yorkshire. By all accounts, his prowess as a fielder was reflected in his goalkeeping abilities:

Well, Ken was a bit like Dave Waddington, if the ball came in, anywhere near, you knew that he'd be there, especially with his height. Nobody'd answer to it in that league. And one outstanding thing for someone of his size was that he could get down to the ball as easy as a much smaller fella. With him behind you, you'd confidence to go forward. If you had a goalie you couldn't rely on, you were all back pedalling; but with him you could go forward, no trouble. (Jack Walker)

Ken Hill was one of two six-footers in the Thackley defensive line-up. Playing at centre-half was David Waddington. Ken Hill is adamant that his skipper contributed more to the Thackley team than his redoubtable aerial domination:

He was good on the ball as well, actually – at school, he scored 50 goals in fifteen games. He weren't a 'crash, bang, wallop' centre-half; he played a bit of football. And he had that bit of time on the ball. He was as good a centre-half as what there was in the area. (Ken Hill)

A third major component of the Thackley defence, Geoff Dennis, is described by Peter Glover as 'a colossus', and by Jack Walker as 'a man mountain, with each leg as wide as my two are now'. Walker regarded both his own and Dennis' roles, at right-half and right-back respectively, as complementary to one another, with the former functioning as a 'holding player' and his colleague as an uncomplicated ball-winner: 'I reckon I was good at stemming the opposition attack. If you were coming towards us, I'd hold you while backtracking until we were set, and then I might go in, or I might say, "Geoff, hit him!"' The left-hand side of the Thackley defence comprised the cool-headed and immensely reliable Terry Wood (left-half) and their former winger, turned overlapping full-back, Colin Binns, who was encouraged to exploit the wide open space available on a pitch reputed to measure 110 by 100 yards. These dimensions were equally tailor-made for the two 'traditional' wingers employed by Thackley: Barry Holmes on the left and Ray Cole at outside-right. Both players were relatively small, tricky on the ball, and lightning fast in the classical manner, and each of them saw their main role as that of servicing the club's main goal-scorers, inside-forward, Frank Edmonson, and centre-forward, John Brentley. According to Cole, the naturally more gifted and two-footed Holmes – a future Halifax Town professional – was equally adept at suddenly cutting inside and letting go a thunderbolt. Cole's own forte involved getting to the byline in order to cross the ball for small but fearless Brentley to head or volley home, or cut it back for the dependable Edmonson to latch onto.

By Peter Glover's reckoning, the Thackley's second inside-forward, John Gunnell, was the star of the side, and arguably the club's best-ever player:

Barry [Holmes] was a very good player – *very* good – and I could name others, but people have asked me over the years: 'Who was the best player that you had at Thackley?' and straight away I say, 'John Gunnell, without a shadow of a doubt.' His touch, his technique, it all came naturally to him. You didn't need to say anything to him because he had far more skill than was necessary in that league. He wasn't big – he was only slight with it – but he had this habit of tracking back and wrapping his leg round the ball and flicking it away from the man in possession without it being a foul. He had vision, speed to burn, exceptional talent. I'm sorry but if he'd been fit all his life, it would have been a crime to have kept him at Thackley.

Undefeated in the league, Thackley's route to the final had been relatively straightforward, save for a closely contested semi-final against Snydale Road Athletic. In the second round, they enjoyed the easy 8-1 home win against Whitwood Mere already referred to in the previous chapter. Two highly impressive away wins then followed: first they defeated their championship rivals, Luddendenfoot 4-2 before crushing Golcar United (Huddersfield) 7-2. In the quarter-finals, they beat Guiseley, of the West Yorkshire League First Division, 2-0 at home, before taking on a Snydale team which had been runners-up in the same league, and were destined to finish as the 1962-63 champions. The semi-final, played at Beck Lane, Heckmondwike, produced a tight, goalless draw. In the replay, however, Thackley ran out more deserving and comfortable winners than the 3-1 scoreline suggests. Goals from Holmes and Brentley secured Thackley a 2-0 half-time lead. Within minutes of the re-start, Nicky Atkinson reduced the arrears, only for Edmonson to score the clincher with a quarter of the match remaining.

Now only Fryston stood between Thackley and the trophy. It is apparent from interviews that the Bradford side may have been guilty of underestimating the quality of the opposition. Asked, for example, whether the Thackley coaching staff had 'done their homework' on Fryston or made any special tactical preparation for meeting them, Peter Glover conceded that:

> Snydale were the only team I was ever remotely worried about. You never knew if they were putting ringers in, and they had a right cracking inside-forward who played with 'em for bloody years. As for Fryston, I thought that, if we simply played as well as we could play, then we'd always win. I mean, take fitness, for example: I was convinced that there was no-one could go for as long as we could. The way that we played, most teams were knackered after 65 minutes, giving us every chance of running them to death by the finish. The higher the team in their league, the more you're inclined to start planning and preparing to meet 'em; but Fryston didn't come with any particular status or reputation, so I never gave them that much consideration, if I'm honest. (Peter Glover)

Ironically, it was Fryston, rather than their more professionally-oriented Thackley counterparts, who engaged in pre-match intelligence-gathering. Jack Sharp recalls how:

> Once we knew who were playing in t'final, some of t'older blokes went to watch 'em a couple o' times. Dick and co were that keen that they popped in a car and went over to watch 'em. And I remember him saying to me, 'Tha'll have to be on thi mettle, old lad!' That winger o' thine is a real bobby dazzler.' The good thing about it, though, was that I didn't know any of 'em personally and was going in without any apprehension. We knew that Thackley were a very good side. We certainly regarded ourselves as

underdogs. We were playing above our weight to be fair because they were regarded as invincible within their own league.

Little did the Bradford team – or, for that matter, the majority of the Fryston players – know at the time, but Dick Foulkes and Chunner Lister were already contemplating a 'secret weapon' with which to outshoot them in the final.

Howard's Midas Touch

David Rotherforth's assertion that he walked away from Fryston five minutes into the second replay against DP and E is disputed by those colleagues who maintain that he was simply dropped for the Thackley final. Whether out of preference or sheer necessity, Fryston turned in their moment of need to a veteran playing out his career in the reserves; none other than the great Freddie Howard. 'My dad told me that it was always his intention to play Freddie, irrespective of whether David [Rotherforth] had gone and shot his bolt,' recalls Ron Foulkes. Agga Mattison appears to bear this out in maintaining: 'Dick thought that Freddie definitely had the Midas touch, especially on the big occasions, and that's why he was ready to bank on him so heavily for one last throw of the dice.'

The teams for the final – at East End Park (Leeds) on Wednesday, 22 May 1963 – therefore read as follows:

Fryston: H. Ward (goalkeeper), B. Wood, J. Sharp, J. Appleyard, H. Mattison, P. Waddington (captain), B. Robinson, T. Templeman, F. Howard, C. Braund and T. Ward.

Thackley: K. Hill (goalkeeper), G. Dennis, C. Binns, J. Walker, D. Waddington (captain), T. Wood, R. Cole, J. Gunnell, J. Brentley, F. Edmonson and B. Holmes.

Among the hundreds of spectators huddled expectantly in the main pavilion that night, there was, ironically, no Dick Foulkes. 'I didn't go to the final,' he explained to Barry Bennett. 'I was on nights and I wasn't going to lose a shift to go.'

As soon as both teams trotted onto the pitch, the Fryston players realised that Thackley represented a daunting proposition:

> They turned up did Thackley and, when you saw 'em, you thought, 'Phew! We haven't got a life on! No way!' They looked just like a professional team. You know how you see pro teams getting into little groups, heading the ball and tapping it to each other keepy-uppie? Well, they came onto the pitch and started doing that – *automatically*! We were stood at one end, hammering the ball into the goal, and they were at the other, *gleaming*, just like Real Madrid. And you thought, 'This is going to be *very difficult, indeed*.' (Trevor Ward)

Against that, superstition dictated that the odds were firmly in Fryston's favour. 'We could have beaten England that night,' maintains Ward. 'There was no way we were going to lose because we played at East End Park! Lucky ground, tha sees?'

Fryston kicked off the match according to a predetermined plan which involved making use of Trevor Ward's height by sending high, pressure-relieving kicks in the direction of his wing:

> And I always remember, they had this stocky right full-back playing against me, so me and Jack decided that we'd have the ball pumped up to me in the air. 'Don't play it on the ground to him at all.' And on the odd occasion that we got the ball – because they absolutely played us off the park for 65, 70 minutes – Jack did just that. Their number eight, Johnny Gunnell, ran the show for 'em. If he wasn't a pro, I don't know who was. He was definitely a class apart. (Trevor Ward)

Without ever finding themselves at risk of being overwhelmed, Fryston nonetheless rode their luck on several occasions in a perilous first half. Ray Cole smashed the ball against the Fryston crossbar, and then Barry Holmes cut inside and clipped the same piece of woodwork with a typical long-range effort. Cliff Braund recalls how Archie Ward seriously fumbled a high lob, only to compensate for his error by trapping the ball with his foot on the goal line: 'Trapped it on the line, he did! Then just bent down casually and picked it up!' Laughing at the extent of his own audacity, Ward also remembered how, 'Earlier on, I'd made a diving save at this bloke's feet, taking man and ball. He went down like a sack and I thought, "Oh-oh! Here we go, that's a certain penalty!" but it was a case of "No, carry on!" I got away with that one!'

Luck was not the only factor working in Fryston's favour. 'You couldn't fault our determination, either,' maintains Pete Waddington. 'I've got to say that our defence, Sharpie in particular, was absolutely rock-solid, and they never really looked like scoring.' Jack Sharp modestly maintains that his side's unshakeable team spirit had never been so significant as in this final: 'We'd got a team there that were a very tight-knit bunch who were prepared to fight for everything. And we needed to 'cos we were under the cosh for most of that game. I know we defended for us lives that day – they hit the bar a couple of times at least. And I do remember having a good game in that final, and so did Agga.'

For all the first-half Thackley pressure, Fryston's half-time team talk reflected a growing mood of optimism: 'I've got to be honest and say that, footballing-wise, Thackley had been a much better side than us,' conceded Brian Wood, 'but, perhaps because they'd one or two misses in t'first half, we felt that today might just be our day, and there was a feeling of "Come on. We aren't doing that bad, we might still get something out of this."'

Cliff Braund remembers how Pete Waddington expressed this sentiment more forcibly: 'I'm sure he was looking at me when he smashed the palm of his hand and yelled, "Come on! We can fucking *win* this! We're *gonna* win this, lads!"' Fryston now needed a crucial moment of good fortune or inspiration if they were to succeed against such a confident and more powerful adversary. When that moment duly arrived, it had all the drama and romance of a *Roy of the Rovers* storyline.

The next edition of the *Express* gleefully reported how:

Playing magnificently, Fryston contained a slick-moving Thackley side for a pulsating 50 minutes and at the end they fully deserved their reward... But spare a thought for their worthy opponents, especially lanky 'keeper Hill who allowed the angled drive of veteran centre-forward Fred Howard to slip from his grasp and into the net... The mistake came midway through the second half.[1]

Opinion varies with regard both to the actual quality of Freddie Howard's successful strike and to the sincerity of his intention. Archie Ward maintained, for example, that 'Freddie got hold of it good and proper', hitting it from just inside the angle of the Thackley goal mouth following a through ball from Jackie Sharp. 'I think it was sheer speed that deceived the 'keeper,' continued Ward. 'Me and Brian Wood went *berserk* when it hit the back of the net.' According to Sharp himself, however, the 'shot' was 'very flukey' and Howard 'didn't get hold of it right'. Cliff Braund's view of the goal was equally circumspect:

> I can't recall the build-up but I do remember Fred hitting it from the edge
> of the box, and my feeling was that he should have buried it because the
> 'keeper was static – rooted to the spot. But he hit the ball a bit tamer than he
> intended, basically straight at the 'keeper who got a good pair of hands on it
> but somehow managed to spoon it into the net. It was a nice enough shot,
> but it wasn't a thunderbolt and the 'keeper should have gobbled it, I reckon.

Thackley interviewees offer a far more charitable and forgiving account of Ken Hill's involvement in the goal. Jack Walker insists that Howard mishit the ball to such an extent that he caused it to spin deceptively through Hill's otherwise capable hands. The goalkeeper will entertain no such excuses on his behalf. He is adamant instead that:

> He [Howard] came into t'penalty area. There were nobody on him. I can't
> remember whether he'd beaten somebody, but he came through on his
> own to the dead-ball line on the Fryston right. And I was stood against the
> post here, covering the post, and he'd be twelve to fifteen yards along the
> dead-ball line, and he crossed it cleanly, and it came dead straight to me. It
> wasn't a shot, no, but it just... it just went through that gap there. It weren't
> spinning, swerving – nowt; it were just dead straight. If I'd have crouched
> down like that and caught it, just like I usually did at cricket, I would have
> saved it easily. Even after I'd let it slip through, I still thought, 'Oh, bloody
> hell, corner kick!' But I turned round and saw it lying there, wrong side of
> the bloody netting. (Ken Hill)

Following this decisive incident, Fryston were forced to contend with unremitting Thackley pressure. Brian Wood recalls how, 'That last ten to fifteen minutes was like the siege of Alamo with them attacking and us devoting absolutely everything to keeping them out.' For all that, Fryston permitted Thackley only one more scoring chance – when Archie Ward injured his wrist in pulling off a spectacular diving save from an oblique shot by Barry Holmes. This final act of Fryston resistance ensured for them an unexpected and famous victory.

The Shipley Times and Express was extremely critical in its post-match analysis of Thackley's performance, insisting that the Bradford side had only themselves to blame for their defeat: 'They were only a shade of their former selves, never getting a grip of the game, and far too often chasing the ball.'[2] The paper maintained that only David Waddington and Colin Binns had played to their customary standard, and found it regrettable that, had Thackley played with anything like their earlier season form, they would undoubtedly have emerged as victors. Slightly uncharitably perhaps, the *Times and Express* remarked that: 'The Fryston team were little better, but their defence was always master of an inept Thackley forward line with Sharp (ex-Halifax Town) at left-back playing a natural copy-book game. He never put a foot wrong which virtually meant that the right-wing pair of Cole and Gunnell were almost snuffed out of the game.'[3] The (Pontefract and Castleford) *Express* was more laudatory in its assessment of Fryston's display. 'They had a cast-iron defence,' it maintained, 'in which "permit" player Jackie Sharp was a strong man and a hard-working forward line never gave up chasing.'[4]

The Thackley players still speak graciously about the merits of Fryston's victory.

> It could possibly have been a draw, 'cos I think we were the classier team, but I think that Fryston generally deserved their win. It was all-or-nothing for them and, in fairness, they played their bloody hearts out. They had their bits of luck and we didn't, but that's the magic of cup football, and I wouldn't want it any different. (David Waddington)

Jack Sharp is the Fryston player invariably singled out for special mention. Ray Cole is adamant that the ex-Halifax Town man was the vital difference between the two sides on the day. 'He was like a miniature battleship,' he laughed, 'with thighs the size of my torso. He was every inch the pro. It was his positional play, his accuracy and sheer know-how. You could spot it a mile away.' Sharp confesses to having felt 'a lot of responsibility on the day', not only to his team-mates but also to his home village, as well. The full-back's pride in his own performance is tempered by the sympathy he still feels for Hill: 'I couldn't have wished anything like that on him,' says Sharp. 'It was a bloody great shame for him, 'cos he was an excellent 'keeper, and it was upsetting to see him in tears after the match.'

The ex-Thackley 'keeper still regards his concession of the Fryston goal as the 'worst moment of my sporting life'.

I mean it's 40-odd years ago, but I can remember it as if it were an hour since. I didn't – I *couldn't* – go for my presentation; I went straight to t'changing rooms, which were just behind us. Apparently, my wife shouted out from t'stand to Dave Waddington to 'Get Ken's medal' because I was too sick to fetch it. Hardly anybody said a word. Frankie Edmondson were best of all. He said, 'Come on, Ken. We'll win it next year,' but I knew it was completely down to me that we'd lost. I had no excuses and, yeah, sports-wise, it were the worst bloody thing that ever happened to me. (Ken Hill)

Fryston veterans of the final prefer to dwell on the more romantic aspect of the winning goal – the fact that it was scored by the club's most celebrated and prolific scorer of all time. 'Freddie Howard did exactly what he was brought in to do for us,' maintains Pete Waddington. 'He confirmed that he was the man for the big occasion.' Brian Wood agrees: 'A lot of people thought that Freddie was too old, but the theory was, if we could just get one good ball to him, he was still likely to do the rest. Freddie didn't do a lot that match, but what he did was vital. I thought that the reason they brought him in was because he always had that magic potential to do the type of thing he did.'

When Fryston won the Cas and District Cup in 1945, the team had been piped back into the village by a military brass band. There was nothing of this nature to commemorate their arguably more prestigious achievement of 1963. Indeed, events happening in the immediate wake of the Thackley final left a lasting sour taste in the mouths of all Fryston players and officials:

Fryston took loads and loads of supporters. Everybody went from t'village and round about, and t'manager, Edgar Williams, were there and he didn't have any interest in football. In fact, there was hell on that day because after we'd been presented with t'cup, he took it back in his car to Fryston club, so we were deprived of the cup in the dressing room! And there was a big to-do about that, even though we were re-introduced to t'cup when we all arrived at t'club an hour or two later. (Jack Sharp)

Freddie Howard's Encore

Fryston still had to win their remaining five league matches in just eight days in order to secure the 'double', so it seemed pertinent to consider whether Freddie Howard's swansong might extend to a few more final bars. In true fairy-tale fashion, Freddie 'responded nobly', as the *Express* put it, and did not let them down. His goals were crucial in Fryston's narrow victories away to Castleford Town (2-1), and home to Airedale Athletic and Pontefract Collieries (each won by two goals to nil).

He got the winning goal at Whitwood on Saturday after Castleford Town, with a stubborn display, had threatened Fryston's championship chances with a first-half goal. A long lob into the goalmouth was mishandled by Archie Ward. After Templeman had equalised, Town's defence, playing very well, regained command and there were only about 10 minutes left when Howard struck the winner. On Sunday, in a game in which Airedale Athletic surrendered ground advantage, Fryston looked anxious until they went into the lead in the second half. It was not until the closing minutes that Howard got the second goal to end all fears. It was a similar story on Monday when Pontefract were the visitors. Again it was an opening goal by Howard before half time which removed the dithers.[5]

Fryston now needed at least a draw against Glass Houghton Welfare to keep their championship hopes alive. However, such a draw would mean them having to 'go for goals' in their final home game against East End Park in order to lift the title on goal average. Fryston did as well as could be imagined, with Fred Howard again playing a vital role in scoring a hat-trick in a 5-2 win against his old club (Robinson and Braund being the other scorers). Only East End Park now stood between Fryston and the title.

This final fixture was somewhat anti-climactic. The *Express* described it as 'a colourless match for [such] a big occasion, chiefly because the home side played just as well as was needed'.[6] Fryston took an early lead with a rare Cobbo Robinson header. Five minutes into the second half, Pete Waddington headed a second from a Terry Templeman corner, and Cliff Braund scored a late clincher that was set up for him by Freddie Howard. The *Express* was fulsome in its appreciation of the latter's belated contribution to Fryston's historic success: 'Although veteran centre-forward Fred Howard might have swelled the total, he can look back on his recall with satisfaction. He notched a hat-trick at Glass Houghton last Thursday, in Fryston's five-two win, to total seven goals in these five final, and vital, games for the club.'[7]

It may have been out of an eagerness to atone that the colliery management subsequently organised a reception for the team, two weeks after their victory over Thackley, at the Spread Eagle Arms in Darrington. Brian Wood recalls how, after an initial round of speeches, Edgar Williams had triumphantly announced that the players could have their first drink 'on the Welfare', but that any additional drinking would have to be undertaken at their own expense. This immediately struck the players as unfair:

> T'bosses carried on drinking and, because we were sure they weren't paying out of their own pockets, we decided that neither were we. So we kept calling t'waitresses over: 'We'll have another bottle of Blue Nun apiece and we'll each have another beer and cigar!' That went on all night! On Monday morning, t'phone rang in t'medical centre and it was only Edgar Williams for Christ's sake! He said, 'Have you got anybody in with you just now? No? Well get thissen over here!' He says to me: 'What were you doing on Friday?' I said, 'What do you mean, Mr Williams?' and he chucked this bill over to me and says, 'What the bleeding hell were you playing at? I don't know what it was you were drinking but you'll never do it again!' (Brian Wood)

The act of 'getting one over' on the management added to the satisfaction of having at last chased down the 'holy grail'. 'You've got to have done it to know what it feels like,' explained Woody. 'For us lads, winning the county cup was akin to lifting the FA Cup for our standard of football. It represented that sort of pinnacle. And, of course, having done it the once, we were determined to do it again.'

Chapter 12
Déjà Vu

Previous page: The Fryston Colliery Welfare team which opposed Thackley in the final of the 1963-64 West Riding County FA Challenge Cup final at Bradford Park Avenue's ground. BACK ROW (from left to right): Brian Wood (not selected), Ronnie 'Chunner' Lister (trainer), Harold 'Agga' Mattison, Johnny Appleyard, Terry Templeman, Keith Mattison, Trevor Ward and Alf Atack (committee member). FRONT ROW: Harold 'Archie' Ward, Barry 'Cobbo' Robinson, Jack Sharp, Pete Waddington (captain), Cliff Braund, Phil Monks and Frank Isles (not selected).

Warming to the Task

Fryston were now back in the First Division of the West Yorkshire League but their return to the top flight initially proved uncomfortable. An opening home win against Ferrybridge Amateurs was followed by four successive defeats, including 5-3 and 5-2 drubbings at Snydale and Guiseley, respectively. Having stopped the rot with a 2-2 draw at Glass Houghton and 3-3 draw at home to Monckton Collieries, Fryston trounced Waddington's Sports 7-0 (with Isles scoring four), and edged out Glass Houghton by the odd goal in five. Tendencies towards roughness and gamesmanship had become established hallmarks of Fryston's game. The *Express* reporter noted that, 'Glass Houghton disliked the tactics of some Fryston defenders and the continual disputing of the referee's decisions.'[1]

One week before mounting their defence of the WRCC Cup, The Colliers were unlucky, by all accounts, to lose 3-1 at home to Methley United. Indeed, 'It was not until those last 20 minutes that United, disrupted by Fryston's splendidly robust game, blossomed and scored the two goals which made them winners… Jack Sharp, at left-half, starred in a Fryston side which gave just about its best performance so far.'[2]

Fryston had received a bye in the first round of the WRCC Cup and the club's 1-0 victory over Guiseley in the second round was not only unexpected, given how heavily they had been beaten by the Bradford team earlier in the season, but also represented the only success achieved by Castleford sides in round two. Emphasising that Fryston were 'Nearly thwarted in [the] last seconds', the *Express* maintained that:

> Their success was just about deserved, though it was almost denied. Pete Waddington, who captained Fryston from left-half when they succeeded Ferrybridge as county cup winners last season, scored the all-important

goal from centre-forward in the dying seconds of the first half. He is, of course, no stranger to that position. Outside-left Trevor Ward, who has been leading the attack, missed an open goal in the second half. It was a chance which, had it been taken, would have spared Fryston the anxiety which their defence suffered because of the possibility of the ball shooting through on a sticky surface. Fryston's attack contrived to create rather more openings than the home line in an end-to-end game, but in the last minute Guiseley went close to equalising.[3]

Fryston's inconsistency was exemplified in their next four games. They followed up their encouraging form against Guiseley with a 3-1 home win over the unbeaten championship leaders, Micklefield Welfare, their third goal being scored by their new signing, the outside-left, Phil Monks, who had just joined them from Great Preston Juniors. Monks' father, Alf, was a miner at Fryston pit and, according to Jack Sharp, had long been pushing for his son to be given a try-out in the colliery team. The Kippax-born Monks arrived amidst rumours that he had been a trialist at several Lancastrian clubs, including Blackburn Rovers, Burnley and Bolton Wanderers.

> We heard a whisper that we were gonna get this new player. He was either gonna come to us or Ferrybridge and he was gonna be a superstar. I think I only played one or two seasons with Phil. He was a nice lad. He looked like a superstar, too. He was dark-haired and good-looking, and very, very fast; absolutely tremendous left leg. He would whack 'em, and whack 'em on the run. And he could get us goals. He *looked like* a professional footballer. (Cliff Braund)

There was an initial feeling in the dressing room that the newcomer was perhaps a shade too arrogant for his own good and needed 'taking down a step or two', as Trevor Ward remembers:

> I first played against Phil Monks when I played with Great Preston Juniors because he played with Micklefield. We played them in the cup and Phil was playing on their left wing and I was playing on our right, and that's how I knew him. He went to Great Preston but they didn't like him, because he had this air about him. Alf, his dad, wanted him to be a professional footballer and he took him everywhere, so he came [to Fryston] with this reputation that he was a cut above. Now, I was on the left wing and what happened was that Dave Rotherforth packed in so they asked me to play at centre-forward and Phil took on my position. The first six or seven games, I don't think he passed to anybody! He'd dribble past three players, only to

210

lose it to the fourth and put us back on the defensive. So we taught him how to play football by the simple method of not passing the ball to him for the next two games. And I'm pleased to say it worked.

In their next match, Fryston suffered an emphatic 4-1 defeat in a their home Cas and District Cup tie against Third Division Whitwood Mere United, for whom Barry Sambrook scored a hat-trick. They were then beaten 2-1 in their home league game against Harehills Amateurs, who had not previously won a match. However, a 5-2 victory over Glass Houghton Welfare in the Greenwood Trophy (including a hat-trick by Trevor Ward) provided a timely boost to their confidence as they looked to continue their defence of the WRCC Cup.

The third-round tie against Huddersfield ICI proved ridiculously easy for Fryston, who thrashed their weaker opposition, 9-0. Huddersfield's cause was rendered even more hopeless by their loss of a player through injury in the first quarter-of-an-hour. Fryston's star performer was Barry Robinson, whose three goals included a penalty:

> I remember that they allowed me to take a penalty in order to reach my hat-trick and I had to take it twice. First off, the goalie saved it, but they said he'd gone too early; and when I took it again, I stubbed my shot and it trickled out of his reach while he dived the wrong way. That was the only hat-trick I ever scored for Fryston. (Barry Robinson)

Of the remaining six goals, Phil Monks and Trevor Ward each scored twice, with Cliff Braund and Harold Mattison grabbing one apiece.

Fryston's next league game, away to Harehills Amateurs, was an extremely poignant affair. Before the game, both sides observed a minute's silence for Harry Mattison, a former Fryston player who had been killed in a pit accident the week before. Fittingly, it was Harry's brother, Agga, who scored for Fryston in their 1-1 draw. The side then secured a comprehensive 5-1 victory at Yorkshire Copper Works in a match played on a treacherous, icy surface.

Another form of extreme weather threatened to disrupt Fryston's progression to the WRCC Cup quarter-finals. Their fourth-round match against Pilkington's Recreation, a mid-table side from the Sheffield County Senior League Division Two, appeared to be in serious jeopardy due to the fact that a thick 'curtain' of fog had descended on the pitch, making it seem certain that the referee would postpone the contest. However, in the words of the *Express* reporter:

> Up went the curtain of fog just when this West Riding Challenge Cup fourth-round game seemed certain to be postponed. And into the murky afternoon 20-year-old painter Phil Monks splashed lots of colour by scoring five of Fryston's six goals. Being an outside-left makes his performance all the more remarkable. And it might have been more exciting still for this Bolton Wanderers discard, who joined Fryston in the autumn, for on my count he was near to scoring on five other occasions. Fryston's other goal came from right-winger Barry Robinson, like Monks an ex-Great Preston Junior.[4]

It had taken Fryston a nervous 30 minutes to open the scoring, before two quick goals in succession by Monks finally released the floodgates. Fryston had a 'spectacular diving save' by Archie Ward to thank for preventing the visitors from being the first team to score against them in this season's competition. Generally speaking, though, 'Home wing-halves, Pete Waddington — a captain who calls for 90 minutes endeavour from his team and sets the example — and Jack Sharp, dominated to such an extent that the rest of the defence had an easy time.' The *Express* reporter maintained that Pilkington's were certainly 'no pushover'; it was simply that their standard of football 'did not compare in speed and thrust' with that of Fryston's, who were looking an even better side than they were when they lifted the trophy a season earlier.

Reading the Runes

A convincing 6-1 away win at Rothwell Athletic in the Greenwood Trophy quarter-finals reinforced the growing impression that Fryston were well-equipped to defend their WRCC title. Early in the New Year, the side received a further accolade when it was announced that Pete Waddington had been chosen to captain the West Yorkshire League XI against Leeds Combination League. The *Express*'s chief sports writer, the Methley-born Norman Elstob, had been writing for the paper since 1952, a period in which he had regularly reported on Fryston matches and earned the profound respect of the club's players and officials. Explaining why he was personally convinced that 'Fryston should do it again', Mr Elstob highlighted the team's inspirational left-half and captain as one of several he regarded as ideal 'men for the job':

For those who look for facts, as well as omens, the scales seem to be tipped Fryston's way. They say a good half-back line is half-way to winning, and Fryston have just that in Jack Sharp (ex Halifax Town and Goole Town), Harold Mattison (ex Frickley Colliery) and Pete Waddington (a skipper who cracks the whip). Behind them Appleyard, Keith Mattison and Archie Ward form a steady trio and up in front the forwards carry more power since Trevor Ward moved to the middle and Phil Monks came in at outside-left. Centre-half in last year's successful team, Brian Wood, is reserve.[5]

Elstob spoke approvingly of Fryston's managerial policy of allowing Chunner Lister and Dick Foulkes to pick the team before presenting it to the committee for ratification. This was considered important insofar as 'it enables a definite team-building policy to be adopted. A settled team is usually happy – and successful.' The writer was optimistic that a Fryston-Thackley final was very much on the cards again, 'providing The Colliers' luck holds and the teams do not meet in the semi-finals'. He concluded with the observation that:

Fryston always have up their sleeve, of course, that wily old bird, Freddie Howard. From behind the scenes, he was recalled to the team for the final last season and scored the only goal of the match – surely the most valuable of the dozens he has struck in the last decade. As a Fryston supporter said to me at the Pilkington match: 'Whoever proposed picking Freddie for last year's final deserved a medal.'[6]

Despite having lost 2-1 at home to Altofts in the preceding week, Fryston were confident of beating a Cooperville White Star team which had lost a game played that same day by 6 goals to 4 to English Electric in a West Riding County Amateur League Division B match. As predicted, Fryston duly overcame their lowly opponents in progressing to the semi-finals:

But they were not at their best in windy conditions on a sloping ground, and the home side, two behind at half time, almost snatched a draw in the last 15 minutes. After eight minutes Fryston put the strong wind and the slope to advantage, centre-half Harold Mattison heading in from a Terry Templeman corner kick. Midway through the half, centre-forward Trevor Ward fired home a second goal from 16 yards, turning, beating an opponent, and shooting splendidly, all in little room. But Fryston's finishing in a ragged match left much to be desired. Robinson once completely miskicked when he could have tapped the ball in. From being all Fryston in the first half, it was all Cooperville later, though they could not open a compact defence. About 15 minutes from the end, however, they scrambled a goal, and seven minutes later, lack of inches prevented the home right-winger heading an equaliser.[7]

Fryston then enjoyed an unbeaten run of eight league matches (five wins and three draws) in the build-up to their WRCC Cup semi-final against Rhodes Street (Halifax) at Beck Lane, Heckmondwike. Indeed, they entered the semi on the back of a morale-boosting 1-0 victory at high-flying Micklefield, where Phil Monks forced the ball home from a Sharp corner. It was Monks who also scored Fryston's much-deserved equaliser in the drawn first match against Rhodes Street:

> Against a side partial to the long, high ball, Fryston were troubled in the first half when facing a sinking sun and inside the half hour were behind. The goal was strongly contested by Fryston, who claimed offside. Rhodes Street did most of the attacking up to half time and almost scored again when left-back Keith Mattison slipped up. But a forward rattled the crossbar from six yards. After the interval, Fryston often promised to win. In the first minutes, Terry Templeman broke through and shot inches over and three minutes later Barry Robinson followed suit. He ought to have scored. But after about 30 minutes Phil Monks made no mistake when Trevor Ward pushed through a pass. Ward created a 'winner' later, squaring across goal to three unmarked colleagues, but Cliff Braund lost control and a chance to cap Fryston's better all-round football was lost.[8]

The semi-final had been played on a Friday evening. On the following day, Fryston were heavily beaten 5-0 in their away match at Monckton Collieries. As the *Express* report rightly put it, 'An energy-sapping West Riding Cup semi-final the previous night and the celebrations which followed (though the match was only drawn!) left Fryston in no shape for this Division One game, on Saturday.'[9]

With their concentration fully restored, Fryston beat Micklefield 2-1 in the quarter-finals of the Embleton Cup (with goals from Braund and Templeman), and Snydale 2-0 (Monks and Templeman again) in the away semi-final of the Greenwood Trophy. They continued this impressive sequence by beating Rhodes Street in their replayed WRCC Cup semi-final at the Bracken Edge home of Yorkshire Amateurs:

It was an excellent match, both sides striving after the finer arts, and there were professional-like touches by Fryston especially in the first half, when they used the open spaces and stroked and chipped some fine passes. Only their finishing caused reservation. Without taking into account good goalkeeping and lucky escapes which thwarted them, they might have had half a dozen goals. Left-winger Phil Monks opened the scoring after 18 minutes, splendidly controlling a long Templeman forward centre. His shot was beaten down, but he recovered to put the ball into an empty goal. But after 65 minutes Monks made the miss of the match, topping that by Trevor Ward in the 41st minute, and the agony of it was that Rhodes Street raced away to equalise and find new life. For a time, Fryston swayed, then followed a series of Rhodes Street escapes, the referee once awarding Fryston a penalty and then, after consulting a linesman, reducing it to a free kick just outside the box. Seven minutes from the end, however, a defender handled needlessly and Sharp hit the winner from the spot, sending the goalkeeper the wrong way.[10]

Fryston briefly came down to earth when they were convincingly beaten 4-0 by Monckton Collieries in the Greenwood Trophy final played at Swillington, their opponents emphasising their dominance with three goals in the last twenty minutes. Marking Trevor Ward that day was the former Doncaster Rovers centre-half, Charlie Williams. The son of a Yorkshire-born mother and Barbadian father, the Barnsley-born Williams began working as a miner at Monckton Colliery, before transferring to nearby Upton, where he played for the pit's first eleven before signing on for Rovers.[11] By 1964, he had already embarked on a semi-professional career as a singer-comedian that would see him eventually become a national star, but at this stage both his face and reputation were unfamiliar to an unsuspecting Trevor Ward:

We were sat in the dressing room beforehand and I think it was Frank who came in and says, 'Hey, you're up against a good 'un today! They call him Charlie Williams, he used to play for Doncaster. I think he's just joined Monckton this season.' I says, 'He can't be all that good, I'm afraid I've never heard of him!' Frank says, 'Oh, he's played a few games, he's all of 38-years-old.' Well, I'm not kidding, he was like greased lightning! He couldn't have weighed above seven or eight stone, and he was six-foot-plus tall; but as for defending, as soon as they played the ball in the air he was right at the side of me, holding my shirt, smothering me for room. He knew all the little tricks. At half time, Jackie came up to me and said, 'Come off him! Drag him around and don't allow him anywhere near you!' But it made no difference whatsoever. He just lived down the back of my shirt and somebody else dropped into where he should have been! (Trevor Ward)

215

Fryston rallied, however, to produce a 4-3 win over Ferrybridge Amateurs in the semi-final of the Embleton Cup. Two of Fryston's four goals were scored by the redoubtable Fred Howard, who was deputising as left-winger for Phil Monks. In the final, Fryston faced Monckton, who had outclassed Fairburn 7-1 in the other semi-final. Fryston edged the game 1-0 with two of their all-time greats having a hand in the goal:

> The goal came after 42 minutes, when a lobbed ball from left-winger Howard was headed by centre-forward Wood. Sharp's was the next header, from inside the six-yard area. Six minutes earlier, Monckton had missed the simplest of the few chances two splendidly compact defences allowed. From less than six yards a Monckton forward shot tamely and goalkeeper Ward thrust out a leg to save. Ward also foiled them two minutes from the end, saving at the foot of a post during a last-ditch Monckton effort to save the game. But in the second half Howard shot straight at the Monckton goalkeeper from 12 yards and Sharp did likewise from a penalty after Howard had gone down.[12]

The Colliers' penultimate game of the season was a home league match in which the defending champions, Snydale, needed at least a point to guarantee retaining their title. Despite being at full strength due to the return of injured players such as Phil Monks, Fryston were no match on the day. It was Monks who established an early lead for the home side but Snydale, not to be denied, ran out easy 5-1 victors. Despite this setback, Fryston still finished a creditable sixth out of thirteen in the league, having won 11, lost 9 and drawn 6 of their 26 matches.

Fryston knew by now that they would be facing their old foes Thackley for a 'return contest' in the final of the WRCC Cup on 5 May at the Bradford Park Avenue ground. Although the Snydale result did not augur well for the return with Thackley, the team were arguably more confident than at the corresponding stage a year earlier:

> Well, we were a better all-round side for a start. We'd played Ferrybridge Amateurs *Reserves* the previous season and lost! In 1963-64 we played their first team and beat them twice. We definitely grew as a team. I won't pretend there was a master-plan or anything but we really did have an exceptionally well-balanced team. (Cliff Braund)

The Return Contest

Thackley entered the final unbeaten in their league, and having hardly drawn breath en route to their showdown with Fryston. A second-round 5-1 home win against Birkenshaw Rovers was followed by easy victories at Yeaden Celtic (3-0) and Liversedge (5-0). Crushing wins were then recorded against Micklefield Welfare, who were beaten 5-0 in a home quarter-final tie, and Bradford Rovers, who were routed 8-0 in the semi-final played at Manningham Mills.

Thackley's more rigorous pre-match preparations for this final included having Fryston 'watched' by Peter Glover and Jack Walker in their semi-final against Rhodes Street, with particular attention being paid to Phil Monks, whom they regarded as Fryston's danger man.

Since the previous year, Thackley had acquired their own 'secret weapon' in the form of the free-scoring centre-forward, John Emmett, whose goal tally already exceeded fifty for the season. Like Fred Howard, Emmett eschewed most other on-field responsibilities in pursuit of scoring goals:

> A goal machine, that's what he were! Very tall, very slim, with no particular skill to brag about, but he were hard, lethal with his right foot and head; and in his determination to score goals, he just trampled through anybody who stood in his way. He were good were John, but only when that ball were in t'eighteen-yard box, otherwise he just stood and picked his nose. He *came* to training, but he didn't *train*, if you know what I mean. But his hunger for scoring goals… I mean, think of the weight of the balls we played with. He were the only fella I saw who stood in the penalty area for a goal kick and headed it straight back past the 'keeper! (Peter Glover)

Emmett replaced the injured John Gunnell from the previous year's team. Geoff Dennis' place in defence was taken over by the slightly smaller, but arguably even more rugged and uncompromising Derek Wyness.

For Fryston, as in the previous year's semi-final against DP and E, controversy was caused by the insensitive way in which the team selection was communicated to the players. Though by no means a regular in the side, Brian Wood had been led to believe that he was playing, only to discover at the last minute that he was not:

I'm on the [team] photograph but they'd got no subs then. I'd got my boots on in the dressing room when Chunner Lister told me I wasn't playing. Right up to t'getting there, I thought I was playing but Chunner it was who told me they were leaving me out. I played in virtually every position that year but they decided on playing Trevor Ward at centre-forward. It was heartbreaking all right. I remember feeling numb up in t'stand at Bradford Park Avenue. (Brian Wood)

There was something almost inevitable about the outcome of the final. Fryston knew that they would have to be at their best to withstand a Thackley side, hell-bent on revenge for their previous year's defeat. It was their opponents who took the lead as early as the seventeenth minute when Ray Cole followed up to score after Johnny Appleyard had stopped a shot on the line. Fryston equalised less than five minutes later when a thunderous trademark Terry Templeman free kick from twenty yards out was deflected into the Thackley net.

Norman Elstob's match report maintains that, 'Without ever looking more than occasionally dangerous Fryston carried most of the play up to the interval.'[13] However, a mere six minutes into the second half, the Fryston defence stood flatfooted as a high, bouncing ball was seized upon by John Edmonson and cracked into the net. Despite the fact that Agga Mattison 'sealed off his penalty area for most of the game', it fell to the prolific John Emmett to wrap up the contest for Thackley with a typically opportunistic shot eighteen minutes from time. There was no Freddie Howard on hand to 'steal' the final from the Bradford club this time.

Sadly, Fryston were not quite up to the task on this occasion. Indeed, given the quality of some of the football they had played throughout the season, they had reason to feel disappointed in a below-standard performance which saw them lose 3-1. Most onlookers felt like Frank Isles that the two-goal margin of victory was no less than Thackley deserved:

I watched it, and they were far better than us on the day. It could have been more than 3-1 in my opinion. They were a really good side and it was evident to me that they really intended putting the record straight after losing the year before. And the ground at Bradford Park Avenue was spacious and really suited their play. (Frank Isles)

Cobbo Robinson remains adamant that Fryston contributed to their own demise – by failing to take similar advantage of the 'acres of space' out wide:

> That's what happened in that second final at Bradford Park Avenue when I never touched the ball – well, I touched it once as far as I can recollect, and then I gave it away through numbness and lack of practice! In fact, whose wife was it, I think it was Johnny App's, they came round to talk to me on t'bloody touch line, seeing as I wasn't getting any ball. (Barry Robinson)

Friends Reunited

Elstob's report placed great emphasis on the fact that the match had provided an excellent opportunity for the senior members of the Fryston party to re-acquaint themselves with an old wartime friend:

> Almost all the Fryston smiles and handshakes at Bradford Park Avenue's ground, scene of the West Riding Challenge Cup final, on Tuesday, were in the stand and for that cheerful Scot, Johnny Downie, the former Bradford and Manchester United player, who shared wartime days down the pit. His ready recognising of a face and his good humour, not to mention some remarkable recollections of daily pit life, softened for supporters the bitter blow of losing the cup to a side from which it was won, by an only goal, last season.[14]

Having left Manchester United for Luton Town in August 1953, Downie had gone on to enjoy spells with Hull City, Wisbech Town, Mansfield Town, Darlington, Hyde United, Mossley and Stalybridge Celtic, before retiring from the game to take on a newsagency in Bradford's Lidget Green. According to his wife:

> We initially had a shop in Manningham on the corner of Church Street and Heaton Road. It was a pokey little shop but we liked it and my sister-in-law started working with us on our very first day, and when we retired, so did she! Then we moved to Lidget Green because we wanted a bigger shop. We had lots of part-time women working for us, because John only turned up first thing in the morning and last thing at night. And why was that? It was because – and anyone will tell you this! – he was supposed to have gone to the wholesalers, but you could bet your life you'd find him on the golf course. We've been very lucky in life. He didn't make a lot out

of playing football but we've never had to starve. And John's always had that knack of meeting people and getting on with them. He'd have sorely missed all that. (Sheila Downie)

Ironically, it was one of the Thackley players, Jack Walker, who continued to stay in touch with Downie long after the 1964 final, due to their shared passion for the game of golf:

He lived at Bull Royd – had a newsagency in Lidget Green – but he moved up to Tynemouth a year or so ago. Lovely man, and he was always playing golf at Bradford. I'll just tell you this. We've got some electric gates up at t'golf club, and when you went forward, got to this line, the gates opened where you are, but John one day went too far and hit t'gates. I tell you what, you've never seen a man so upset in your life! He virtually stopped driving. Perhaps that explains why you always saw him walking. He walked absolutely everywhere, even though he'd be in his eighties. Me and t'wife would see him all over t'place, but never casual like we are now; always with a jacket and tie on – a proper gentleman. (Jack Walker)

It is with such obvious high regard and deep affection that Mr Downie, who died on 19 February 2013, will always be remembered by those who knew him well.[15]

Thackley's Subsequent Progress

Thackley's progress since their second WRCC Cup final has been impressive to say the least. Having previously resisted overtures from the West Yorkshire League, they entered its Premier Division at the start of the 1964-65 season, and finished third (on 30 points from 20 matches) behind Guiseley (top) and Snydale (runners-up), who each obtained 32 points. In the following two seasons, though, Thackley were crowned as champions, losing only once in the 1965-66 campaign and twice in 1966-67. The 1966-67 season also saw them regain the WRCC Cup, thanks to a 3-0 victory over Ferrybridge Amateurs. David Waddington, Derek Wyness, Ray Cole and John Emmett were the only surviving members of the team that had defeated Fryston.[16]

There was now no limit to Thackley's ambition. At the start of the 1967-68 season, they entered the Second Division of the Yorkshire League and were immediately promoted to Division One. They were just as soon demoted, though, and it was not until the 1973-74 season that they truly hit their stride by taking the Second Division championship and capping a truly remarkable year by also lifting the 1974 West Riding County Cup by beating Farsley Celtic 1-0 in the final. (This competition is a senior version of the WRCC Cup, with entry limited to sides playing in the Yorkshire, Midland and Northern Premier leagues.) The following season, Thackley successfully defended their county triumph by repeating their 1-0 victory over Farsley Celtic at Bradford City's Valley Parade. Though it would have seemed inconceivable at the time, this was to be Thackley's last major honour for 37 years.

This is not to suggest that the club had been 'failing' in the meantime. Having been founding members of the Northern Counties East Football League in 1982, Thackley are the only club to have retained their Premiership status since the league's inception. In 2010-11, Thackley came desperately close to winning the West Riding County Cup once more, when they were beaten 4-2 in the final at Valley Parade by their old rivals, Guiseley. One year later, however, Thackley's four-decade wait was ended when they won the 2012 Baris Northern Counties East League Cup, beating Shirebrook Town 3-1 in the final.

Chapter 13
Twilight of the Gods

Previous page: Under the continuing influence of their 'ex-pros', Agga Mattison (pictured with cup) and Jack Sharp (with plinth), Fryston enjoyed great success in the West Yorkshire League in the mid- and late-1960s.

Lords of the Manor

In the close season that followed their defeat by Thackley, Fryston applied unsuccessfully for membership of the West Yorkshire League's Premier Division. Their application was rejected due to the perceived shortcomings of their ground and accompanying facilities. The club therefore remained for two more years in the First Division where they enjoyed a major rivalry with Ferrybridge Amateurs.

From the start of the 1964-65 season, the club lacked the services of their erstwhile skipper, Pete Waddington, who had signed for the reigning First Division champions, Snydale Road Athletic, having fallen out with the Fryston committee:

> It had something to do with washing t'team kit. I'm pretty sure it was. My wife, Mary, used to wash t'kit for bugger all payment but they came back and said they thought she should do it for nowt, what with me being captain; and I'm afraid I wasn't having it. (Peter Waddington)

The challenge for the title was a two-horse race between Fryston and Ferrybridge. Despite taking only one point in their head-to-head meetings with Ferry, and losing to them 2-0 in the semi-final of the Cas and District Cup, it was Fryston who wrested the league title. They also claimed the 'double' by beating Queensbury Youth 5-1 in the final of the West Yorkshire League (Division One) Cup. Any thoughts that Fryston might have entertained of appearing in a third successive WRCC Cup final evaporated at the quarter-final stage when they surrendered a 1-0 half-time lead (secured by a great Terry Templeman volley) to the Premiership leaders, Snydale, who eventually won 3-1.

The 1965-66 season saw a resumption of the rivalry between Fryston and Ferrybridge. When both teams brought 100 per cent league records to their match at Ferry Fryston in November, it was The Colliers who triumphed 4-0. The opposition team had a familiar-looking outside-right in its ranks, in the shape of Cobbo Robinson, who had left Fryston the previous season in a self-confessed fit of pique:

How it came about: we were beating Knottingley five-nowt – it must have been, what, 1964, 1965 – and I walked off because I weren't being involved enough for my liking. In t'first half of that match I weren't in t'game, so I came out for t'second period eating a bag of crisps. That made no impression and about ten minutes, a quarter-of-an-hour from t'end, I thought 'I've had enough!' and walked right off! (Barry Robinson)

Fryston's subsequent runaway lead was briefly trimmed back as a result of Ferrybridge's 3-1 win over The Colliers the following April, a game in which Robinson narrowly avoided paying the price for scoring against his old club: 'I remember Johnny App tried to take my head off with a haymaker, but luckily I saw it coming and I ducked!' Nevertheless, two losses over the Easter period put nails in the Ferrybridge coffin. Fryston enjoyed the further satisfaction of ending Amateurs' unbroken run of appearing in every final of the Cas and District Cup since 1954. Their 5-1 semi-final win set up a 3-0 victory over Fairburn in the final. In a re-run of the previous year's West Yorkshire League Cup, Fryston comfortably defeated Queensbury 3-1, but Ferrybridge gained some degree of revenge for earlier setbacks by easily defeating Fryston 5-2 in the final of the Embleton Cup.

Fryston proved incapable once more of emulating their recent success in the WRCC Cup. Having overcome Neville Sports 4-1, they then lost away to Liversedge in a closely fought contest:

There was little to choose between the teams throughout, but Liversedge, top of the County Amateur League, were a shade more constructive and had a vital lucky break. Fryston were ahead early, Harold Mattison heading home from a corner kick. Defences dominated, but four minutes before half time a long ball down the middle hit a rut on the icy pitch and bounced off Fryston goalkeeper Archie Ward for an equalising goal. When Sharp was brought down in the second half, Fryston called vainly for a penalty and the match looked booked for extra time until Liversedge hit an out-of-the-blue winner with five minutes left. The ball went into the net from about 20 yards, like a rocket.[1]

Fryston's renewed application for Premiership status was accepted in a close season during which Cobbo Robinson returned to the club after a one-year absence. ('I didn't really know the players and the crack weren't the same as at Fryston, so that's why I went back.') In the next two years, the club set about establishing themselves among the elite clubs of West Yorkshire. In 1966-67, they came fourth in a league dominated by their old rivals, Thackley, to whom they lost 2-1 away and 2-0 at home.

Fryston lost a 4-3 thriller to Manningham Mills in their only match in that year's WRCC Cup. The final was contested by Thackley and a Ferrybridge side including Pete Waddington at centre-forward, who had joined them from Snydale via a season spent with Methley United. Amateurs had finished a very modest fifth in Division One that year (eighteen points adrift of the champions, Queensbury Youth); and although their side contained three members of their 1962 cup-winning team in Milner, Wright and Sands, the match was even more one-sided than the 3-0 score-line suggests. Thackley could easily have doubled the three goals John Emmett actually planted in the net.

Fryston started the 1967-68 season as if there would be no stopping them. A five-goal haul from new centre-forward, Pearson, was the centre-piece of their 7-1 drubbing of title favourites, Snydale, in the opening match of the season. With their midfield strengthened immeasurably by the acquisition of Heseltine from Pontefract Collieries, Fryston maintained an astounding 100 per cent league record through to March. By this time, however, they had been unexpectedly knocked out of the WRCC Cup. Following home wins against Holmes-Holset (3-1) and Neville Sports (7-1), Fryston were held 2-2 away to the leaders of the Leeds Red Triangle League, Farnley. The Colliers' impressive league form was already making them one of the favourites to win the county cup.

But Fryston, who only narrowly evaded defeat at Farnley, the first side they had failed to beat, were never happy in treacherous conditions [in this replay] at Elmete Road and only centre-half, Harold Mattison, was anything near normal form. Farnley, surprisingly sure-footed on the ice, scored midway through the first half after home outside-left Scalfe was dispossessed. Later, Fryston escaped when a shot struck the crossbar. Though Fryston twice might have snatched goals, they created no clear-cut opening before the interval. In the second half, however, when they dominated more than Farnley had done before the break, Heseltine shot over from four yards with only the goalkeeper to beat – the kind of chance he usually eats. With a Templeman shot striking the foot of a post and the goalkeeper turning another of his efforts over the top, Fryston had done enough in the end to have deserved a third chance.[2]

Fryston's first league defeat of the season – 1-0 at Methley in early March – heralded the loss of seven points in four games, a poor run which threw the title race wide open. They were also beaten by Methley in the semi-final of the Premier Division League Cup. The Colliers' 5-1 home win against Guiseley in the last week of April, and Snydale's 2-1 defeat of Methley United in their penultimate match, set up a tightrope situation requiring them to at least draw their last match of the season at Snydale, who would otherwise beat them to the title. The outcome was agonisingly close for Fryston. Snydale were two goals up with 68 minutes played when Braund was brought down in the area and Appleyard scored from the spot. Then, with only minutes remaining, the home 'keeper dived at Appleyard's feet to save a certain goal, and in so doing rob Fryston of the title.

Breaking Up is Hard to Do

Without knowing it, Johnny Appleyard's heroic performance even in defeat was to prove his fitting finale. During the close season (June 1968), the popular, raw-boned half-back was playing at a Coal Industry Social Welfare Organisation (CISWO) seven-a-side competition held in Goldthorpe, near Barnsley. Having comfortably made it to the final against Monckton, Fryston had already established a 1-0 first-half lead when Appleyard suddenly tripped while running and fell forward onto his face. According to the on-looking Trevor Ward:

> It was right odd because he was just chasing back towards our goal when an opposition forward ran across his back and just clipped his leg, causing him to go down, head-first; and, of course, he never got up. Well, Woody [Brian Wood] came running out of his goal to gather the ball, but on seeing that Johnny was in some sort of distress, he just kicked the ball away as if to say, 'That's the least of my concerns.' I think it was Brian who shouted, 'Can we get some help here?' because he could see that Johnny wasn't moving. Initially, two medics came on and then the ambulance arrived more or less straight away… The match carried on in his absence. We came off at half time and it was then that we discovered he'd died. There was no way we were carrying on, but their team manager came into our dressing room

228

just as we were getting changed. He said, 'They've told us the trophy's ours by right, but we've said that we're not accepting it,' because we [Fryston] were winning 1-0 at the time and they thought we were the ones who deserved it.

When Charlie Williams heard about the tragedy, he put together a special concert for the benefit of Appleyard's widow, Carol, and the pair's two young children, David (aged two) and Janine, who was only a few weeks old. 'On top of that,' remembers Trevor Ward, 'we had a charity match against Monckton Colliery. We kicked off at half-past-six and, turned eight o'clock, they piled into the Welfare and he put us all these turns on. They took a collection from the audience, but all five turns put a show on for nothing. He [Williams] had us all in stitches – just like Johnny would have wanted.'

The loss of Johnny Appleyard soon proved part of a larger turnover of Fryston personnel in readiness for the 1968-69 season. Cliff Braund moved to Swillington Welfare and Trevor Ward to Pontefract Collieries, while Agga Mattison took the decision to retire. The team photograph for Fryston's 3-2 home win against Methley in late September included only Cobbo Robinson from the county cup-winning team of 1963. This did not prevent them from making an impressive start to the season which saw them unbeaten going into the WRCC Cup first round at home to Knottingley Albion. Fryston soon established a 2-0 lead over their Division One opponents, only for Knottingley to force a draw by virtue of two second-half goals. In the replay, the former holders were comprehensively defeated as Albion struck three times in the first fifteen minutes of the second half and finally ran out 4-0 winners. A fatal rot had now set in. Despite the return of Sharp, Templeman, Archie Ward and Brian Wood, and the acquisition of a fine centre-forward in Bateson, Fryston began an alarming descent which saw them win scarcely any of their remaining league matches, and finish eleventh out of fourteen in the table.

The Colliers made an abysmally poor start to the 1969-70 season. By now, they had lost another talismanic mainstay of the county cup-winning side in Terry Templeman, whose career was cut short by a debilitating back problem. Beginning with a 6-1 setback at Monckton, where Brian Wood ended up in the Fryston goal after Archie Ward was injured, Fryston endured seven consecutive defeats before finally registering a 2-1 win against Micklefield. By this stage, Agga Mattison had been temporarily coaxed out of retirement in a bid to stiffen the defence. Having received a bye in round one of the WRCC Cup because Armthorpe could not raise a team, Fryston came a cropper against Firth Sports of the West Riding County Amateur League, who beat them 4-2. Fryston's malaise was exemplified by the fact that, for their 4-2 setback at Salts (Saltaire), they could only summon up eight regular players and were forced to hunt around desperately in order to make up a team. A dismal record of only three wins and two draws out of their 24 matches saw Fryston propping up the Premier League and grateful for the fact that there was no automatic relegation.

The dawning of a new decade saw Cliff Braund taking up the position of coach with the Dunedin City Football Club in New Zealand. This unexpected twist of fate occurred in the early winter of 1969, when the 25-year-old Braund and his 22-year-old wife, Elaine, came across an article in the local *Echo Final* (the 'Green 'Un'), asking for anyone who might be interested in playing and coaching football in New Zealand to get in touch with a local agent for Dunedin. The club's interest was reinforced by the contents of the scrap book that Braund's mother had been keeping of his career progress.

> I then talked it over with Elaine and she said, 'Do it!' on the basis that, if I didn't, I'd regret it for the rest of my life. I think I gave four days' notice [to the Leeds-based Yorkshire Copper Works, where he was working as an accountant] and left on the Monday. It was a very expensive airline ticket they bought me. I worked out that the fare of £800 was the equivalent of two years' wages. The contract I signed promised me a job and accommodation but nothing else. I left on the Monday, arrived on the Wednesday and played in the team at the weekend! (Cliff Braund)

The Derek Stokes Revolution

Fryston now turned for much-needed support to the ex-Bradford City, Huddersfield Town and England Under 23 international centre-forward, Derek Stokes, in the hope that he might inspire a reversal of recent fortunes. Born in nearby Normanton on 13 September 1939, Stokes had initially played in the West Yorkshire League for Snydale Road Athletic, before joining Bradford City as a left-winger and soon converting into a star centre-forward.[3] Among the 25 league and ten cup goals he scored for The Bantams during the 1959-60 season was the second goal in their famous 2-2 draw with high-flying First Division Burnley in the fifth-round FA Cup tie at Valley Parade.

Stokes was then bought by Huddersfield Town for £22,500 in June 1960, and played alongside future England internationals, the winger, Mike O'Grady, and the 1966 World Cup-winning left-back, Ray Wilson. The highlight of his first season with the club was Town's third-round FA Cup tie against holders and Division One leaders, Wolves. Although they were bottom of Division Two, Town forced a 1-1 draw, thanks to a goal by Stokes. The replay, in which a crowd of 46,000 witnessed the first-ever floodlit match at Leeds Road, was won for Huddersfield with goals by Stokes and O'Grady. During his five-year spell with Huddersfield, Stokes won five Under 23 caps for England (scoring goals against Belgium and Greece) and played alongside such legendary full internationals of the future as Peter Bonetti, George Cohen, Alan Mullery, Brian Labone, Martin Peters, Roger Hunt and Ian Callaghan.

Stokes had a brief second spell with Bradford City between 1965 and 1967, before spending three successful seasons with Dundalk in the Irish League. When the Yorkshireman took the decision to return to the Normanton/Castleford area, friendship and working relations played a part in his decision to manage Fryston:

> When Stokesy came, he was the first manager who actually *managed* the club. With knowing him at Hickson's, our Jack [Sharp] was big mates with Stokesy. He was at Bradford City while Jack was at Halifax. They played against each other a couple of times. He used to watch us a lot, did Derek. He was over in Ireland, you know, and when we asked him to play for us, they wanted a couple of grand. He couldn't play for a year even after he'd started as manager. He put a bit of weight on. He spent a lot of time in t'club and he'd brought this dolly bird with him, but he knew how to get the players trained and he single-handedly picked the team. He was lucky that he also had a good side to come to. He managed us for about four or five good years. With him being an ex-pro, people wanted to come and play for him, so he brought in all the good players from round about. (Frank Isles)

Stokes' impact was immediate. Having taken seven games to win their first point a season earlier, Fryston got off the mark at the first attempt in 1970-71, with Cobbo Robinson scoring their goal in a 1-1 home draw with Whitkirk Wanderers. Among several new signings were the Ferrybridge centre-forward, Johnny King, and the talented Trevor Winter, an inside-forward from Methley. Stokes had also persuaded Jack Sharp to resume playing for his former club. Stokes' methods soon produced dividends. In commenting on Fryston's 2-0 win at East End Park in the second week of September, the *Express* maintained how Fryston 'seemed to have the edge in the first half and gradually tightened their grip as they out-ran a capable home side. The secret behind Fryston's fitness is the work of their new coach, Derek Stokes, the former Bradford City and Huddersfield Town forward.'[4]

A long, unbeaten start to the season was ended in late November when Monckton Collieries beat Fryston 4-2 to replace them at the top of the table. Monckton reinforced their superiority by knocking Fryston out of the Premier League Cup before going on to become league champions. The Colliers were eliminated from the WRCC Cup in the first round, when Methley beat them 2-1 after extra time, with Trevor Winter hitting the post against his former club. Fryston also lost 4-0 to Grimethorpe in the final of the Embleton Cup, but drew some consolation by beating Altofts 1-0 in the Pontefract Infirmary Cup final.

Within Touching Distance Again

In the next two seasons, Fryston consolidated their progress under Derek Stokes by launching two determined attempts at the Premier League title and making spirited attempts to regain the WRCC Cup. Johnny King's class was highlighted by the two early season hat-tricks he scored in Fryston's 3-1 home win against Ardsley Celtic and 7-1 away thumping of East End Park. It was another astute Stokes signing – that of Agga Mattison at centre-half, who allowed himself to be coaxed out of retirement once more – which proved equally invaluable to Fryston:

> I'd already made a big impression on him! I remember playing against Derek [Stokes] when he played for Snydale – it must have been 1956 or thereabouts – and we collided into each other going for a loose ball and he came off the worst of it. He was all dazed up so they sent for an ambulance as a precaution. They said to Derek's dad, 'Are you going in the ambulance with him?' and he told 'em, 'No, he can go on his own!' (Harold Mattison)

It was good performances by Mattison and Terry Bacon (a midfield trialist with Bradford City) that helped ensure Fryston a 2-0 win over their closest rivals, Altofts, in mid-February. The scorer of Fryston's second goal that match, Trevor Winter, also scored in the 1-0 win over the same opposition that secured Fryston the Premiership title at the end of April. Altofts gained sweet revenge by beating Fryston 3-0 in the Premiership League Cup final, but Fryston enjoyed the considerable consolation of beating Ferrybridge Amateurs 3-2 in the replayed final of the Cas and District Cup, thanks largely to commanding displays by Sharp in midfield and Mattison at centre-half.

It was in the WRCC Cup campaign that Fryston strove hardest to make their mark. In the first round of the 1971-72 competition, a Johnny King hat-trick proved decisive in their 5-4 win at Farnley. King and Derek Stokes each contributed two goals in Fryston's 4-1 second-round win at Allerton Rovers of the Bradford Red Triangle League, in a game in which Fryston also hit the woodwork four times. Fryston led virtually from the off in their 7-0 home win in the third round, in which King helped himself to another hat-trick. Things were much tighter in the next round, however, when Trevor Winter scored his second goal of the game two minutes from time to secure a 2-1 win over Swillington Welfare.

Goals by Sharp, Stokes and Winter gave Fryston a well-deserved 3-1 quarter-final victory over Ovenden at Ferry Fryston.[5] In their semi-final tie, Fryston shared four goals with Liversedge in a game they should easily have won:

> Derek Stokes got the first Fryston goal, finding the corner of the net from 25 yards, and though Liversedge equalised during a brief spell of pressure, Fryston took the lead again when King latched onto a rebound after Stokes had hit the bar. With perhaps their only shot of a second half dominated by Fryston, Liversedge equalised and held on until the end. Centre-half Mattison and outside-left Bateson, who frequently tested the Liversedge defence with long penetrating runs, were outstanding.[6]

In the replay at East End Park, Sharp and Price dominated the midfield for Fryston in a game that nonetheless went into extra time before a 25-yard screamer from Winter settled matters, and put Fryston through to the first-ever final exclusively to involve two local teams.

Fryston's opponents in the final were Pontefract Collieries. A crowd of 700 turned up for the Friday-night contest at Glass Houghton Welfare's ground. It was Pontefract who established what seemed like an insurmountable 2-0 lead. Fryston's chances took a further dive when Derek Stokes was taken to hospital with concussion. Fortunately for them, however, in the second half Pontefract lost the influential Pete Jacobsen (who had hitherto kept a tight rein on Jackie Sharp) through injury:

> Jacobson's absence gave Sharpe [sic] all the room he needed and slowly he coaxed Fryston into a game they looked to have lost in the first 20 minutes. Ten minutes into the second half Bateson pulled a goal back for Fryston and after a number of near misses [Melvin] Rotherforth flicked home the equaliser.[7]

The final was replayed a week later at Glass Houghton. The heavy, incessant rain, which had turned the ground into a mud bath, forced a ten-minute interruption of the game: 'Collieries, with Jacobson dominating the middle of the field, were not affected by the conditions, however, and frequent long balls often had the Fryston defence in trouble.'[8] The Pontefract striker, Heseltine, made most of an uncharacteristic hesitancy in the Fryston defence, to help himself to five goals as his side handed out a 6-0 drubbing to the West Yorkshire League Champions. Hard as Bateson and Rotherforth tried for an otherwise ineffectual Fryston team, 'they had no-one to match the industrious Jacobson, outstanding throughout. Once again he kept a tight hold on Sharpe [sic] and still found time to venture upfield in attacking sorties.'[9]

In 1972-73, Fryston set out to supersede what had been one of their most successful post-war seasons by striving, not only to win the Premiership title but also the WRCC Cup. They overcame the early handicap of losing 3-0 to Pontefract Collieries on the first day of the season, to gradually overtake a strong Monckton team and win the league. Pontefract were responsible for eliminating Fryston from the West Yorkshire League Cup and Cas and District Cup, but the county cup holders were knocked out of that year's competition 5-3 at the quarter-final stage by the Bradford team, Luddendenfoot.

Since starting out with an emphatic 8-0 win over Battyford Wanderers in round two, Fryston had confidently progressed to the semi-final at East End Park, where they easily defeated Leeds Catholics

5-1 for the right to meet Collieries' conquerors in the final, again at East End Park. It was Fryston who did all the early running. However, Luddendenfoot increasingly turned to the attack and, just before half time, they opened the scoring amidst Fryston appeals for offside.

Spiritedly, the Castleford area side fought back and a shot from Winter just went wide. Fryston's efforts were rewarded early in the second half when Lethbridge forced the ball home after a goalmouth scramble. Another good save by Kelsey thwarted Luddendenfoot but all the time they were gaining control and from a neat build-up they headed in a second goal. Undaunted Fryston fought back and got the ball into the net only to have the goal disallowed, Lethbridge nipping in after a defender had headed towards his goal. The referee awarded the goal in the first place but after appeals by Luddendenfoot he consulted his linesman and cancelled out his earlier decision. More pressure came from Fryston as they forced several corners with Bateson floating over some delightful centres. He sent over one cross which went into the net only for the referee to again deny the goal, ruling it offside. Just before the end the issue was settled when Luddendenfoot's centre-forward crowned a good solo effort with a third goal.[10]

The 1973-74 season was one in which Fryston ceded local supremacy to Pontefract Collieries. Despite beating their great rivals 2-0 away (with two goals from Trevor Winter) in the second match of the season, Fryston lost the return fixture 3-0 and Collieries went on to win the title. They also beat Fryston 6-4 in the semi-final of the West Yorkshire League Cup, with the ex-Fryston star, Johnny King, contributing two goals to Fryston's defeat. Fryston also performed poorly by recent standards in the WRCC Cup, where they were knocked out in the third round by Brackenhall United.

The pendulum swung back decisively in Fryston's favour in 1974-75, as a team blending established stalwarts like Trevor Winter and Derek Stokes with an influx of teenage talent (like Graham Riley and Derek Whipp) from the successful Centre XI Youth Club, proved literally invincible in the league. Part way through the season, Fryston's challenge was strengthened by the acquisition of the powerful sharpshooter, Johnny Nicholls, from Ferrybridge Amateurs. It was his hat-trick which helped demolish Pontefract Collieries in Fryston's 4-1 away 'showdown' match in late February. By the time the two sides met for the return match (in which Fryston cancelled out two first-half Johnny King goals to force a 2-2 draw), The Colliers had not only beaten their Pontefract rivals 3-2 in the West Yorkshire League Cup semi-final (from which they went on to beat Whitkirk Wanderers 1-0 in the final), but had also secured the league championship by remaining unbeaten in the process.

Fryston made relatively sure-footed progress to the semi-finals of the WRCC Cup for the right to meet a Gascoigne Wood side that had previously accounted for Pontefract Collieries. However, the semi was a disappointing affair in which Fryston conceded an early goal and were severely disadvantaged by a succession of controversial line-keeping decisions:

> Playing with much of their usual composure, Fryston pressed hard to draw level, Riley making a run and [Alan] Dickinson forcing his way past several defenders to score. Fryston became plainly rattled at some of the ruling of the touch judge who did not interfere when a United player was offside and Gascoigne went on to take the lead again. Fryston appealed for offside again after the restart, but again the man with the flag did not stop play and United increased their lead. An eight-man defence bottled up Fryston when they tried to get back into the game and it was during one of these attacks that Alan Bateson was badly fouled, an incident which the linesman ignored and United broke to score another goal. Throwing caution to the wind by putting everything into the attack, Fryston left themselves wide open with the result that Gascoigne added a fifth goal. And to add to Fryston's tale of woe 'hot shot' Derek Stokes missed from the penalty spot.[11]

In Fryston's last season in the West Yorkshire League, both they and Pontefract Collieries were overshadowed by newcomers to the Premiership in the shape of Silsden from Keighley. A regular supply of goals from the likes of Winter and Nicholls (the former hit four in 6-1 at Walton; the latter likewise in 6-2 victory at Carlton Athletic) ensured that Fryston continued their long unbeaten run until late November. It was at that point that they went down 2-1 at home to Silsden. The two sides remained neck-and-neck at the top of the league. However, at the turn of the year, Silsden put together a long run of twelve successive victories, culminating in a 3-1 win over Fryston, that put paid to The Colliers' hope of retaining their title.

Fryston drew Pontefract Collieries at home in the fourth round of the WRCC Cup and, in what proved to be yet another titanic confrontation between them, Collieries established a two-goal lead despite playing into the wind.

Ten minutes after the change round, Fryston pulled one back when, after the woodwork had been hit several times, Price cracked the ball through a bunch of players to score. Fryston kept up the pressure and five minutes from the end Stenton latched onto a clearance and lobbed the ball over the defence for the equaliser. By extra time the wind had died down and both teams produced some sparkling football, but the goalkeepers were well up to their job, keeping the score sheet clear of further goals.[12]

The replay was characterised by end-to-end football, in the course of which Fryston took a first-half lead when the Collieries goalkeeper allowed a Rotherforth free kick to slip though his hands and into the net. Winter fired home Fryston's second after half time and, thereafter, 'Pontefract threw everything into attack but Fryston's defence, especially Hewitt who brought off an amazing save, kept them in check.'[13]

Fryston then had to negotiate a difficult quarter-final tie at home to Almondbury United. The Colliers twice took the lead in normal time through goals by Winter and Nicholls, only for the opposition to equalise each time. The visitors dominated the first period of extra time, but it was Riley who gave Fryston the lead. Mills extended Fryston's advantage in the second period. However, Almondbury pulled back a late goal, and it was only a 'magnificent point-blank save'[14] in the last minute by Hewitt which saw Fryston through to the semi-final, where they met Bradley Rangers.

It was probably against the run of play that Fryston established a 2-0 first-half lead against Bradley, through an opposition own goal and an opportunistic strike by Johnny Nicholls. However:

Rangers hit back a minute before half time from the penalty spot after the linesman had signalled a corner. The referee was unsighted and ruled that Stenton had handled when Fryston claimed the ball had hit his thigh. The second half was only two minutes old when Bradley equalised at a goal mouth scramble, and from then on goalkeeper Hewitt was kept busy trying to keep the goal-hungry side at bay. Another harsh decision proved costly for Fryston, who appealed for offside as Bradley scored. In vain the Castleford area side threw everything into the attack but Bradley held out.[14]

Fryston were subsequently beaten 2-0 by Pontefract Collieries in the semi-final of the Cas and District FA Cup, leaving their 6-3 demolition of Royston Inn Cross in the Embleton Cup final (a game in which Nicholls scored a hat-trick) as their only success that season. Plans were disclosed shortly afterwards for a facelift for the stand and a widening of the playing area in support of their application to join the Yorkshire League next season. This move ended Fryston's association with the WRCC Cup for the next sixteen years – as a senior league team they would compete in the West Riding County Cup instead.

Back in the High Life Again

In August 1976, Fryston returned to the Yorkshire League for the first time in 50 years. It took the club only three years to progress from the Third into the First Division, however they were relegated back down after just one year. It was during their only season in Division One (1979-80) that Fryston enjoyed easily their best-ever run in the West Riding County Cup, when they overcame Liversedge 2-0 in the semi-final for the right to face Guiseley in a final played at Bradford City's Valley Parade. Fryston entered the final already certain of relegation. However, they played with commendable spirit early on, and with Terry Bacon playing a blinder in midfield, opened the scoring on nine minutes when Whitehead hammered home a 25-yard shot. As the game progressed, Guiseley gradually asserted their superiority and the final score of 3-1 was no less than the Bradford team deserved. Following their immediate relegation back into Division Two, they languished in the lower reaches of the second tier, finishing fourth from bottom in 1980-81 and in last place the year after.

The Yorkshire and Midland leagues were merged in 1982 to form the Northern Counties East. Fryston finished the first two of their eleven seasons in this league in mid-table positions, which appeared to vindicate a forward-looking youth policy that had seen the recent introduction of the talented young goalkeeper, Mark Smithson, and the equally gifted teenage strike-force of Dave Penney, Carl Sprago and John Hannah. It was in the second of these seasons (1983-84) that Penney (a future Football League professional with Derby County) really came into his own.

His growing footballing stature was emphasised in what turned out to be Fryston's only sustained West Riding County Cup run during their time spent in the NCEL. Having scored both goals in Fryston's

2-1 first-round victory at Ossett Albion, Penney then found the net six times in Fryston's subsequent 7-0 league win over Brook Sports, their highest score since leaving the West Yorkshire League. It was another Penney goal that proved decisive in the second round, when Fryston overcame a previously unbeaten Yorkshire Amateurs side, 1-0 away. In the quarter-finals, Fryston had the misfortune to draw the eventual cup winners, Farsley Celtic of Division One. After Farsley had taken the lead against the run of play on 20 minutes, Fryston replied eleven minutes later when Chris Waite latched on to a Penney overhead kick. The Colliers were eventually overcome as Farsley added two more to their total, but this was only after Penney had been thwarted by two last-ditch saves, Alan Arlotte had struck a post and their player-manager, Trevor Winter, the angle of the upright and crossbar.

Winter had previously asserted that the failure by Fryston pit management to adequately invest in the maintenance and development of club facilities was making it difficult for him to attract or hold onto top quality players.[16] As if to prove this point, in the spring of 1984 Penney moved to Pontefract Collieries, leaving Fryston to lose five of their remaining six games. Worse still, five disastrous seasons then followed in which Fryston finished bottom (or close to the bottom) of the league and were regularly on the receiving end of fearsome batterings in the West Riding County Cup (most notably, their 10-0 and 8-0 defeats by Guiseley in 1985-86 and 1987-88, respectively). The appointment in 1985-86 of Pete Waddington as manager and Jackie Sharp as his assistant was just one of several measures which failed to arrest Fryston's demise.

Almost inexplicably, the 1988-89 season represented Fryston's best-ever season in the NCEL. Their 2-1 home win against Winterton Rangers in early November saw them temporarily top a league in which they eventually finished a highly creditable fourth, and narrowly lost out 1-0 at Thackley in an early round of the West Riding County Cup. The club was not quite able to sustain this form during 1990-91, though, when they slipped back to eighth out of thirteen in the league. However, in what proved to be their final appearance in the county cup, they lost out, 4-0 in round one, in what the *Express* described as a 'battling display'[17] at home to Armthorpe Colliery.

Bringing it All Back Home

In the following year (1991-92), the club slipped into the Central Midlands Premier League (North) where they found the standard of opposition less daunting. Their first four league games were won at an average of over five goals per game. Having now returned to the West Riding County FA *Challenge* Cup competition, Fryston recorded a 3-1 first-round victory over Upper Armley Old Boys. The Colliers were perched on top of the league when they encountered Hebden Royd Red Star in their second-round home tie – a fact which made the 3-1 defeat they suffered all the more surprising. The club's march towards the league title continued undeterred. By the New Year, they had stretched their unbeaten run to ten games and their championship lead to ten points; and by early March, the title was already theirs.

How strange, then, that this high note should have heralded Fryston's subsequent demise. This all came about when planning restrictions prevented the club from making the requisite developments to the ground for promotion to the Central Midlands League Supreme Division. This outcome led to the resignation of the team manager, Jim Kenyon, and several key players, the upshot being that the committee disbanded and the club's days as a major force in the Castleford district were now over.

At the start of the 1994-95 season a re-branded Fryston Miners AFC, containing a host of talented young players, entered the Second Division of the Castleford and District FA Sunday League. Success was instantaneous: back-to-back promotions in 1995-96 and 1996-97 saw Fryston leapfrog the First Division straight into the Premier League, where they stayed for six seasons before suffering relegation back into the First Division in 2001-02.

A corresponding move to re-establish Fryston as a 'Saturday side' (in Division Two of the West Yorkshire League) was attempted in the 2000-01 season. The newly-formed 'Fryston Miners' Welfare' fared poorly in their inaugural season, winning only one and drawing another of their 24 matches. They initially performed much better at the start of the following year's campaign, winning their first four games, but three straight defeats thereafter, culminating in a shattering 9-1 setback against Sherburn White Rose, put paid to any further progress, and the club immediately folded amidst reports of player apathy.

At the root of Fryston's demise as a Sunday football team had been the problems provoked by an exodus of their best players to the rival Glass Houghton FC. In 2003-04, however, a change of management encouraged the return of key personnel from Glass Houghton, the upshot being that Fryston were immediately returned to the Premier Division. A year later, the club enjoyed their best-ever season, winning the pre-season Embleton Cup and finishing as runners-up in the league. Inexplicably, however, they plummeted to second-bottom a year after; and, amidst chronic disillusionment, folded only a few games into the season.

Two years later, following a determined effort to recruit high-quality local players, another version of the club, Fryston AFC, entered the Castleford and District FA Sunday League. This recruitment policy immediately paid dividends, allowing Fryston to gain promotion to the First Division, which they proceeded to win the following year. Having finished fifth in the Premier Division in 2010-11, the team narrowly missed out on the title a year later, losing out to by a single point. There was consolation in the fact that Fryston lifted the Oakworth Open Cup to finally break the hoodoo of having appeared in six cup finals without success, since re-forming in 2008-09.

Club officials were now clearly looking to their rich local heritage as a source of further inspiration. Fryston's annual awards for the 2010-11 season were presented by The Colliers' skipper from the 1963 final, Pete Waddington, and a year later by Dave Penney. The club's appearance in the 2012-13 West Riding County Football Association Sunday Cup competition provided a timely and potent reminder that the fiftieth anniversary of their momentous win over Thackley was now imminent. If ever there was a time to reclaim and draw inspiration from such a heritage, surely it was now.

Chapter 14
Out of the Ashes?

Previous page: From (goal) poacher to gamekeeper! Freddie Howard (pictured here with his daughter, Susan) turned to refereeing once his playing career was over.

Unprecedented and Unsurpassed

The famous cup-final victory which this book has sought to commemorate represents a key symbolic milestone in the shared history of a village and a football team. The preceding chapters set out to show how the sporting and cultural significance of Fryston Colliery Welfare's 1963 West Riding County FA Challenge Cup win over Thackley can only be fully appreciated by delving back into a combined social, industrial and sporting history in which patterns of conflict, styles of management, and population change are intermeshed with, and inseparable from, the exploits of great local football teams and the skills and heroics of the players who once represented them.

In my earlier publication, *One Road In, One Road Out: A People's History of Fryston*, I made the point that, by the early 1980s, the miners at Fryston Colliery represented one of the most 'militant' branches in the Yorkshire Area of the National Union of Mineworkers, and that they were among the most ardent supporters of the 1984-85 national miners' strike.[1] It therefore makes it all the more ironic to discover that it was particular late-nineteenth-century patterns of industrial conflict and population change (involving, to some degree, the migration of strike-breaking labour) which helped shape Fryston's development as a mining community and encouraged the rapid evolution of a vibrant and intensely competitive local football culture. The social isolation of the village, the harshness of the associated everyday working life, and values imported from such established sporting bastions as the Staffordshire coalfields appear to have been key factors in the generation of a tough-minded footballing ethos which was first manifested in attempts by Fryston-based teams at the turn of the twentieth century to win the newly-instigated West Riding Cup.

Fryston's involvement in organised league and cup competitions remained fleeting and sporadic until the formation of Fryston Colliery AFC in 1910 – the point at which the club became viable contenders for the WRCC trophy. In 1912, they narrowly lost out in the semi-final to the eventual winners, the legendary Mirfield United; and in 1914 and 1915, they were beaten finalists against Horsforth (Leeds) and Goole Town, respectively. Fryston's expulsion from the Leeds and District League following the final against Goole underscored their enduring reputation for roughness, gamesmanship and intimidation, as well as their consummate football skills.

The club had to wait until 1925 for its next appearance in the final of the WRCC Cup – a disappointing affair in which Fryston (now playing in the Yorkshire League) were outplayed by the less fancied Harrogate Town. Fryston had succeeded, one year earlier, in defeating the neighbouring Castleford Town of the more senior Midland League in the preliminary rounds of the English Cup, only to then find themselves disqualified for fielding an unregistered player. The club's propensity to combine aggression and gamesmanship with more 'legitimate' footballing skills was personified by the scorer of Fryston's winner against Castleford, the Pelsall (Staffordshire) born Dick Foulkes, who would subsequently coach the 1963 cup-winning team. Like their predecessors of the pre-First World War era, Fryston's Yorkshire League teams invariably comprised hybrid forms of local-grown talent and 'imported', non-colliery personnel, some of whom were ex-professionals. The impact of these latter players was to reinforce the skilful, but tough and uncompromising, approach traditionally associated with Fryston.

Patterns of colliery ownership and management, as well as national economic and political considerations, may well be important in helping to explain variations in Fryston's success. The Fryston sides of the 1910s and 1920s emerged in a period in which the mines were privately owned. While conflict and exploitation were undoubtedly rife at these times, there are signs that the Fryston pit managers of these eras (Soar and Purcell, respectively) set out to nurture and encourage the success of the colliery football team. The onset of the 'Great Depression' of the late-1920s and 1930 brought massive coalfield unemployment and poverty. Workers at Fryston Colliery saw the corresponding introduction of a more cynical and exploitative form of pit management. In such a climate of economic under-resourcing and managerial indifference, the football team became weakened to the point of eventual collapse.

The wartime era of the 1940s could hardly have been more propitious in comparison. The newly-appointed Jim Bullock shared the view of preceding Fryston pit bosses like Soar and Purcell that football could be 'used' to management's benefit and therefore did everything to encourage his team's success. The club could count itself especially fortunate, not only in the respect that mining was a 'reserved' occupation and that many of his 'star' players were therefore not obliged to go to war, but also to the extent that Fryston played host to many professional footballers (notably from Bradford Park Avenue) who had entered the mines as 'Bevin Boys'. Bullock also made the inspired decision to persuade Dick Foulkes to return to Fryston Colliery as the team's football coach. In due course, he also employed Dick's brother, the Fryston-born and ex-Stockport County professional, Jabie Foulkes, with the intention of having him spearhead the team's attack.

The Fryston team of the 1940s was an essentially 'home-grown' unit, drawing together a core of Fryston and Airedale-based players alongside men from more 'peripheral' localities like Brotherton and Pontefract, under the captaincy of the Foulkes' cousin, Freddie Astbury. Although the players were inherently talented in their own right, it is also indisputable that the 'professional' influence and advice they received, not only from the Foulkes brothers, but also the recently entered Bevin Boys, was crucial to their success. The colliery team proved capable of taking on and beating such all-comers as the Leeds United and Huddersfield Town reserve sides. However, it was their misfortune in the 1945 WRCC Cup final to come up against the extremely talented Bradford Park Avenue 'nursery team' and reigning champions, East Bierley, who Freddie Astbury subsequently rated the best opposition he had ever encountered.

The conclusion of the war and the retirement of Jabie Foulkes and other star players disinvested Fryston of many of the above advantages. The capacity for colliery managers like Jim Bullock to act as patrons of their football teams was also tightly constrained by the nationalisation of the mines in 1947. Other unknown factors may also have been involved, the combined effect of which was to temporarily bankrupt the side and force it to slide steeply backwards into the Second Division of the Pontefract and District League. Bullock remained Fryston's pit manager until 1954, by which time Fryston were well on their way to re-entering the top flight of the West Yorkshire League. He was succeeded thereafter by a colliery boss whose highly directive management style and resolute unwillingness to show any 'favouritism' towards the footballers on his books was a salient feature of a late-50s period which saw Fryston struggling to hold on to, and then finally losing, their First Division status.

By the 1962-63 season, Fryston could therefore point to an extremely distinguished but fading past in which their prospects of ever achieving a WRCC Cup final victory appeared to have receded beyond recall. Not since their contest with East Bierley, eighteen years earlier, had Fryston been in serious contention for the trophy. Nor had they been capable of securing a permanent foothold in the First Division of the West Yorkshire League. Now was the time to change all that, as Fryston not only hauled themselves out of the Second Division as champions but also triumphed in their historic encounter with Thackley.

Where the team my father captained was undoubtedly similar to its predecessors was in its subscription to the traditional local football values of toughness, togetherness, and an irreverent commitment to 'getting one over' the opposition, referees, and other members of the game's 'establishment'. There was an element of continuity with the past in the fact that the old, Staffordshire-born warrior, Dick Foulkes, remained the Fryston coach, and the hard-bitten Chunner Lister his 'right-hand man'. The players, all being local, came along already socialised in terms of such values. Even those like Cliff Braund who entered the team in relative naivety were given crash courses in the 'dark arts' of how to play to win. None of this is to pretend that Fryston had a local monopoly of these qualities in league competitions in which other tough, working-class teams were prevalent. However, there is no doubt that The Colliers were also mindful of the particular type of reputation and tradition they were under an obligation to uphold.

One thing which arguably made this team so different from their predecessors who had played in previous finals was that they did not regard themselves as representatives of the 'colliery', per se. They, like thousands of other Yorkshire miners of this era, were far too alienated from the industry and its management[2] for that sort of identification to have existed in reality. The majority of the players undoubtedly regarded themselves as playing on behalf of the 'village' (and there is no disputing that this fundamentally 'local' character of the side made it distinctive from its predecessors); but there was also a wider appreciation of the fact that it was the team's complementary range of skills and abilities, their compatible personalities, and shared ethos, that made them 'more than the sum of their parts' and gave them that special 'something'. Thus there are those who, like Trevor Ward, are apt to take the almost fatalistic view that the team was somehow 'blown together' as if their success was simply 'meant to be'.

Almost without exception, the Fryston players harboured dreams of 'getting away' – of seizing an opportunity to enter the professional game. Those individuals who, like Jack Sharp and Freddie Howard, were blessed with the requisite talent and opportunity were not so enamoured of professional football as to allow themselves to become wholeheartedly attached to it. Jack Sharp would only commit himself to playing part-time for Halifax Town, while Freddie Howard chose to forego entirely the chance of playing for York City. Agga Mattison was arguably more ambitious than both of these but did not quite have the ability to progress beyond reserve team football. Other members of that side could justifiably point to close encounters with future or ex-professionals as evidence of their own potential. However, this was a Fryston team which 'played hard and worked hard', but did not train or 'plan moves' with anything like the dedication of the Thackley team which opposed them in the final. The dominant ethos was avowedly amateur. In addition to the tactical and technical skill involved, it was the weekly opportunity to exhibit the working-class occupational values of toughness, irreverence and loyalty that made the game so undoubtedly intoxicating.

Inherently ironic in all of this is the fact that Fryston's winning goal against Thackley was scored by perhaps the one Fryston player who was unequivocally rejecting of the club's traditional emphasis on physical toughness and intimidation. Through his entire career, Freddie Howard eschewed the robust tendencies of the traditional English centre-forward in favour of the more subtle skills of the arch 'goal poacher'. While such nonconformity to the more recognisable Fryston approach occasionally proved a source of considerable tension between Howard and Dick Foulkes – and provoke the former's temporary departure (or expulsion) from the club – there is no doubt that both the latter and the other Fryston players considered the talismanic, free-scoring, veteran centre-forward a sporting 'genius' with a proven temperament for the big occasion. It was therefore with all the romance and flourish of a fairy tale that Dick Foulkes called on Howard to re-emerge from reserve-team football and answer Fryston's need to produce something special in the face of more fancied opposition.

We have seen how the victorious Fryston team of 1963 was unable to emulate their success in the following year's 'repeat contest' against Thackley. Nor have Fryston won the trophy since then. Even the excellent Fryston side managed by Derek Stokes in the 1970s fell short of regaining the trophy by losing three semi-finals and the 1972 final to Pontefract Collieries. It is clearly impossible to say whether the now legendary Fryston team captained by Pete Waddington would have been any match for the teams of 'invincibles' who donned the club colours with such great and lasting distinction in 1910, 1945 and 1974. What certainly is irrefutable, however, is that the 1963 victory was unprecedented in Fryston's history and remains unsurpassed. Given the uniqueness and enormity of their achievement – which, like England's 1966 World Cup success over West Germany, appears to be growing in significance with every passing year – and the poor prospect of anything like it ever happening again, it is apposite to ask: what became of the 'heroes of '63'?

The Best of Times: What Became of the Heroes of '63?

Of the eleven players appearing in that final, the majority would consider themselves happily retired. Brian Wood, for one, is now 'enjoying a quiet life' in South Kirkby, near Pontefract, following a career spent in the mines. 'Woody' temporarily departed Fryston pit to take up the role of basic underground instructor at the National Coal Board's Area Offices in Allerton Bywater: 'I was there about two years before I got a job back at Fryston as Assistant Training Officer. Then, in 1983, I moved from Fryston to the Selby Complex to set up training for their computer systems at Wistow, which was the first mine to [produce] coal [at the Selby Complex].'

Woody's day-to-day working life occasionally crossed paths with that of Terry Templeman's. The latter's career as a 'belt man' below ground was cut short by a chronic spinal condition which forced him to occupy what he refers to as a 'button job', first at Fryston, and subsequently at Allerton Bywater. The ever-genial 'Tempy' now lives on the 'Four Lane Ends' estate between Whitwood and Methley, and enjoys a weekly rendezvous with Jackie Sharp, who lives just on the edge of Castleford town centre, and Agga Mattison, who resides in Ferry Fryston.

Sharp is yet another ex-Fryston miner and footballer who moved to nearby Allerton. Having initially left Fryston to spend a ten-year spell at the Hickson and Welch chemical company, Sharp briefly resumed working at Fryston, where he stayed until it closed in the immediate aftermath of the 1984-85 miners' strike. He then spent three years at Allerton before moving into the job of postman, at which point he suffered a heart attack. 'Sharpie' nonetheless remains as sprightly and gregarious as ever.

Given that Agga Mattison is commonly considered to be part of Fryston's triumvirate of 'born leaders' (the others being Jack Sharp and Pete Waddington), it should come as no surprise to discover that he holds the distinction of having become Fryston's youngest-ever pit deputy, at the unusually tender age of 25. During his long career in the mines, Mattison also served as delegate, president and secretary of Fryston Colliery's NACODS (National Association of Colliery Overmen, Deputies and Shotfirers) branch, before moving, like Wood, to the Gascoigne Wood pit in Selby in the wake of Fryston's closure. He is the second of three ex-Fryston players to have suffered a heart attack. His was incurred in 1990.

Fryston's 'official' team captain, Pete Waddington, is recovering well at the time of writing from a quadruple heart bypass operation. By the time he took over as Fryston's team manager, Waddington was working as caretaker of the Thomas A Beckett school in Sandal, Wakefield. Waddington's brief spell as a Fryston miner was followed by a long and enjoyable career at the Glass Houghton Coking Plant, the closure of which in the late 1970s induced his move to Wakefield, where he continues to live in retirement in central Horbury.

The 'fifth Beatle', Barry 'Cobbo' Robinson, went on from working at Fryston to become a contract worker at Ferrybridge power station. On entering his second marriage, he and his wife sought greater stability by first looking into the possibility of running a public house, before eventually taking over their fish shop and sandwich bar in Bradford:

> We went to look at a pub in Goole but somebody who I knew from contracting nipped in before us. Shortly after, she saw this fish shop advertised in t'paper and said we should go and have a look at this one. And God, what a dive it was! Mice everywhere! We had to get Rentokill in to get 'em sorted out! But we bought if for 30-odd thousand pounds, spent over twenty years in it, built it up, and eventually tagged a sandwich shop onto it which used to be a storage place for t'potatoes. (Barry Robinson)

The career trajectories of Fryston's other flying wingman, Trevor Ward, and his lifelong pal, Cliff Braund, could hardly have been more discrepant. Ward spent a total of 27 years at the NCB prior to being made redundant in 1988. He then enjoyed four years as a driving instructor, but was forced to change career because of the government's pit closure programme, which robbed him of his main client base, the local miners. Ward therefore became a member of the security staff at Leeds University, where he worked from 1992 until his retirement in 2009.

Cliff Braund's life story since leaving Fryston for New Zealand merits detailed description. When Braund initially left to begin a new life at the other side of the world, his wife, Elaine, initially stayed behind with the intention of selling their house. However, after four months passed by without success, she and Cliff took the decision that she should go out join him and leave it to her father to expedite the sale. The difficulty was that the club would only pay for Elaine to take the cheaper option of travelling by sea. Cliff was due to meet her in Wellington, only to be told that the ship would be arriving a day or two late due to a dockers' strike in Sydney. As luck would have it, Braund had a friend who was already visiting Wellington, and he kindly agreed to meet Elaine off the boat and escort her down to Dunedin:

> They flew down as far as Christchurch and the plan was for them to drive down from there to Dunedin, where I'd throw a welcoming party for her in the lodge where I lived. Unfortunately, they never made it as he fell asleep at the wheel, so she woke up in hospital where they kept her in for around four months. And when she eventually came out, she decided she wanted to go home. That put me really in the crap because I'd still got sixteen months

left on the contract, plus I'd got the accommodation to pay for on top of the mortgage on the house back in England – *plus* her expenses because she wasn't covered by medical insurance. (Cliff Braund)

This episode placed great strain on the couple's relationship and they soon decided to separate and were eventually divorced.

Finding himself increasingly prone to homesickness, Braund had been contemplating resettling in England but the premature death of his mother put paid to all that and he ended up becoming a senior supervisor for a major New Zealand bank. The ex-Fryston player continued to play at an impressive standard of football, turning out as a 'converted' midfielder for the Otago provincial team against such touring English professional teams as Stoke City and Sheffield United. Braund's match against the latter was especially memorable:

> I had a bit of a punch-up with that guy Len Badger! I never liked him as a player, even when I saw him on telly, and I liked him even less in real life! We had a bit of a scuffle and then they came back to our lodge – the accommodation was a tourist lodge with a nice restaurant and swimming pool out the back. They came back for a beer and we had another go. I got pissed with Tony Currie, who was a really nice lad. But best of all, I played against the full Welsh team and they beat us 6-1, but we really made them work for it. (Cliff Braund)

Braund remarried in 1974 and now has three grown-up daughters. After spending over twenty years with the bank, he spent the remainder of his career as a consultant for PriceWaterhouseCoopers, before taking early retirement. Within eighteen months, he contracted bladder cancer, and suffered a heart attack soon after. In 2012, he incurred a minor stroke following a heart bypass operation. However, he has made a good recovery and is back to his cheerful best.

The same, alas, could not be said for Braund's fellow migrant, Harold 'Archie' Ward, who had also carved out a new life for himself in neighbouring Australia. When interviewed in November 2010, Archie explained how he had been resident in his adoptive country for going on 45 years:

> I came out with the wife and three kids and settled in Sydney. But then I got divorced. I played soccer until I was forty, even though I lost a couple of fingers in an accident at work, steel works. Then I refereed for a while

before I started strapping – doing first aid. I gave up refereeing when I was handling an Under 16s final and got hit on the head with a full can of Coke. Next thing I knew I was waking up in hospital with seven stitches in the wound. That was it. No more for me, mate. I walked away from it forever. The legs play me up a lot now, but just as long as I can walk down the pub I'm happy! (Harold Ward)

By this stage, Harold was enjoying an extremely happy relationship with his partner, Anne Field, a popular retired schoolteacher and local councillor of nine years' standing, who was busy writing a history of her local racecourse. Ms Field recalls how:

Harold had a recognisable Yorkshire accent and kept it. I always remember being on Green Island (off Cairns) Great Barrier Reef in maybe 2004. A British Naval destroyer had stopped off Green Island en route to Sydney for naval exercises. The sailors were brought in by tender to the island. Harold went to the end of the wharf and in a loud voice called out: 'Any Yorkies here? Follow me to the pub lads!' I was decamped to the beach with some American ladies for some substantial time! (Anne Field)

Not unusually for someone so sociable and gregarious, Ward was a heavy smoker, and Ms Field believes that it was this habit that ultimately proved his undoing. Sadly, Ward was diagnosed with lung cancer on 28 July 2011 and died on 30 September. Anne Field considers it cruelly ironic that on the equivalent date eleven years earlier, she and Ward had enjoyed one of their happiest and most memorable moments together, as they sat behind the goal posts to watch the gold medal play-off between Cameroon and Spain at the 2000 Sydney Olympics.

Ward would have been proud to know that, in March 2012, his partner was honoured with a Notice of Motion in the NSW Parliament (Legislative Council), congratulating her on her services to public education and the community. With typical regard for the contributions of others, Ms Field was instrumental in the instigation of a memorial 'Harold Ward Rookie of the Year Award' that henceforward would be presented to the Under 21 player at the newly-launched Dapto Dandaloo Football Club who had 'exhibited the most promise, sportsmanship and generally good attitude to the code'.

Freddie Howard's Ashes

With the exception of Johnny Appleyard, whose untimely and tragic demise was referred to in the previous chapter, the only other player not so far mentioned is Fryston's goal-scoring hero of their final with Thackley, Freddie Howard. The story of what became of the extraordinary striker in the wake of Fryston's victory is certainly deserving of our final word. Sadly, it was not too long – in 1974 to be precise – that Howard joined Appleyard on the death-roll of Fryston heroes.

Howard had been working in Doncaster as a bus driver. By now, his playing days were over but, much to the amusement of his daughter, Susan, he had embarked on a subsequent 'career' as a referee. 'He was always scrupulously fair,' she proudly maintains. 'He never showed any prejudice to one side or the other. I remember seeing him in his black uniform. He used to say, "I've got better legs than you!"'

It was while Howard was out driving his bus one day that he started to experience chest pains. So, according to his brother Stan, 'He quickly took the bus straight back into the depot, and immediately set off home; but he hadn't been in the house too long when he suddenly collapsed and died. He was only 43.'

Judged by any standards, the funeral was a poignantly memorable affair. Such was Howard's popularity among his colleagues that they chartered one of the company's buses to take them to his service and ensured that all the traffic was halted while en route:

> And all the bus drivers that were out on duty got out of the buses and they all stood there with their heads bowed as it went by through Doncaster with the coffin, right away past the depot where he worked, and all the staff were outside: office staff, garage staff, everybody were outside – even the traffic wardens were out as it passed through, and took him to t'crematorium – as a mark of affection and respect. (Stan Howard)

What followed next was more romantic than any fiction writer could surely dare to imagine:

> All I know is that, when my dad died and my mam came over here, she said 'I'm making arrangements to have him scattered over at Fryston football field,' and she got in touch with the Welfare, and they gave her permission to do it. My mam and maybe a couple of sisters went, and a couple of

committee men went, and then they scattered him. I used to go up and throw carnations on his birthday. Now I've just got a crystal glass with a plaque on which, needless to say, I treasure. (Susan Jackson)

We have already seen how the 'hat-trick' goal scored by James Lister in Fryston's 6-0 win over Queensbury in the 'Sunday County Cup' was eerily reminiscent of Freddie Howard's immortal strike against Thackley. Unfortunately, the club's challenge for county honours petered out when they suffered a tame 3-0 home defeat in the next round against Stannington Albion; but it is imperative that they do not allow this setback to deter their general progress. The ashes of the legendary centre-forward who scored the most important goal in their club's entire history lie literally all around them. It is hopefully from such physical and mythical manifestations of this precious heritage that these and future Fryston players will draw suitable inspiration – and one day rise again.

Acknowledgements

This book might never have been written at all had it not been for the vital encouragement and support volunteered by numerous key individuals and/or the organisations they represent.

First and foremost, I wish to express my profoundest gratitude to the ex-players of Fryston and Thackley – and in some cases, their wives, partners or widows, and other relatives and friends – for having kindly consented to be interviewed. On the 'Fryston side', the relevant list comprises: Charlie Barnett, Cliff Braund, Anne Field, Ronnie Foulkes, Stan Howard, Frank Isles, Susan and Trevor Jackson, Harold Mattison, Barry Robinson, David Rotherforth, Jack Sharp, Terry Templeman, Mary and Peter Waddington, Harold Ward (now deceased), Carol and Trevor Ward, Brian Wood and Carol Woolley. The corresponding 'ex-Thackley' interviewees were the former players, Ray Cole, John Gunnell, Ken Hill, Barry Holmes, David Waddington and Jack Walker; and the man who was their coach at the time of their 1963 and 1964 cup finals against Fryston, Mr Peter Glover.

Two important respondents not so far mentioned are the ex-Bradford Park Avenue and Manchester United star, the late Johnny Downie and his wife, Sheila, to whom I am also very grateful for having talked to me. I am equally indebted to the former Fryston Colliery Welfare club secretary, Barry Bennett, who generously agreed to let me use the contents of an interview he conducted with the former Fryston, Frickley Colliery and Bradford City player, Dick Foulkes, back in the 1980s.

Club officials from Fryston and Thackley, and the secretaries of local amateur football associations, have greatly assisted me in my efforts. For example, the Thackley club secretary, Chris Frank, was extremely instrumental in helping me make contact with relevant former players, while few people could have been more generous in their general support and encouragement than the Fryston AFC treasurer, Stuey

Leach. I also have good reason to be grateful to Patrick Monaghan, secretary of the Castleford and District FA Sunday League, and Kevin Parkinson, secretary of the West Riding County Football Association, who each kindly responded to my request for relevant information.

During the lifetime of this project, I occasionally turned, for role models as well as practical support, to such well-known and highly-respected local football historians as Ronnie Wharton (and his son, Ian) and Rob Grillo, who have written extensively about the amateur game in Bradford and Keighley, respectively. Rob, in particular, is famous, both for his compendious knowledge of local sport and his commendable willingness to share whatever invaluable information he may have at his disposal. It was in keeping with this reputation, that he was constantly on hand with information and advice. I have also benefitted from wise counsel kindly provided by corresponding historians and chroniclers of the professional game, such as Tim Clapham, co-author (with Malcolm Hartley) of *All About Avenue: The Definitive Bradford Park Avenue AFC*, and Andrew Leonard, who is editor of the *About Man Utd: The Manchester United Football Club Resource* website.

Given the importance of local newspaper archives to this research, I have been very fortunate in terms of the co-operation and support I have received from staff in the local studies sections of relevant libraries. I have particular reason to be grateful for the immense patience and practical assistance afforded me by staff at Pontefract Library, where I spent long periods trawling through back-copies of the *Pontefract and Castleford Express*. However, I would also like to express my gratitude to staff based in the local studies departments of the Goole and Bradford central libraries, who proved ready and willing to dig out archival information on request. This was especially true of Mick Birdsall, a Team Leader at Bradford Central Library, who cheerfully extended me numerous favours of this nature during the period of research.

This kind of archival information would obviously be of no value without the corresponding authorisation of its use. I am therefore most grateful for the permission granted me by the editors of the *Pontefract and Castleford Express* to quote the numerous extracts from match reports which illustrate this study. The photographs presented in this book are provided courtesy of the *Express*, the *Bradford Telegraph and Argus*, and the *Yorkshire Evening Post*, as well as the following parties:

Ray Cole, Anne Field, Ronnie Foulkes, Ken Hill, Frank Isles, Terry Templeman, David Waddington, Peter Waddington, Fryston AFC, Wakefield Council, and the families of Jim Bullock and Jack Hulme. I am grateful to them, one and all, for allowing me to use their pictures.

I take great pride and satisfaction from the fact that this book is being published by Route, and feel incredibly flattered that they have agreed to do so. It was always important to me that the eventual publishers would show genuine respect for the book's fundamental subject matter and not be driven by a purely commercial motivation. Route have more than justified my faith in them. Moreover, Ian Daley has exercised his unrivalled editorial skills in such a way as to add quality and refinement to my own preliminary drafts. The book I would select if ever chosen to appear on *Desert Island Discs* would be Ian Clayton's *Bringing It All Back Home* (which is a Route publication). I therefore feel honoured in a way that mere words cannot describe that Ian has written such a warm and genuine Foreword to this book.

Last but not least, I want to express my heartfelt appreciation to particular members of my own family. My brother Paul, and daughter, Laura, gave me huge practical support in the early days of the project – especially in helping me gather in and edit *Express* match reports from the 1960s. My wife, Joanna, is a senior administrative assistant whose typing, computing and organisational skills have been invaluable to me at various stages of the research. Every bit as important, though, has been the fact that, knowing the emotional significance that this study has for me, she has cheered and willed me on, right from beginning to end. So, too, have my mam (Mary) and dad (Peter). They know, as I do, that this book would have meant a great deal to my dad's late brother, Melvin, which is another reason why I was so determined to see it through.

When I wrote *One Road In, One Road Out: A People's History of Fryston* in the late 1980s, I dedicated it to the memory of my maternal grandparents, Sam and Edie Holmes. In this instance, I would like to pay tribute to the footballing (Airedale) side of my family by dedicating the book to the loving memory of my paternal grandma and granddad, Edie and Tommy Waddington, and beloved 'Uncle Melv'.

Notes in Chapters

Introduction: In Pursuit of the Ultimate Prize

1. Waddington, D. (2008) *One Road In, One Road Out: A People's History of Fryston*. London: PAVIC.
2. *Express,* 29/08/2002.
3. Hattenstone, S. (2006) *The Best of Times: What Became of the Heroes of '66?* London: Guardian Books.
4. Connor, J. (2007) *The Lost Babes: Manchester United and the Forgotten Victims of Munich*. London: HarperCollins.
5. Berry, N. (2007) *Johnny the Forgotten Babe: Memories of Manchester and Manchester United in the 1950s*. London: Brampton Manor Books.

Chapter 1: Strikers and Substitutes

1. *Express,* 8/11/2012.
2. See, for example, Hulme, J., van Riel, R., Fowler, O. and Malkin, H. (eds) (1990) *World Famous Round Here: The Photographs of Jack Hulme*. Glass Houghton, Castleford: Yorkshire Art Circus.
3. See *Yorkshire Post,* Magazine, 2 June 2012.
4. *Yorkshire Evening Post,* 17/3/1986.
5. Padgett, L. (1988) *Castleford and District in the Olden Time*. London: Williams-Brown/Pritchard.
6. *Wakefield Express,* 16/4/1873.
7. Baylies, C. (1993) *The History of the Yorkshire Miners, 1881-1918*. London: Routledge.
8. Ibid.
9. Waddington (op. cit., pp. 2-3).
10. Belcher, S. (1993) 'Home ownership and miners' housing on Cannock Chase in the late nineteenth century', in J. Benson (ed.) *The Miners of Staffordshire, 1840-1914*. Keele: Centre for Local History, Keele University, p. 66.
11. Machin, F. (1958) *The Yorkshire Miners: A History, Volume 1*. Barnsley: National Union of Mineworkers, p. 248.
12. Baylies (op. cit.).
13. Baylies (op. cit., p. 117).
14. See, for example, Machin (op. cit., p. 248).

15. *Leeds Mercury,* 26/9/1885.

16. *Leeds Mercury,* 2/2/1886.

17. See, for example, *Sheffield and Rotherham Independent,* 16/2/1886.

18. *Yorkshire Evening Post,* 24/3/1898.

19. Baylies (op. cit., p. 206).

20. *Yorkshire Herald,* 9/2/1899.

21. *Sheffield Daily Telegraph,* 29/9/1903.

22. *Express,* 30/1/1904.

23. Baylies (op. cit., p. 188).

24. Waddington (op. cit., pp. 3-4).

25. Barstew, B. (n.d.) Barbara's Website. Available at: http://barstew.wordpress. com/fryston-colliery-village-from-1903/.

26. Fryston woman, quoted by Waddington (op. cit., pp. 3-4).

27. Altofts AFC (n.d.) *Club website.* Available at: http://www.pitchero.com/clubs/ altoftsjuniors/a/history-9709.html.

28. Ibid.

29. *Yorkshire Evening Post,* 20/1/1897.

30. Grillo, R. (2001) *100 Years On: The First Bradford City FC, the Early Years of Bradford (Park Avenue) and Other Stories.* Manchester: Parrs Wood Press, p. 2.

31. *Express,* 27/3/1902.

32. Grillo (op. cit., p. 44).

33. Wharton, R. (1987) *The Best of Bradford Amateur Football: A Series of Articles on Famous and Legendary Football Teams from Past to Present.* Stanningley, Pudsey: Allanwood Press, p. 7.

34. Pelsall History Society (n.d.) Pelsall History Society Website. Available at: http://www.pelsall-history.co.uk/fryston.htm.

35. Bullock, J. (1972) *Them and Us.* London: Souvenir, p. 58.

36. Baylies (op. cit., p. 18).

Chapter 2: Fryston's Colliery Association

1. *Express,* 5/8/1910.

2. *Express,* 2/9/1910.

3. *Express,* 10/2/1911

4. *Express,* 17/2/1911.

5. *Express,* 10/3/1911.

6. *Express,* 21/4/1911.

7. *Express,* 15/11/1911.

8. *Express,* 23/2/1913.

9. *Express,* 8/3/1912.

10. *Express,* 29/3/1912.

11. *Express,* 22/11/1912.

12. *Express,* 3/10/1913.

13. *Express,* 9/1/1914.

14. *Express,* 13/3/1914.

15. *Express*, 27/3/1914.
16. *Express*, 17/4/1914.
17. Ibid.
18. *Express*, 30/10/1914.
19. *Express*, 26/3/1915.
20. *Express*, 9/4/1915.
21. *Express*, 23/4/1915.
22. Ibid.
23. Ibid.
24. Ibid.
25. Ibid.
26. *Express*, 30/4/1915.
27. Ibid.
28. Ibid.
29. Ibid.
30. Ibid.
31. Ibid.

Chapter 3: Between the Wars

1. *Express*, 20/8/1920.
2. *Express*, 17/9/1920.
3. *Express*, 10/12/1920.
4. This brief summary of Millership's professional career is drawn from the Leeds United supporters' 'Oz White' website. Available at http://www.ozwhitelufc.net.au/leedscityprofiles.php/MillershipH.php.
5. *Express*, 12/10/1923.
6. Ibid.
7. Ibid.
8. Ibid.
9. Ibid.
10. *Goole Times*, 19/12/1924.
11. *Express*, 19/12/1924.
12. *Express*, 15/4/1925.
13. *Express*, 9/1/1925.
14. *Express*, 13/3.1925.
15. *Express*, 15/5/1925.
16. See, for example, Farman, C. (1974) *The General Strike, May 1926: Britain's Aborted Revolution*. London: Panther.
17. *Express*, 6/5/1927.
18. *Express*, 28/12/1927.
19. Bullock (op. cit., p. 108).

Chapter 4: War and Glory

1. Bullock (op. cit., p. 113).
2. Bullock (op. cit., p. 102).
3. See, for example, Hickman, T. (2010) *Called Up, Sent Down: The Bevin Boys' War*. Shroud: The History Press. Second edition.
4. Bullock (op. cit., p. 113).
5. Hartley, M.L. and Clapham, T. (2004) *All About Avenue: The Definitive Bradford Park Avenue AFC*. Nottingham: Tony Brown, p. 57.
6. Malam, C. (2004) *Clown Prince of Soccer? The Len Shackleton Story*. Compton, Newbury, Berkshire: Highdown, pp. 48-49.
7. *Express*, 14/4/1944.
8. *Express*, 6/10/1944.
9. *Express*, 9/2/1945.
10. *Express*, 16/3/1945.
11. Wharton (op. cit., p. 47).
12. Ibid., pp. 47-48.
13. *Bradford Telegraph and Argus*, 23/4/1945.
14. *Express*, 27/4/1945.
15. Ibid.
16. Ibid.
17. *Express*, 4/5/1945.
18. *Express*, 18/5/1945.
19. Ibid.
20. Greenwood, R. (1984) *Yours Sincerely*. London: Willow Books, p. 117.
21. *Express*, 11/5/1945.
22. *Express*, 11/1/1946.
23. Ibid.
24. *Express*, 10/5/1946.
25. Ibid.

Chapter 5: Post-War Reconstruction

1. The Huddersfield-born Farrell signed for Avenue in May 1940 and made 157 wartime appearances for the club, mainly in his preferred position of left-back, scoring sixteen times in the process. He also made four guest appearances for Huddersfield Town and one for Leeds United. His career at Fryston pit is not as well documented as those of Stephen and Shackleton, who worked, side-by-side at the colliery.
2. Quoted in Malam (op. cit., p. 49).
3. Shackleton, L. (1955) *Clown Prince of Soccer*. London: Nicholas Kaye, pp. 61-62.
4. Malam (op. cit., p. 61).
5. *Express*, 25/11/1946.
6. Bullock (op. cit., p. 134).
7. WYAFL Minutes, 16 May 1947.

8. WYAFL Minutes, 6 June 1947.
9. Bullock (op. cit., p. 140).
10. See Waddington (op. cit., chapter 11).
11. *Express*, 2/5/1952.
12. *Express,* 9/5/1952.
13. *Express*, 5/12/1952.
14. *Express*, 1/5/1953.
15. *Express*, 8/5/1953.
16. *Express*, 1/5/1953.

Chapter 6: Freddie Howard's Heyday

1. *Express*, 25/9/1953.
2. *Express*, 19/2/1954.
3. *Express*, 12/3/1954.
4. *Express*, 30/4/1954.
5. *Express*, 15/10/1954.
6. *Express*, 12/11/1954.
7. *Express*, 26/11/1954.
8. 'Obituary – Willie Watson: Sportsman Capped by England at Cricket and Football', *The Independent*, 26 April 2004.
9. Ibid.
10. *Express*, 7/1/1955.
11. *Express*, 11/3/1955.
12. *Express*, 15/4/1955.
13. *Express*, 22/4/1955.
14. *Express*, 29/10/1954.
15. *Express*, 11/2/1955.
16. *Express*, 22/4/1955.
17. *Express*, 20/5/1955.
18. *Express*, 23/9/1955.
19. *Express*, 13/5/1956.
20. *Express*, 27/1/1956.
21. *Express*, 24/2/1956
22. *Express*, 2/3/1956.
23. *Express*, 9/3/1956.
24. *Express*, 16/3/1956
25. *Express*, 23/3/1955.
26. *Express*, 11/5/1956.

Chapter 7. Falling Apart at the Seams

1. *Express*, 31/8/1956.
2. *Express*, 5/10/1956.
3. *Express*, 23/6/1957.

4. *Express*, 6/9/1957.
5. *Express*, 20/8/1957.
6. *Express*, 4/10/1957.
7. *Express*, 18/10/1957.
8. *Express*, 8/11/1957.
9. *Express*, 28/3/1958.
10. *Express*, 3/4/1958.
11. *Express*, 14/8/1959.
12. *Express,* 12/2/1960.

Chapter 8: Like Pieces of a Jigsaw

1. *Express*, 23/9/1960.
2. *Express*, 11/11/1960.
3. *Express*, 2/12/1960.
4. *Express*, 6/1/1961.
5. *Express*, 9/12/1960.
6. *Express*, 13/1/1961.
7. *Express*, 28/4/1961.
8. Express,14/4/1961.
9. *Express*, 8/9/1961.
10. *Express*, 6/10/1961.
11. *Express*, 27/10/1961.
12. *Express*, 8/12/1961.
13. *Express*, 12/1/1962.
14. *Express*, 16/2/1962.

Chapter 10: Bound for Glory

1. *Express*, 19/11/1962.
2. Ibid.
3. *Express*, 7/12/1962.
4. *Express*, 15/3/1963.
5. *Express*, 5/4/1963.
6. *Express*, 11/4/1963.
7. *Express*, 26/4/1963.
8. *Express*, 3/5/1963.
9. *Express*, 17/5/1963.

Chapter 11: Sharp's Triumph

1. *Express*, 24/5/63. (Headline:'Drastic Slip Gives Fryston WR Cup').
2. *The Shipley Times and Express*, 24/5/1963.
3. Ibid.
4. *Express*, 24/5/1963.

5. *Express*, 24/5/1963.
6. *Express*, 31/5/1963.
7. Ibid.

Chapter 12: Déjà Vu

1. *Express*, 17/10/1963.
2. *Express*, 31/10/1963.
3. *Express*, 7/11/1963.
4. *Express*, 9/1/1964.
5. *Express*, 23/1/1964.
6. Ibid.
7. *Express*, 6/2/1964.
8. *Express*, 16/4/1964.
9. Ibid.
10. *Express*, 23/4/1964.
11. For a biography of Charlie Williams, see: Smith, S.S. (1998) '*Charlie':The Charlie Williams Story*. Barnsley: Neville-Douglas.
12. *Express*, 30/4/1964.
13. *Express*, 7/5/1964.
14. Ibid.
15. See, for example, 'Obituary: Johnny Downie, footballer', *The Scotsman*, 25 February 2013. Available at: http://www.scotsman.com/the-scotsman/obituaries/obituary-johnny-downie-footballer-1-2809635.
16. Out of all the former players, left-winger, Barry Holmes, enjoyed the greatest subsequent success. After a brief spell with Ossett Albion, he signed on as a professional for Halifax Town and played 90 league matches between 1966 and 1973. The undoubted highlight of his career occurred on 31 July 1971, when he turned out for The Shaymen in a pre-season charity tournament, the Watney Cup, at home to a Manchester United side which included George Best, Bobby Charlton and Dennis Law. Halifax triumphed 2-1 and, although he did not score, Holmes came incredibly close to doing so: 'I let rip with a thunderbolt,' he proudly recalls, 'and [the United goalkeeper] Alec Stepney was beaten all ends up, but it struck the corner of the post and crossbar! I can still see it rebounding back into play!'

13. Twilight of the Gods

1. *Express*, 9/12/1965.
2. *Express*, 18/1/1968.
3. For a brief summary of Derek Stokes' professional career, see the Huddersfield Town supporters' 'Barmy Army' website. Available at: http://www.thisisthebarmyarmy.co.uk/htafc_legends_derekstokes.htm.
4. *Express*, 17/9/1970.
5. Two weeks before their semi-final tie against Liversedge, the Fryston team was

saddened to hear of the death Norman Elstob (who by then had become the *Express*'s Sports Editor). Elstob was fatally injured in a car crash on the A1 near Fairburn, from which his wife and twelve-year-old son fortunately survived. He was only 43-years-old.

6. *Express*, 27/4/1972.
7. *Express*, 25/5/1972.
8. *Express*, 1/6/1972.
9. Ibid.
10. *Express*, 17/5/1973.
11. *Express*, 10/4/1973.
12. *Express*, 8/1/1976.
13. *Express*, 15/1/1976.
14. *Express*, 12/2/1976.
15. *Express*, 8/4/1976.
16. E.g. *Express*, 16/9/1982.
17. *Express*, 20/12/1990.

14. Out of the Ashes?

1. Waddington, D (op. cit., p. 83).
2. See Allen, V.L. (1981) *The Militancy of the Miners*. Shipley: The Moor Press.

Bibliography

Allen, V.L. (1981) *The Militancy of the Miners*. Shipley: The Moor Press.

Banks, W.S. (1871) *Walks in Yorkshire: Wakefield and Its Neighbourhood*. London: Longmans, Green, Reader and Dyer.

Baylies, C. (1993) *The History of the Yorkshire Miners, 1881-1918*. London: Routledge.

Belcher, S. (1993) 'Home ownership and miners' housing on Cannock Chase in the late nineteenth century', in J. Benson (ed.).

Benson, J. (ed.) (1993) *The Miners of Staffordshire, 1840-1914*. Keele: Centre for Local History, Keele University.

Berry, N. (2007) *Johnny the Forgotten Babe: Memories of Manchester and Manchester United in the 1950s*. London: Brampton Manor Books.

Bullock, J. (1972) *Them and Us*. London: Souvenir.

Clapham, T. (2012) *Avenue at War: Bradford (Park Avenue), 1939-1946*. Nottingham: Tony Brown.

Connor, J. (2007) *The Lost Babes: Manchester United and the Forgotten Victims of Munich*. London: HarperCollins.

Daly, J. (1985) *Four Mitres: Reminiscences of an Irrepressible Bishop*. Published by the author.

Fairweather, H.R. (1975) *The Development and Growth of Castleford as a Coal Mining Town*. Leeds: James Graham College.

Farman, C. (1974) *The General Strike, May 1926: Britain's Aborted Revolution*. London: Panther.

Greaves, P.C. (1938) *Black Diamonds: Gleanings of Fifty Years in the West Yorkshire Coalfield*. Published by the author.

Greenwood, R. (1984) *Yours Sincerely*. London: Willow Books.

Grillo, R. (1999) *Glory Denied: The Story of Association Football in Keighley, Volume 2*. Manchester: Empire Publications.

Grillo, R. (2001) *100 Years On: The First Bradford City FC, the Early Years of Bradford (Park Avenue) and Other Stories*. Manchester: Parrs Wood Press.

Grillo, R. (2012) *Keighley's Soccer History*. Published by the author.

Hall, T. (1981) *King Coal: Miners, Coal and Britain's Industrial Future*. Penguin: Harmondsworth.

Harding, J. (1985) *Football Wizard: The Story of Billy Meredith*. Derby: Breedon Books.

Hartley, M. and Clapham, T. (2004) *All About Avenue: The Definitive Bradford Park Avenue AFC*. Nottingham: Tony Brown.

Hattenstone, S. (2006) *The Best of Times: What Became of the Heroes of '66?* London: Guardian Books.

Hickman, T. (2010) *Called Up, Sent Down: The Bevin Boys' War*. Shroud: The History Press. Second edition.

Hulme, J. (1986) *A Photographic Memory*. Glass Houghton, Castleford: Yorkshire Art Circus.

Hulme, J., Van Riel, R., Fowler, O. and Malkin, H. (eds) (1990) *World Famous Round Here: The Photographs of Jack Hulme*. Glass Houghton, Castleford: Yorkshire Art Circus.

MacFarlane, J.E. (1987) *The Bag Muck Strike: Denaby Main, 1902-1903*. Doncaster: Doncaster Library Service.

Machin, F. (1958) *The Yorkshire Miners: A History, Volume 1*. Barnsley: National Union of Mineworkers.

Malam, C. (2004) *Clown Prince of Soccer? The Len Shackleton Story*. Compton, Newbury, Berkshire: Highdown.

Padgett, L. (1988) *Castleford and District in the Olden Time*. London: Williams-Brown/Pritchard.

Pope-Hennessy, J. (1949) *Monckton-Milnes. The Years of Promise: 1809-1851.* London: Constable.

Pope-Hennessy, J. (1955) *Lord Crewe. The Likeness of a Liberal: 1858-1945.* London: Constable.

Shackleton, L. (1955) *Clown Prince of Soccer.* London: Nicholas Kaye.

Smith, S.S. (1998) *'Charlie': The Charlie Williams Story.* Barnsley: Neville-Douglas.

Waddington, D. (2008) *One Road In, One Road Out: A People's History of Fryston.* London: PAVIC.

Wassell, J. (2009) *A History of Airedale with Fryston and Guide to Holy Cross Church.* Ferrybridge, Yorks: Pen2Print.

Wharton, R. (1987) *The Best of Bradford Amateur Football: A Series of Articles on Famous and Legendary Football Teams from Past to Present.* Stanningley, Pudsey: Allanwood Press.

Fryston captain, Pete Waddington, receiving the WRCC Cup.